Beyond Accommodation

Beyond Accommodation

Everyday Narratives of Muslim
Canadians

JENNIFER A. SELBY, AMÉLIE
BARRAS, AND LORI G. BEAMAN

UBCPress · Vancouver · Toronto

27 26 25 24 23 22 21 20 19 18   5 4 3 2 1

Printed in Canada on FSC-certified ancient-forest-free paper (100% post-consumer recycled) that is processed chlorine- and acid-free.

Library and Archives Canada Cataloguing in Publication

Selby, Jennifer A., author
Beyond accommodation : everyday narratives of Muslim
Canadians / Jennifer A. Selby, Amélie Barras, and Lori G. Beaman.

Includes bibliographical references and index.
Issued in print and electronic formats.
ISBN 978-0-7748-3828-3 (hardcover). – ISBN 978-0-7748-3830-6 (PDF). –
ISBN 978-0-7748-3831-3 (EPUB). – ISBN 978-0-7748-3832-0 (Kindle)

1. Muslims—Religious life—Canada.   2. Muslims—Canada—Social conditions.
3. Islam—Social aspects—Canada.   4. Religious minorities—Canada.   I. Beaman,
Lori G., author   II. Barras, Amélie, author   III. Title.

FC105.M8S45 2018   305.6'970971   C2018-903270-7
                                                            C2018-903271-5

Canadä

UBC Press gratefully acknowledges the financial support for our publishing program of the Government of Canada (through the Canada Book Fund), the Canada Council for the Arts, and the British Columbia Arts Council.

This book has been published with the help of a grant from the Canadian Federation for the Humanities and Social Sciences, through the Awards to Scholarly Publications Program, using funds provided by the Social Sciences and Humanities Research Council of Canada.

UBC Press
The University of British Columbia
2029 West Mall
Vancouver, BC V6T 1Z2
www.ubcpress.ca

If we are able to choose positive words [...] it's possible to create an affirmative myth for the future that contrasts the negative myth currently prevalent in society.

– Lídia Jorge, on her book *Les Mémorables*[1]

Contents

Acknowledgments

The seeds for this book were planted in lively conversations in coffee shops in St. John's and Montreal, Canada. One late afternoon in March 2010, Lori Beaman and Jennifer Selby met with a dozen women who were members of the Muslim Association of Newfoundland and Labrador at a café in downtown St. John's. Together they began discussing the kernel at the heart of this book: What about thinking about "positive" experiences and social interactions? We thank all those present for their generosity (even paying for coffee! Selby had awkwardly locked her wallet and Beaman's in her car kilometres away). We are especially grateful to Faiza Ennany, who died in 2012, for her encouragement; she is deeply missed. We built on this initial idea during a conversation with Barras on a January 2012 morning in a Montreal coffee shop on Notre-Dame Street. Our collaboration began. This book is the product of hundreds of conversations like these ones.

First and foremost, our deepest gratitude goes to our interviewees who have made this book possible. We are grateful for your patience, time, and willingness to share details about your lives with us. Your stories have made us think differently about diversity in Canada, and we hope that we succeeded in conveying these narratives here. Particular thanks go to Ayse Sule, Amrah Pirzada, Kamrul Islam, Haseen Khan, Fatime Khan, and Mahmoud Haddara. We also sincerely thank Richard Awid for generously sharing his historical research on the Al Rashid Mosque, as well as Kassem Abouchehade and Katherine Bullock for helping us fill in some gaps in our historical overview.

The research undergirding this book and its publication was generously supported by the Canadian Social Sciences and Humanities Research Council, the Religion and Diversity Project, the Swiss National Science Foundation, and the Canadian Awards to Scholarly Publications Program. Beaman would also like to acknowledge the ongoing financial support of her research through her Canada Research Chair in Religious Diversity and Social Change. We thank our respective departments, as well: the Department of Religious Studies at Memorial University of Newfoundland (Selby), the Department of Social Science at York University (Barras), and the Department of Classics and Religious Studies at the University of Ottawa (Beaman).

Our arguments were sharpened thanks to invited talks and conferences, including the Religion and the Exercise of Public Authority workshop (Osgoode Law School, 2014), for the University of Waterloo's Department of Religious Studies (2014), the Osgoode Colloquium on Law, Religion and Social Thought (Osgoode Law School, 2015), the Winter Research Talks (Department of Social Science, York University, 2016), the Islam on the Prairies conference (University of Saskatchewan, 2016), the Groupe Sociétés, Religions, Laïcités (CNRS, Paris, 2016), and the European Conference on Politics and Gender (Lausanne, 2017). We are grateful for our colleagues' engagement and helpful feedback at each of these occasions. Three anonymous reviewers also made thoughtful detailed comments on the manuscript, for which we are very appreciative.

Others who helped shape this book include Florence Rochefort, Abdie Kazemipur, Sobia Shaikh, and participants at the "Re/Posing the 'Muslim Question'" workshop held at Memorial University in June 2014: May Al-Fartousi, Valérie Amiraux, Nadia Fadil, Aizza Fatima, Mayanthi Fernando, Matteo Gianni, Julie Macfarlane, Géraldine Mossière, and Sherene Razack. Thank you.

We also acknowledge the graduate students who participated in assembling this book. Caitlin Downie and Jennifer Williams met with us to think and rethink our interview schedule. They conducted some of the interviews, took on transcription, and wrote their own Master's theses drawing on our shared data. Alexandra Caron, Julia Carpenter, and Maude-Marie Salin de l'Etoile also undertook careful (and we know, sometimes tedious!) transcription. We thank Marianne Abou-Hamad, Elena Fenrick, and Cory Funk for their editorial assistance.

We are grateful to our editor at UBC Press, James MacNevin, for his enthusiasm and his sound advice, as well as to Katrina Petrik, our production editor, for her detailed work and patience.

Four children were born to us over the course of researching and writing this book: Alanna, Nour, Leah and Julien. We hope one day you might read this book or at least this acknowledgment. Lastly, we extend thanks and love to our partners, Óscar, Karim and Derek, for genuinely supporting our years-long conversation.

***

Some of the interviews featured in this book have previously appeared in "Le jeu des figures et ses règles: le role des figures musulmanes masculines dans la vie quotidienne des musulmanes canadiennes" in the *Revue Anthropologie et Sociétés* (2018); "Reasonable Accommodation" and "Muslim Canadians" in *Exploring Religion and Diversity in Canada: People, Practice and Possibility* (edited by Catherine Holtmann, 2018); *Deep Equality in an Era of Religious Diversity* (2017); "Muslimness and Multiplicity in Qualitative Research and in Government Reports in Canada" and "Exploring the Intricacies and Dissonances of Religious Governance: The Case of Québec and the Discourse of Request" in *Critical Research on Religion* (2016); "No Mosque, No Refugees: Some Reflections on Syrian Refugees and the Construction of Religion in Canada" in *The Refugee Crisis and Religion: Secularism, Security and Hospitality in Question* (edited by Luca Mavelli and Erin Wilson, 2016); and "In/Visible Religion in Public Institutions: Canadian Muslim Public Servants" in *Religion and the Exercise of Public Authority* (edited by Benjamin Berger and Richard Moon, 2016).

Beyond Accommodation

Introduction

Sabah, the Building Manager, and the Swimming Pool

I live with my younger sister. We rent; we share an apartment. And [*pis*[1]], in this apartment building, there's a swimming pool, there's a sauna, etc. The owner is so so nice ... that I didn't really need to negotiate. I only talked to him once. I explained my conviction. I explained my religion: that I cannot swim with the veil. He told me, "Well me, I respect this a lot [*Ben moi, je respecte beaucoup ça*], and I don't have a problem because after 8:00 p.m. the pool's normally closed," he told me. "I'll give you the key. You can make a copy of the keys," he told me, "but with the condition that you do not show everybody that you have a copy." He added, "You have the right to use [the pool] starting at 8:00 p.m." And that works for me. It works out well because I'm free [after work]. Sometimes I go to the pool, to the sauna. I even have sisters that live on the West Island who also come sometimes.

Sabah, aged thirty-eight, told us this story in a café on a cold November evening in 2012, in Montreal, Quebec, at a time when there were intense debates about a proposed state ban on visible religious garments.[2] At the time of our conversation, Sabah has lived in Montreal for almost twelve years, settling in the province's largest city after a brief stay in Germany following her departure from her native Algeria, where she completed studies in engineering. Part of her family had already settled in the city. Their presence and her fluency in French influenced her decision to stay. "Going door to door," she says, she quickly found work with an engineering company and now manages twelve employees in the same company. Active and gregarious, Sabah considers herself to be a practising Muslim.

Exercise is important to Sabah. She told us the pool story in the midst of a longer description about her sporting life. The women's-only gym she attends does not have a pool and sauna, so she decides to approach her apartment's building manager in the hopes of finding a solution. In her description of their interaction, the "very kind" manager acknowledges the sincerity and importance of her beliefs. She remembers that he said, *"Ben moi, je respecte beaucoup ça* [Well me, I respect this a lot]," *ça* referring to her religious beliefs that shape her need for sex-segregated swimming. Responding to her predicament, he offers a generous solution: to give her the master key to duplicate so she can access the pool and sauna space in the evening, after he normally locks the doors. In telling us this story, Sabah stresses the facility and simplicity of their conversation: "I only talked to him once." The manager responds quickly with a solution. She shares the space with "sisters," her female Muslim friends in a similar predicament. At the same time, the arrangement puts the manager in a vulnerable position; he must trust her discretion and asks her not to show the key to other inhabitants in the building. In giving her the key, he becomes responsible for anything that could happen when she uses the pool.

In retelling this story, we are not interested in determining whether giving Sabah the key was the best solution or whether her request for pool access was "reasonable." Rather, our point in considering this mostly unremarkable story is that Sabah's pool access was negotiated without fuss. We think the interaction that took place between her and the building manager is worthy of analysis because such everyday moments of negotiation have been generally overlooked by scholars who prefer to focus on memorable conflicts. And yet negotiations happen all the time. Our interviews are replete with incidents like that described by Sabah, which reveal the fabric of everyday life in both its richness and its mundaneness.

In this book we take moments like this one seriously in order to analyze the negotiation of religion in the public sphere from a different and a new vantage point. We were inspired to consider these mundane interactions in light of recent scholarly knowledge production on the constraints and complications faced by Muslim minorities in contexts in which discrimination and Islamophobia are on the rise. As the reader is likely well aware, social scientific research on Muslims in Western Europe, Canada, the United States, and Australia has exploded in the last fifteen years. Almost invariably, this scholarship focuses on problems – integration, failed political participation, undesired headscarves, problematic halal foods,[3] and unreasonable requests of all kinds (see Modood 2005; Cesari 2006, 2013; Bader 2007; J.R. Bowen 2007; Lamine 2014; Göle 2015; Jouili 2015). Specific to the Canadian context, these interactions have been most recently conceived and framed (in law, policy, and public discourse) by the notion of "reasonable accommodation." Drawing on data from ninety interviews with self-identified Muslims, this book invites critiques of this model. We analyze and situate moments in which religiosity is "worked out," sometimes so casually and subtly that we have described them as "nonevents" because they are not memorable or remarkable. One academic commentator on our work stated, "There is no such thing as a 'non-event' for Muslims." This point, in fact, is contrary to what the vast majority of our interviewees told us. Many of our participants indicated that overemphasis on problems contributes to a pejorative foregrounding of their religious identities that they found unrepresentative and tiresome. There is no question that our study participants experienced racism and/or Islamophobia. Sometimes these moments were blatant, as with the experience of one participant, whose front steps of her home were defaced in what she described as a hate crime, or less blatant, as was the case for participants positioned by non-Muslims to be the resident workplace experts on Islam. Our aim is not to negate these experiences or to deny the exhaustion and pain that comes from attempting to deal with racism and ignorance. In the simplest terms, we seek to shift our gaze to these nonevents while, at the same time, being attentive to the layers of power relations that characterize these nonevents. The sociopolitical climate in which we conducted these interviews was also a factor. In Sabah's case, we interviewed her during a period in Quebec when a bill to ban religious symbols in the administration and reception of public services had been tabled in the provincial legislature, so her hijab was under particular scrutiny. In September 2013, the then provincial government introduced Bill 60 to the Quebec National Assembly.[4] The bill, entitled *Charter affirming the values of State secularism and religious neutrality and the equality between women and men, and providing a framework for accommodation requests* (popularly called the Charter of Secularism), developed a specific framework for the settlement of religious reasonable accommodation and de facto differentiated visible religiosity as a special case requiring specific accommodation rules. It also proposed to prohibit public servants from wearing visible religious symbols, as well as to prevent access to public services to individuals who cover their faces. The government was defeated in a provincial election in April 2014 before the bill was passed, but in October 2017 the current government passed Bill 62, *An Act to foster adherence to State religious neutrality and, in particular, to provide a framework for religious accommodation requests in certain bodies*, which similarly outrightly poses a specific framework.[5]

In our research, we encountered an overall desire to "get on with it" within an incredibly wide range of religious practices and negotiations that we have not seen in most contemporary social scientific treatments on Islam. The ways that people effectively negotiate in their day-to-day lives have remained largely invisible and have not been empirically and systematically studied. In part, therefore, this project was born out of a desire to chronicle these often excluded or forgotten narratives of religious beliefs, practices, and negotiations. This book focuses on the ways in which Muslims negotiate and navigate everyday life, a distinction we elaborate upon in a moment.

It is from this vantage point that we aim to rethink the reasonable accommodation model currently referenced in the management of religion and diversity in Canada and increasingly embraced by scholars and policy-makers in Western Europe. The notion of reasonable accommodation moved from its original location in employment-related religious discrimination and human rights law[6] to a broader application in the 2006 Supreme Court of Canada *Multani v Commission scolaire Marguerite-Bourgeoys* decision, a case about a young Sikh student's request to wear his ceremonial dagger (kirpan) at a Montreal public school.[7] The Supreme Court ruled that allowing the student to wear his kirpan, provided that it was sealed and secured under his clothing, constituted "reasonable accommodation" of the student by the school. The notion has since circulated and been subsequently referenced[8] and affirmed through public discourse, notably with the 2007 Bouchard-Taylor Commission and its recommendations in Quebec (Bouchard and Taylor 2008; Lefebvre and St-Laurent 2018). Over six months, the commission referenced the concept to determine which demands made by religious minorities were reasonable and worthy of accommodation within the sociopolitical parameters of Quebec. The model has since been lauded internationally for acknowledging difference, both as a legal concept and as a social framework for managing diversity. Our research does not focus on the legal concept of reasonable accommodation, though to be sure there is a link between the two, with the legal concept arguably being evidence of law's influence over everyday life. That is not, however, our focus. As a social framework, reasonable accommodation circulates in everyday language as an organizing force. Moreover, as we will demonstrate, our participants' narratives reveal significant fissures and power imbalances in how reasonable accommodation is translated and put into action.

Inspired by our on-the-ground narratives, one of the overarching objectives of *Beyond Accommodation* is to question the reasonable accommodation model as well as to propose an alternative approach that better captures the subtleties of how individuals work out their religious needs in their everyday lives. First, we are concerned about how reasonable accommodation is undergirded by (neo)colonial and often racialized power imbalances that ignore indigeneity and intersectionality, similar to how other authors have critiqued notions of tolerance (Jakobsen and Pellegrini 2004; Beaman 2011; Barras 2016). Individuals who feel compelled to make requests for reasonable accommodations are often members of religious minorities who may find themselves in a vulnerable position. In other words, the accommodation mandate proclaimed as reasonable and designed to foster inclusion and equality can negatively impact practical negotiations and lived identities and represents a barrier to achieving these laudable goals in everyday life. Religious minorities are often required to vocalize and simplify their religious need(s) to make it legible to those in charge of deciding whether the need is worthy of accommodation. In so doing, in addition to being flattened, homogenized, and de-theologized, their religious practice becomes the de facto object of close scrutiny.

Second, and partly as a consequence of these imbalances, the framework implicitly distinguishes and solidifies certain forms of religiosity as non-normative. Because of sometimes invisible structures ingrained in the fabric of Canadian society, not all expressions of religiosity require accommodation and determination of their reasonableness. In other instances, these structures encourage an assessment that too much accommodation exists. In effect, the everyday experiences of our participants point to how reasonable accommodation tends to require that they make their "Muslimness" visible (see Amiraux 2016, 2017, on mechanisms that maintain this identity). Even if they are comfortable with this precondition, doing so may also shelter a Christian normativity that permeates Canadian society. In many ways, therefore, our participants' stories provide insights into what reasonable accommodation produces and overlooks and whom it privileges. Lastly, we are concerned that public discourse tends to focus on rare, litigious, and emotional cases where religion appears rigid and inflexible, while ignoring positive and productive moments like Sabah's interaction. Her story offers innovative and rich insights into how individuals craft a place for their religion in Canadian society through the processes of negotiating and navigating relationships with others.

In reaction to these and other concerns, *Beyond Accommodation* invites the reader to consider an alternative approach to religious difference to better consider the richness and intricacies of everyday lived religion: a navigation and negotiation model. Each term captures different facets of these interactions. *Navigation* reflects an internal juggle of how one enacts and lives religious ideals. Sabah thought about swimming, an activity she enjoys, and decided she no longer wanted to swim in mixed-gender pools. More practically, before speaking with the building manager, she weighed the pros and cons of approaching him about her swimming predicament. Should she ask him for a women's only swim period? If yes, how and when should she ask? How should she introduce and frame her desire for a sex-segregated space so that he, as a non-Muslim, could hear her? *Negotiation* reflects how one interacts with others: Sabah describing her situation, listening to and assuaging the building manager's concerns and, eventually, going to a hardware store to have his key cut and discreetly use it after hours. Internal navigation was present in all the accounts we heard, regardless of whether participants embarked in a negotiation with others. We explore these multitudinous processes concretely through sites identified by our participants, from ski lifts and grocery stores to sports centres.

When we take these perspectives into account, a few neglected aspects of the reasonable accommodation approach become visible: first, few Canadians (religious or not) ever make formal accommodation requests. Most work out informally with themselves or/and with others a place for their needs. Second, religiosity is rarely rigid. Rather, it is lived as changing and dynamic, adapting to the complexity of life.[9] Third, while the navigation/negotiation model does not eliminate the power dynamics inherent in the reasonable accommodation model, it does acknowledge them insofar as requesters are not immediately positioned in a defensive or passive mode. By drawing our attention to how negotiation is internalized or navigated before an individual engages with someone else, our framework captures the dynamism and, as one participant said, the *délicatesse* (finesse) involved in crafting a place for religion in everyday life. It also shows how respect is a key motivating factor in the decision-making processes and internal or external dialogues in which participants engage. As they navigate and negotiate, participants seek to balance, combine, and assemble different values, responsibilities, and registers. Again, this does not mean that there are no incidents of Islamophobia, racism, prejudice, misunderstanding, and disappointment. However, contrary to the dominant narrative of conflict, demands, and dissatisfaction, the stories we heard involved a mutual and sometimes "agonistic" respect we thought was important to consider more fully. These moments can foster an agonistic relationship, where one "absorbs the agony of having elements of [her] own faith called into question by others, and fold[s] agonistic contestation of others into the respect that [she] convey[s] toward them" (Connolly 2005, 124).

With these critiques of reasonable accommodation in mind, drawing on Sabah's short description of her interaction with her building manager, the remainder of this chapter details the methodological shift we propose with this study and the two cities where we conducted interviews. Finally, we provide a brief map of the chapters and structure of the book.

Methodological Attention to "Unremarkable" Moments

Cognizant of how methodology shapes results, we agonized over how to ask questions that did not replicate assumptions about piety or reify religious identities and how to best locate and think about ongoing moments typically not granted attention. This approach posed certain methodological challenges. Because it proved cumbersome, and we wanted to include a larger sample, we ruled out asking participants to record their interactions (with a daily diary, phone call, or through video) and relied on their retelling. But even their recall could be a challenge. Because of their ordinariness, unremarkable moments can be difficult to locate and study. They are often fleeting – a meeting between friends, dinner with colleagues, interactions between coworkers, exchanges between private and government service providers and clients, playdates, neighbourhood activities – and are not necessarily memorable or exceptional. In hindsight, their unremarkableness is perhaps why few theorists have examined these not-easily-recovered, yet important and recurring, moments. There is counterexample research (see Deeb and Harb 2013; Turam 2015). Sociologists Valérie Amiraux and Javiera Araya-Moreno (2014: 111) suggest that to best consider how religious minority issues become the focus of public debate in relation to radicalization, one should focus on everyday interactions: "By looking at ordinary unease, at the day-to-day emotions emerging in the course of interactions in a pluralistic society, between people ignorant of or unfamiliar with another's moral universe, we seek to avoid the classical and exclusive emphasis on pathological trajectories of radicalization and the functionalist modes of explanation." In this spirit, we did not specifically inquire about our participants' thoughts on their hijabs, why they grew beards, whether they fasted during Ramadan, or what they believed as Muslims. We did not inquire abstractly about their beliefs and practices by relying on a typology of the "five pillars" – a declaration of faith, daily prayer, charity, fasting in the month of Ramadan, and pilgrimage to Mecca – which is a common construction of the traditions of Islam. Rather, we asked participants about their beliefs and practices in relation to particular contexts and situations. Referencing Kim Knott's (2005, 2009) work on the centrality of space in shaping the lived experience of religiosity, we deliberately directed our interviewees to describe and to reflect on their social interactions in different places in their everyday lives, such as at restaurants, on buses, in mosques, at work, in grocery stores, at the dinner tables of friends, at public pools, at community events, and so on. In other words, instead of asking, "How do you express your Muslimness?" we could ask, depending on their work and social status, "How do you express (or not) your religiosity when you are invited by [a friend, colleague, Muslim, or other] to their home?" "What specific steps do you take (or not) at work to feel comfortable and express your religiosity as you would like?" We hoped that such precision and spatiality would bring us closer to how Islam is lived through individual lenses.

For this reason, we have sought to underscore a "lived religion" approach, both in our research design and in our discussion of it here. As we completed interviews and began our analysis, we spent some time thinking about the "arithmetic" or the processes present in our interlocutors' descriptions of these unremarkable moments and interactions in their everyday lives. We sought to untangle their descriptions of what took place – physically, emotionally, linguistically – in these moments of exchange. Social scientists have long been interested in considering lived realities, both through the lenses of what has been called the everyday (following Goffman 1956; de Certeau 1984; D.E. Smith 1987; McGuire 2008) and through recent social scientific research on Muslim realities (Schielke 2009a, 2009b, 2015; Deeb 2015).

We also draw on these everyday moments to demonstrate and decentre the notion that there is one Islamic orthodoxy or truth, a common misunderstanding about Islam and Muslims. This aim may not seem to be particularly original. And yet, from our vantage point, despite the recognition that Muslims live out their practices in myriad ways and come from Sunni, Shi'ia, Sufi, and other backgrounds, branches, and sects, this observation is rarely translated in scholarship. We recognize the danger of going too far with this moderate social constructionist approach (following Beckford 2003); we may find ourselves in a position of there being "no there there," or no fixed Islam, as anthropologist Abdul Hamid el-Zein (1977) proposes. Our more modest aim is to consider how our participants navigate and negotiate what they define as Islam or practices related to being a Muslim, recognizing that being Muslim is not their only point of reference. Despite an imagined Islam that is made up of the five pillars mentioned above, and despite a tendency to measure practice by these and other standards of orthodoxy, as with any religious group Muslims practice in innumerable ways.[10] Examination of their stories of quotidian life reveals this multiplicity.

This is not to say that religion is not important to the people we interviewed. To many, it is. But for the most part, as for Sabah, religious commitments do not define all that they are.[11] These moments speak to the porousness of boundaries between identities and to the idea that religious practices are not fixed but often evolve in function of context for those who are highly observant and for those who are not. Our sample in Montreal, Quebec, and in St. John's, Newfoundland and Labrador, included mostly Sunnis, a half-dozen Shi'ias and about 15 percent who identified as "cultural Muslims" in that they felt Muslim related to their ethnic or cultural background rather than to their religious practices (see Gans 1994; Eid 2007; Duderija 2008; and Moghissi, Rahnema, and Goodman 2009).[12] Unless pertinent to their narratives, we do not identify participants by ethnic groups, the most common way Canadian mosques and community groups self-identify or are located. We did ask participants to specify their sectarian identities within Islam in our initial identifying questions, but given that it came up in only one narrative (Hassan, who made clear he was Sunni and whom we will meet in Chapter 3), we chose not to identify individuals using these categories. Indeed, we point to other scholarship on Muslim Canadians that confirms this insight, that these sectarian differences are less important than readers might expect (see Chapter 2; Bunting and Mokhtari 2007; Saris and Potvin 2010; Macfarlane 2012b; Selby 2016b). This is not to say that we did not encounter diversity. While identities and theologies can be characterized by a certain discursive coherence, we found that this coherence shifts when translated into practice and when confronted with the diversities, ambivalences, contradictions, and respect that underlie these interactions. For these reasons we take a lived religion approach in our examination of the experiences of the self-defined Muslims we interviewed in Montreal and St. John's. As we show in our review of the scholarship on Muslims in Canada, to date there have been few empirical studies that take account of these moments in mosques and Muslim associations, but even fewer that also include more mundane places.

More generally, we come to this project with related but differing interests and perspectives and with training in the disciplines of anthropology, law, political science, religious studies, and sociology. Amélie Barras comes from a political science background. She is particularly attentive to documenting the interactions between modes of religious governance, religion, and gender. Lori Beaman's background is in law and sociology. She is interested in religious diversity and how it is cast as a problem to be managed. Jennifer Selby has a religious studies and anthropology background and also relies on qualitative methods – particularly interviewing and participant observation – to think about Muslim lives and their expression amidst putatively secular countries like Canada and France. The amalgam of these disciplinary realms has, we hope, fostered a constructive dialogue between us, which translates into our approach to the interview data we collected.

And lastly, in a more self-reflexive move, in our research design and analysis we aim to locate our situatedness as researchers and as white, perceived-Christian women. In addition to the socioeconomic and political climate in which our study was undertaken, as with all qualitative research (see M. Fischer and Abedi 1990; Bourdieu 1977), our identities (and perceived identities) as researchers invariably shaped the data we collected, including the voices and stories that we heard and those we highlight. As Aaron Hughes (2015: 39) reminds us, "How we bring our data into existence, the rhetorical moves we make to re/present it are not, simply put, natural acts." Our intention here is to attempt to name potential asymmetries (our statuses, gender, privilege, funding to undertake this research, and so on), not to eliminate them but to remain reflexive about how they may impact the premises and outcomes of this project. We are tenured and tenure-track faculty members who are encouraged to undertake research. We are not Muslim and are not racialized. But unlike some scholars, we do not necessarily believe that our nonmembership excludes us from undertaking this research.[13]

Montreal, Quebec, and St. John's, Newfoundland and Labrador

The narratives we examine are drawn from ninety interviews we conducted with self-identified Muslims. In 2012–13, Beaman and Selby conducted interviews in St. John's and Barras in Montreal. All participants were over eighteen years of age, and just over half were women. Reflecting the overwhelming similarities we found in our combined data, our analysis is not comparative, a decision made following our collection and analysis of the data. Given the political moment in which we conducted interviews in Montreal and the differences between Montreal and St. John's in their geographies, size, immigration histories, percentages of visible minorities, and sociopolitical make-ups (including Quebec's language politics and sovereignty debates and Newfoundland's geographic isolation and relative ethnocultural homogeneity), we expected greater difference. Initially we saw St. John's as a counterspace to Montreal because it is not in the province of Quebec and also because it is not one of Canada's larger and more diverse cities to which scholarly discussion regarding diversity tends to be relegated. It was an opportunity to conduct research outside the four Canadian cities where most research on Muslim Canadians has been conducted (Toronto, Montreal, Vancouver, and Edmonton).[14] We hope to show how the similarities in the data point to something about the Canadian context that shapes the everyday negotiation of religious identities in ways that cannot be ignored.

Interviews in Montreal were conducted in the midst of a debate on the Charter of Secularism, so that many of our Québécois participants were especially aware of their perceived or visible religiosity. Questions of visible religiosity in Quebec are part of a long, publicly debated history. Anticlericalism fostered the Révolution Tranquille (Quiet Revolution) in the early 1960s, which sought to shift the province's earlier Catholic influence to a putatively secular one.[15] The rapid shift towards secularization, as well as the possibility of political sovereignty in two referendums that posed the question of independence, continues to impact Muslims living in the province of Quebec. Other international geopolitics have further compounded the visibility of Québécois Muslims, as in the remainder of Canada. But minority politics in Quebec are configured differently and shape sharp critique of the country's broader multicultural ethos, which explains why some scholars have promoted an ethos of *interculturalism*, a paradigm that emphasizes social cohesion and integration in Quebec through common values (see Bouchard and Taylor 2008: 19–20, 120–21).

There are other visible differences between these cities. Montreal is 65 percent francophone (up to 82 percent province-wide), and St. John's is 98 percent anglophone. There are more Muslims per capita in Montreal than in St. John's. According to 2011 data, almost 6 percent of Montreal's population lists itself as Muslim, while 0.05 percent of St. John's population does. Another significant difference is that in contrast to Montreal's 20.3 percent visible minorities, approximately 3 percent of St. John's population constitutes visible minorities.[16] Muslim Canadians are not necessarily visible minorities, but these figures reflect a more general sense of diversity and how it might be experienced in these places. Almost half our Montreal participants were born in Canada, signalling the longer settlement of Muslims in that province. Only two of fifty-five, or 4 percent, of our St. John's participants were born in Canada, both of whom converted as adults. A slightly higher number of participants in Montreal were of North African origin. Still, in both cities our participants were born in twenty-five different countries, including Canada, demonstrating the heterogeneity of their origins no matter whether they live in Montreal or St. John's.

Nevertheless, overall we found the similarities in our participants' narratives remarkable, so much so that a comparative analysis would be neither illuminative nor compelling. Although there are occasional differences to which we draw the reader's attention, for the most part the geographic location was irrelevant. In part this was because many of our participants have lived in multiple locations and told their stories drawing on the wealth of their experiences across geographies. Like most Muslims in Canada, the majority of our interlocutors were born outside of Canada. In both cities we interviewed self-identified Sunnis, Shi'ias, Sufis, cultural Muslims, and nonpractising Muslims. We suspect that the overwhelming similarities are also tied to the predominantly

Catholic population of Quebec and to the largely Protestant population of Newfoundland and Labrador, which result in a Christian normativity that permeates the lives of our respondents, an observation that echoes scholars who have argued there is a Christian hegemony present in Canada (Beaman 2008; Berger 2010; Klassen 2015).

Also, in both cities, our interlocutors live in a Canadian climate of heightened surveillance and securitization of Muslims and those perceived as Muslim. A number of studies have demonstrated how this climate impacts Muslim Canadians, some of which we detail more closely in Chapter 1.[17] For example, a 2004 study by the Council on American-Islamic Relations–Canada found that 43 percent of participants knew of someone of Arab origin and male who had been questioned by the Royal Canadian Mounted Police (RCMP), the Canadian Security Intelligence Service (CSIS), or local police.[18] The detainment, ten-month imprisonment, and torture of Maher Arar, who was later acquitted of all charges, is one of the most dramatic examples in recent Canadian history of this kind of profiling (see Zine 2012a: 16), not to mention the Omar Khadr case, which we turn to in greater depth in the next chapter. In sum, contemporary securitization and Islamophobic-inspired attention on the lives of Muslim Canadians shape our interlocutors' daily lives, no matter their age or gender.[19]

Given that fewer than half of our participants attend mosque regularly, a figure that correlates with quantitative studies on mosque attendance,[20] participant recruitment varied. In the St. John's case, because there are two formal Muslim associations – the Muslim Association of Newfoundland and Labrador and the Muslim Students' Association in the city's one university – we approached both organizations to recruit participants. In Montreal, we recruited through associations, including Muslim Students' Associations on university campuses. In both cities, we relied on personal networks and snowball methodology to ensure we did not overemphasize institutional or association membership as a reflection of Muslimness. This approach also reflects our strategy to imagine ways of being religious that might not be immediately visible or accessible (see Jeldtoft 2011: 1139–40; Gökariksel and Secor 2015). Sabah, whom we met at the beginning of the Introduction, was recruited through a friend whom we also interviewed.

Chapter Overview

In the five chapters that follow, we explore facets of the narratives of our participants that contextualize and forefront their negotiation and navigation of religion in everyday life. Chapter 1 interrogates the context in which these negotiations take place. It is framed by our experience on a local radio program about Muslims in Newfoundland. Drawing on the dynamics of the on-air interview and linking them to the broader literature that critiques the social construction of Muslims (e.g., Mamdani 2004; Shryock 2010), we problematize the radio host's insistence on rendering Islam and the four Muslim guests as "peaceful" and his "welcome to the province" discourse that conjures the figures described below. We show the pervasiveness of these constructs, whether through overt discrimination or more subtle microinequities in interlocutors' narratives. We focus on what we have conceptualized as five central figures – the Terrorist, the Imperilled Muslim Woman, the Enlightened Muslim Man, the Foreigner, and the Pious Muslim – in the Canadian social imaginary and how they are manifest in the lives of our participants. Sometimes these figures appear as spectres, invoking fear or moral outrage or a more subtle reversion to "our values." At other times they appear as reassuring presences (like the Enlightened Muslim Man), often in tandem with a spectre. Even though the figures are shaped, produced, and reproduced through discourse, their impact on the lives of our participants is real. They drive the creation of laws and policies that heighten religious difference, sanction securitization, and fuel public fears. Through more than a dozen evocative stories, we map our interlocutors' (re)production, their (re)appropriation, and refusals to engage with them, in part to understand Islam in Canada. We also consider how the figures were present in our research design.

Chapter 1 also considers contemporary knowledge production on Islam, with attention to social scientific scholarship on Muslims. Obviously, the kinds of questions we pose, the ways in which we collect data, and the knowledge we create do not exist in a vacuum. We consider the implications of the post-9/11 boom in scholarly literature attentive to Islamic revivals or pious Muslims and the related context of a heightened securitization where Muslimness remains politicized and ostracized in Canada and elsewhere. The abundance and relatively limited focus of this post-9/11 scholarship may protect and project stereotypes that pigeonhole Muslims as apologists (at best), as only pious, or as extremists (at worst), where piety is identified as *the* overarching identity, therein overlooking the multiplicities and complexities of daily life.

In contrast, Chapter 2 invites readers to understand the lives of Canadian Muslims through a different lens. Here we chronicle the historical settlement trends of Muslim Canadians by drawing on two stories of immigration – a Lebanese family to Northern Alberta and a Moroccan family to Montreal – that capture some of the sociocultural and political variances in which Muslims settle in Canada. We draw out differences in the stories to illustrate the shifting political, social, and economic landscapes of settlement from the late nineteenth century to the 1990s and 2000s. A consideration of the scholarly work on Muslims in Canada appears alongside this historical account. While there is a pervasive idea that there is little written on Islam in Canada before the 1990s, we found the opposite to be the case. We conclude by highlighting a lack of empirical in-the-field research that, even if inadvertently, contributes to a narrow narrative of Muslim life in Canada. While we are aware of its normative trappings, it is in part to address this lacuna that we chose, with a lived religion approach, to chronicle more mundane moments of Muslim realities in Canada, like Sabah's experience with her apartment manager.

Chapter 3 turns to our participants' myriad experiences of encountering (and, at times, enacting) the secular, including at Christmas parties, with prayer in public spaces, and with expectations around handshaking and physical embrace in social interactions. We draw on scholarly literature on secularism and note how its contours are folded into and interwoven with a host of other normative notions that are managed and protected through the delimitation and location of the religious. This theoretically driven scholarship tells us a great deal about the political systems at work, the coconstructed relationships between secularism and religion, and the historical conditions that have shaped and promoted the secular. Even though Canada has no constitutional separation of church and state, it is often understood as a secular and religiously neutral space. Our participants suggest that it is not lived as such. They live within a country they recognize as intrinsically Christian.

Church bells ring on Sunday mornings, prayers are said before municipal council meetings, oaths are sworn on bibles, Christmas lights adorn public streets in December, and "ethics and values" courses in public schools retain a decidedly Christian narrative. Yet, these are imagined to be "cultural"; they are part of "our heritage." These assignations demarcate those bodies, to quote Stuart Hall (1996: 612), that "participate in the idea of the nation as represented in its national culture" and those bodies that do not.

In relation to religion, while mainstream Christianity is imagined as being successfully privatized, invisible, and confined to the private realm, minority religions (especially Islam) are constructed as being inherently visible and public. Our interlocutors' stories reveal how this silent privileging of Christianity on the one hand and the hypervisibility of Islam on the other are experienced and lived. They identify a number of locations where this interplay unfolds, including at the annual Christmas or holiday parties in many workplaces. Some readers might stress that attending this annual party has nothing to do with Christianity. We are not interested in assessing whether these spaces are intrinsically or symbolically Christian. We *are* interested in how our interlocutors may have experienced the holiday party as such. It is precisely this instability that constitutes and reconstitutes the power of this secular model.

With this analysis of the Canadian context in mind, in Chapter 4 we ask: How do our participants navigate and negotiate religion in their everyday lives? We describe how the narratives we heard called us to move away from the prevalent language of accommodation and demand to a language of navigation and negotiation. This chapter presents a navigation/negotiation lens that comes out of our interviews and, we believe, better conveys the complexity of how participants work out and balance their religious practices with other self-identified important areas of their lives, which we situate in relation to theory on working consensus (drawing on Goffman 1956), moral registers (Schielke 2009a; Deeb and Harb 2013), and cobbling (James 1998). We see our participants' descriptions of their quotidian navigations and negotiations as challenging dominant narratives of conflict that often underpin the notion of demands for accommodations and dissatisfaction with visible religious difference (whether through hijabs or through various requests). Though much emphasis is placed on conflict and, at times, on formal resolution of accommodation needs, the analysis in this chapter points to how differences are more often than not worked out informally.

Power dynamics remain ingrained in our proposed model. As sociologist Dorothy Smith (1987: 89) reminds us, the everyday and the writing about it are replete with power relations. Even insisting on examining the everyday lives of Muslims comes with its own normative assumptions. Unremarkable events like the scene described by Sabah are fragile and occur in the midst of such power asymmetries. One can easily imagine alternate resolutions under other circumstances or for different individuals. The apartment manager could have responded negatively or disrespectfully. He could have dismissed the religious or gendered elements of her appeal or the request altogether. He could have been empathetic but offered no concrete solution. While her situation is the result of skewed power relations – she could not locate women's-only pool hours in a large multireligious city – recovering her internal and external dialogue also sheds light on how religious diversity is lived and negotiated.

Building on the exploration of negotiation and navigation we introduce in Chapter 4, Chapter 5 considers the often overlooked respect undergirding these moments. Focusing on our participants' stories about food and dietary requirements, we consider the conditions that both facilitate and impede mutual respect. The narratives we examine illustrate how social circumstances require flexibility and an appreciation for the porousness of boundaries between identities. They also build on the idea that practices (including religious practices) are not fixed but often evolve in function of context. Taking mundane interactions as our point of departure, we examine narratives about unexceptional fleeting moments.

Respect is central to these interactions but is often not easy. In most cases, our interviewees seek to protect their interlocutors from discomfort, embarrassment, or exclusion, approaches that can necessitate the suspension of a sense of truth, even if they foster a kind of "agonistic respect" (Connolly 2005: 124). Significantly, we also found that they are typically more process oriented than outcome based (Van Quaquebeke, Henrich, and Eckloff 2007). In other words, rather than approaching recognition as an end in itself, we situate navigation and negotiation as mechanisms that, in addition to often being fragile and complicated, also include care, generosity, respect, even playfulness, and fun. These interactions are constitutive of how pluralism and coexistence are worked out in contemporary societies. At the same time, in documenting their fragility, flexibility, and creative potential, we draw attention to situations where mutual respect falls apart. Our emphasis is on the potential to imagine alternatives based on stories from the everyday.

Our Conclusion argues for the importance of considering all these narratives alongside one another for a more sophisticated and balanced characterization of what we heard from our participants. We describe the significance of our methodological approach to get to sometimes mundane and often forgotten moments when religiosity is worked out – when, from our interlocutors' perspective, it is successfully navigated and/or negotiated. All our readers might not agree with these determinations. One scholar who heard Tobias's story of how he negotiated the end-of-year Christmas staff party at his workplace – having his assistant purchase alcoholic and nonalcoholic beverages (see Chapter 3) – deemed this outcome far from positive. We have left the determination of a "positive" experience with our interlocutors. Tobias is a practising and self-described devout Muslim. He laughs as he shares this Christmas party story in our interview and appears not to see his facilitation of an at-work social drink as undermining his religious self, as our scholarly interlocutor assumed. At the same time, the conclusion revisits how, in general, these moments are fragile and changing and require parties to listen and interact with one another while withholding judgment. Lastly, we return to our critique of reasonable accommodation in Canada.

***

One of our central goals in this book is to take seriously the narratives of our participants with attention to religion in their everyday lives. Their stories reveal complexity and flexibility and depict examples of the shaping and workings of contemporary pluralism. Sabah's description of her navigation and negotiation regarding the pool in her apartment building with which we opened this Introduction is a case in point. Delving into this brief interaction reveals dynamics that are too often overlooked or silenced when we ignore the mundane. And yet, as we have argued, this moment is rich. First, it speaks to the dissonance between how a language of accommodation situates Muslim practices and how most Muslims actually work out their religion in their everyday lives in informal ways that legal regulatory frameworks both miss and dismiss. Second, while Sabah's religious identity is important to her and motivated her decision to approach the building manager, her narrative also shows the importance that her love of swimming played in her decision. Her religious identity in this story is not all-encompassing. Rather, it is entangled with her multiple other intersectional identities as a swimmer, neighbour, friend, and so on. Third, her negotiation with the manager is devoid of difficulty: the situation is worked out with a generosity and flexibility that characterizes many of the situations described by the participants in our study. And yet, fourth, Sabah and the manager's arrangement speaks to the fragility and trust that are constitutive of these moments. Sabah is vulnerable when she shares her beliefs about sex segregation and swimming with the building manager. These are intimate details about her beliefs and practices that she does not readily share with male nonrelatives. The conversation carries the possibility that her beliefs will become subject to discussion, criticism or, worse, contempt, or discrimination. Sabah also has to be ready to deal with how their conversation might impact their future relationship. And in taking her needs seriously and finding a concrete solution, the manager too is put in a fragile position vis-à-vis other tenants and the owner of the building. Still, while their interaction is delicate, we invite the reader to also see how mutual trust and respect shaped their interaction and its outcome.

Situations like Sabah's may be worked out without great fuss, but that does not mean these moments are devoid of power relations. On the contrary, power relations are constitutive and ingrained within everyday life and mark the fragility of these moments. Sabah finds herself in a position, like many of our participants, where she feels that she has to approach her manager to negotiate a place for her faith. This disruption is partly because she has been unable to locate swimming facilities in Montreal that offer women-only hours. In addition, the manager has the authority to decide whether an arrangement is possible and to dictate its terms. In fact, as we will discuss at a greater length in Chapter 5, one of the reasons why this moment is worked out is perhaps precisely because both parties are aware of and acknowledge these power asymmetries. Both are concerned by the feelings of the other and take care to protect each other from discomfort. They *both* navigate and negotiate.

Attention to these power dynamics is part of recognizing the complex terrain in mapping when religious life appears in the everyday. As will become clear, some of our participants, particularly women who wear headscarves, undertake far more navigations and negotiations in Canadian society than others do. Their everyday lives are marked by colonial and neocolonial politics, coloured by secular mores that problematize visible religiosity, and shaped by global Islamophobic discourses and racialized images. More generally, it should be clear that Muslims in Canada are often required to negotiate their religious difference (see Jamil and Rousseau 2012; Barras 2016). And yet, we propose to do more than simply unravel these asymmetries: our methodological shift reveals how these power relations are lived, played out, and, in many cases, worked out in daily interactions. This perspective invites us to be attentive to the richness and intricacies of diversity as it is lived, elements missed by the pervasive scholarly and popular perspective on reasonable accommodation.

Figures That Haunt the Everyday   **1**

"Being Muslim" on the Radio

Leaving a local radio station during a bleak January snowstorm, I wondered what just happened in there. Four of us – three members of the Muslim Association of Newfoundland and myself, as a researcher – had been invited to speak about "being Muslim in Newfoundland" for a local AM talk-radio program. After the hour-long show, as we settled into a fellow guest's car and buckled our seatbelts (due to the snowstorm, she had generously offered me a ride home), our conversation fell into a familiar exchange about the forecast. Despite our easy chatter, I felt unsettled about what had taken place inside. On the surface, the mood of the radio program had been friendly and upbeat. In the pitch for the station's bimonthly round-table program, the show's producer explained that the station wanted to promote knowledge of Islam for their listeners, who they expected knew little and/or mostly sensationalized accounts. Yet, even if its overall aim was well intentioned, a number of troubling assumptions undergirded our discussion. (Selby, fieldnotes)

The talk radio experience described here encapsulates a number of archetypical figures that, it turns out, appeared throughout the daily lives of our participants, as well as throughout public and political discourse about Muslims in Canada. To be clear: we did not ask our participants specifically about the ways in which Islam is essentialized or misrepresented in everyday life. These themes emerged organically through the interviews as they unfolded. Their recurring presence across our participants' experiences impelled us to consider them and the contexts in which they emerged. We have chosen to consider them at length because we see them as reflecting the contexts and forces that shape the navigation and negotiation of religiosity for our participants. We will identify the personalities of these figures shortly, but first, back to our radio program:

> Sitting comfortably around a table in the studio with each of us facing individual microphones, the two male hosts were relaxed and talkative. As the red light turned on, one of the co-hosts began reading a pre-written list of media-frenzied events purportedly involving Muslims, including the events of 9/11, recent terrorist actions of ISIS [Islamic State of Iraq and Syria], and the attacks at Charlie Hebdo in Paris. He then paused for effect and asked us to describe how, in contrast, "Islam is *really* about peace." We all nodded silently in agreement. But, how could we disagree? The guest sitting to my left responded by defining jihad not as a holy war, but as an internal struggle. The guest to my right referenced Hadith that demonstrate the peace-loving nature of the Prophet Muhammad.[1]
>
> The conversation then turned to our backgrounds: When had we come to Newfoundland? How did we find Newfoundlanders? One invitee responded by telling humorous anecdotes incorporating the local dialect. Another told a well-circulated narrative of flowers left at the door of the mosque on September 12, 2001. Innocuous at first glance, the questions reminded listeners of the three Muslim guests' foreignness and reinforced other subtexts: that Newfoundlanders are friendly and welcoming; that everyone should want to live in the province; that Muslim children integrate easily; that there are no other more pressing problems around employment and discrimination for local Muslims.[2] The host then asked us to "tell the listeners something about Islam." In response, one of the women began reading a prepared script outlining the "five pillars" of Islam – a statement of faith, prayer

five times per day, charity, Ramadan fasting, and pilgrimage to Mecca – typically considered to reflect normative Islam. She had prepared several single-spaced pages punctuated by "Peace Be Upon Him" following references to the Prophet, which she read uninterrupted. Her overview would be familiar to listeners who had taken a nonconfessional introductory course to world religions or were themselves Muslims.[3] The request for a concise overview specifically related to the Qur'an also seemed to force her to perpetuate an Orientalist assumption that actions performed by Muslims are overdetermined by text. (Selby, fieldnotes)

Using this radio program experience as a point of departure, we examine the broader narratives of our participants with a view to identifying figures whose presence is largely ignored and yet is simultaneously, perhaps paradoxically, invoked. We use the term *figure* to indicate that these images are discursive constructions that haunt late modern imaginaries.[4] Building upon feminist scholar Sherene Razack's (2004: 129) conceptualization of a triad of "Imperilled Muslim Women, Dangerous Muslim Men and Civilized Europeans" as well as on the work of scholars who propose binary typologies (Guénif-Souilamas and Macé 2004; Guénif-Souilamas 2006; Shryock 2010; Hajjat 2012), we explore figures whose presence was persistent throughout our interview data. This chapter focuses more specifically on five figures: the Terrorist, the Imperilled Muslim Woman, the Enlightened Muslim Man, the Foreigner, and the Pious Muslim. But there are more figures, and sometimes, as we describe in this chapter, the presence of one of those five figures in our participants' narratives activates another figure (e.g., the Imperilled Muslim Woman or the Enlightened Muslim Man is often evoked in tandem with the Patriarch). Some of them, like the Terrorist, are rather predictable, both in their presence and in the harm that they do. Others, like the Pious Muslim, are more complex, appearing in altered form depending on context. Sometimes the figures appear as spectres, invoking fear or moral outrage, or they appear as a subtle reversion to "our values." At other times they appear as reassuring presences, often in tandem with a spectre. Thus, the Imperilled Muslim Woman appears with the Liberated Muslim Woman (who never seems to wear a niqab).[5]

All do a particular kind of work that draws from a repertoire of scripts and works within a specific stage set. The figures resemble archetypes in a *commedia dell'arte* play who are ascribed well-defined, almost clichéd characteristics. The pervasiveness of these constructs is remarkable, and as with the radio show, they shape power relations in day-to-day life. Moreover, they are produced and reproduced not only at the levels of the local and relational, but also through social institutions such as the media, law, policy, and education. Their hegemony is amplified by their mobility. They are quickly erected and dismantled.

In conceptualizing these figures, we would be remiss if we did not mention Erving Goffman's classic sociological work, *The Presentation of the Self in Everyday Life* (1956), which in part has informed our analysis here. As with Goffman, by referring to figures and to a set we are in no way implying disingenuous "acting." We all draw on scripts and sets to present ourselves to others and, indeed, to ourselves in daily life. As Goffman (1956: 11) points out, there is a range of positions in relation to the figure being played, from complete belief to cynicism. Goffman recognized the ways in which a performance is "moulded and modified to fit into the understanding and experiences of the society in which it is presented" (22). The figures we present embody those social expectations. They represent the possibilities and constraints for presentation of self. We examine the ways in which they are coproduced by a variety of actors, including the multiple ways in which our participants react to their presence through their (re)production, (re)appropriation, and, in some cases, a refusal to engage with them.

In what follows, we outline how we draw from and expand upon previous scholarly conceptualizations of putative Muslim figures. We then identify a cast of figures, which appeared in the presented-as-benign discussion at the radio station and in our participants' narratives of everyday life, to think about the impact of their presence, to challenge their hegemony and, by way of conclusion, to press for their reconfiguration through insights from our participants. In a self-reflexive move, we also briefly discuss how the figures are present in our own research. We conclude by considering the ways in which they infiltrate, produce, and reproduce.

Beyond the Good/Bad Muslim Binary

In addition to the host/guest, local/immigrant, and racialized hierarchies present in the studio (issues of class were less pronounced, likely as the three other guests spoke English fluently and all held medical or doctoral degrees), the aforementioned St. John's radio host rhetorically stated, "Islam is peace," engaging in what Mahmood Mamdani (2004) calls "culture talk," which he views as an essentializing binary discourse which was heightened in the post-9/11 West. Mamdani pins the intellectual origins of culture talk on Samuel Huntington's (1996) *Clash of Civilizations and the Remaking of World Order* and Bernard Lewis's (1990) "The Roots of Muslim Rage," which both infamously and influentially positioned a unified, de-historicized Islamic civilization with a "surge of hatred" in battles with a civilized West (20–24). Mamdani (2002: 766) explains that pervasive and persuasive frameworks like Huntington's and Lewis's collapse identities – particularly Muslim ones – into a unitary pejorative religious experience and "define cultures according to their presumed 'essential' characteristics, especially as regards politics." For Mamdani, this highly simplistic discourse anchors a recurring Good Muslim/Bad Muslim binary.[6] These simplistic categorizations are widespread historically, dating from the Crusades to the colonial period and contemporarily (Allen 2010; Hajjat and Mohammed 2013; Werbner 2013). The binary remains powerful because, as our participants show, it has become normalized in innumerable situations and locations, including those that purport to be neutral, like in the oversimplication of the traditions of Islam to be only inherently peaceful. Post-9/11, Mamdani shows how the binary is ubiquitous, including in influential mainstream media. For example, Mamdani (2004: 24) notes how "even the pages of the *New York Times* now include regular accounts distinguishing good from bad Muslims: good Muslims are modern, secular, and Westernized, but bad Muslims are doctrinal, antimodern, and virulent."[7] In addition to its Islamophobic, racist, and colonialist inflections, Mamdani argues, culture talk fosters moral panic about the threat Muslims supposedly pose to national and international orders.[8] Generally, these not-always-subtle, narrow, and often racist characterizations of Muslimness bolster already present narratives of nonintegration on the one hand and imperilled Muslims on the other.[9]

In short, the replication of the binary has significant impacts, including for our interlocutors.

Along similar lines to Mamdani's theory, anthropologist Andrew Shryock (2010) elaborates on the Good Muslim/Bad Muslim binary by drawing attention to what he argues is one result of its presence. Accompanying the figure of the Good Muslim is the construction of a specific script that includes a selective imagining of Muslims as peaceful, all-loving, and always completely compatible with the so-called secular West. Shryock calls this *Islamophilia*, which he argues is a strategy employed to combat Islamophobia. Shryock elaborates on some of the common stereotypical features of the Good Muslim, who

> tends to be a Sufi (ideally, one who reads Rumi); he is peaceful (and assures us that the jihad is an inner, spiritual contest, not a struggle to "enjoin the good and forbid the wrong" through force of arms); he treats women as equals, and is committed to choice in matters of hijab wearing (and never advocates the covering of a woman's face); if he is a she, then she is highly educated, works outside the home, is her husband's only wife, chose her husband freely, and wears hijab (if at all) only because she wants to. The good Muslim is also a pluralist (recalls fondly the ecumenical virtues of medieval Andalusia and is a champion of interfaith activism); he is politically moderate (an advocate of democracy, human rights, and religious freedom, an opponent of armed conflict against the U.S. and Israel); finally, he is likely to be an African, a South Asian, or, more likely still, an Indonesian or Malaysian; he is less likely to be an Arab, but, as friends of the "good Muslim" will point out, only a small proportion of Muslims are Arab anyway. (10)

The radio host in St. John's does not wade into waters and stereotypes quite this murky. But in seeking to only positively portray the invited guests, the host evokes jihad as an inner struggle, Islam as peace, women's choices as sartorial, and the non–Arab Muslim majority as "positives." Even while the intentions and the tone of the conversation are seemingly friendly, framed in this way, the conversation sets an inescapable trap. The figure of the Bad Muslim remains ever present through the constant assurance that *these* nice, educated, and tax-paying Muslim radio guests are peaceful Newfoundlanders. Ironically, therefore, bolstering positive elements (e.g., the Good Muslim), in fact, serves to reify the binary and maintain the figure of the Bad/Terrorist/Foreign Muslim as a shadowy presence that defines the actual conversation. In addition, the figures rarely appear as sole actors, but cast multiple shadows over the negotiation and navigation of everyday interactions for our participants, adding to the figures' power.

Mamdani's (2004) theorization on the Good and Bad Muslim binary and his charting of its pervasiveness resonates with the narratives we heard, in which the shadowy presence of these figures framed social relations. Shryock's (2010) theory similarly effectively locates neo-Orientalist politics in prevalent binary depictions of Muslims, and Abdellali Hajjat (2012) usefully shows how in their usage the binary is in constant flux. However, in relation to our data, both theories' dichotomies are too flat to adequately consider what we heard from our participants. To more adequately address the racialized and gendered underpinnings of these constructs, which we found to be central within the narratives of our male and female participants, we aim to complicate their presentation. The figures do not always work in opposition. Some figures are related but not necessarily opposed to one another. In some cases, however, a particular figure (e.g., the Terrorist) activates another related but not necessarily dichotomous one like the Imperilled Woman or the Foreigner, rather than the Enlightened Muslim Man.

Nacira Guénif-Souilamas and Eric Macé (2004) and Razack (2004) develop a more nuanced gender analysis in their discussions of Muslim figures. Guénif-Souilamas and Macé (2004), who describe an "urban white feminist" and a "suburban Arab boy" in contemporary French headscarf debates, are revelatory in how values around constructions of race, geography, and feminism are woven into the figures.[10] Razack (2004) similarly underscores the genderedness of prevalent post-9/11 figures in characterizing the power dynamics present in the aforementioned triad of the white Civilized European's maintenance of the Dangerous Muslim Man and his central co-protagonist, the Imperilled Muslim Woman. Razack sees these three figures as central to American justifications for the "War on Terror's" so-called liberation of burqa-wearing women in the name of feminism,[11] as well as more generally for the contemporary regime of surveillance of Muslim communities, to which Muslim men are particularly subjected (130; see also Hirschkind and Mahmood 2002; Razack 2008). Gendered norms and racism enable the activation of these figures. A second point we aim to mobilize through our overview on Razack's work on Muslim figures is how they emerge in representations by non-Muslims and Muslims.[12] As we examine in the next section, our participants are subjected to these stereotypes, but also react to their presence in (re)producing and (re)appropriating them.

Even though the figures are shaped and (re)produced through discourse, their impact on the lives of our participants is real. In the contemporary Canadian context, these essentialized, simplistic, and inaccurate lenses on Muslimness drive the creation of laws and policies that heighten religious difference, sanction securitization, and fuel public fears of a tidal wave of pre-modern fundamentalists who taint the image of the Peaceful Muslim, another figure created by this discourse.[13] As discussed below, they operate in the quotidian lives of our participants to produce both overt discrimination and more subtle microinequities, evidenced through gestures, looks, and changes in tone.

To think about the persistence of such figures in the Canadian imaginary even in the face of facts (particularly social scientific research) that could and should displace the figures or reduce their credibility, we find Valérie Amiraux's (2016, 2017) work helpful. Islamophobic narratives create "evidence" of an imminent threat by the Terrorist (and perhaps other pejorative figures like the Patriarch), who is imagined to lurk everywhere and anywhere, including in our own homes, as with the "homegrown" Terrorist. In her analysis of the public sphere discussion of face- and head-coverings in France, Amiraux (2016: 44) argues that "authoritative declarations" about head- and face-coverings are "reminiscent of the social function of gossip. Gossip betrays secrets and perpetuates rumours." Gossip, argues Amiraux, creates a "sort of authority, regardless of the initial source" (see also Amiraux 2017). For example, even though a large body of research finds minimal evidence that women are forced to wear head coverings, and, indeed, in some cases their husbands/fathers ask them not to, the notion that Muslim women are impelled by their male relatives to cover their heads and faces persists. Our interview with

Raja, aged fifty-two, is a good illustration of debates on the meaning of headscarves, including within Muslim families. During our meeting, her son, in his late teens, came home, and she shouted out to him from the living room, "You don't like it when I wear hijab, do you?" referring to how she recently adopted the garment after her mother's passing. According to Raja, her teenage son felt uncomfortable as he did not like images associated with the headscarf. As a figure, the Imperilled Muslim Woman has a large presence in the public imaginary, which often seems to override evidence to the contrary. All the figures our participants identify have similar larger-than-life presence and influence.

To think about the persistence of these Islamophobic and Islamophilic figures and some that encapsulate both, the next section begins by introducing our participants' narratives, considering ways in which the figures relate to one another, and tracing ways they have been theorized.

The Figures

The Terrorist

Mahmood, aged thirty-eight, is a gregarious and good-humoured doctoral student who travels regularly. He first migrated solo from Sierra Leone to Winnipeg, Manitoba, in the early 2000s. After one long winter, he moved again, to Vancouver, where he pursued his studies. Mahmood has thus lived in Canada only in the post-9/11 period, in which a series of securitization laws continue to frame Muslim life in specific ways. The Terrorist figure is present in his daily life but particularly when he is required to officially identify himself. In this passage, he describes how he hesitates to attend places of worship when he visits relatives in the United States:

> So I can imagine sitting down next to some guy [at a mosque] who has been on the radar. Maybe he's from Afghanistan or from one of those places where there's a lot of terrorists. Maybe from Somalia. And then sitting next to him at the mosque and then maybe shaking hands and *Asalaam Alaykum* [a greeting that can be translated literally as "peace be upon you"]. And this is me, who has been stopped a couple of times [at airports], and I happen to sit down next to some

high-profile terrorist that I don't know about and I'm supposed to be; my name is flagged. It's, it's not ... I don't think that it can help me in any way. So I said to my mom, "Mom, I don't think going to Friday prayers is anything I would like to do."

Mahmood fears that he may be wrongly accused if he accidentally speaks to an individual already being watched, given that he is Muslim, male, and regularly interrogated at airports. Mahmood maintains an aura of coolness in most situations, but he cannot shake the Terrorist figure. Not only does Mahmood have a common name, but he also shares his first and last names with an individual on the North American no-fly list.[14] This situation means that he is inevitably interrogated and often misses connecting flights. In consultation with friends who are similarly racialized and stigmatized because of their names and perceived Muslimness, he tries to book his travel far in advance and makes sure to request frequent flyer points, a strategy to try to further distinguish himself from other young men of the same name.

Most of our racialized participants have had a negative airport security experience where the Terrorist figure looms. The Terrorist emerges at times in explicit ways, particularly in the lives of male interviewees of all ages and backgrounds. Though the genealogy of the figure of the Terrorist is complex, its current manifestation continues to be significantly shaped by Orientalist thinking.

The figure of the Terrorist is far from limited to airport spaces. Sometimes it appears through more subtle channels like jokes and humour. Akeem, aged twenty-nine, is a graduate student from, as he describes it, a "traditional" family of Kuwaiti origin. Despite pointed attempts to circumvent the Terrorist figure, he reflects on the Terrorist's infiltration in his daily life. Akeem was recruited to this research through snowball sampling. He was reluctant to be interviewed, believing his experiences would not be representative because he had avoided attending a mosque since moving to Canada five years earlier. He recalls once "accidentally" going to a Muslim Students' Association event, which he erroneously thought was a social gathering for Middle Eastern-origin students.

So-called humour in his workplace overtly zeroes in on his undesirable imposed Muslimness and foreignness when his labmates "jokingly" nicknamed him Osama, an indisputably terror-filled Bad Muslim reference. Akeem explains how he came to know about the nickname: "They [labmates] said, like, 'We are telling you now because we know that you are OK with it, because it's a joke.' And I was, like, 'Yeah, of course. It's funny.' But I was thinking, like, hmmm, they didn't stop doing that. They started [the slur], even after I told them I'm not religious." Like the Peaceful Muslim figure, this "joke" places Akeem into an essentialized trap, falsely cushioned by the tone of delivery. Through humour, the figure of the Terrorist emerges and is difficult to contest and dislodge. We are reminded here of domestic relationships characterized by violence in which the abuser says, "What's wrong? Can't you take a joke?" This is a classic strategy of abuse, in which a joke, defined as such by the abuser, is used as a springboard to abuse or to maintain or create unequal power relations. The recipient of the joke is in a no-win situation. In the case of Akeem, he would appear to be overly sensitive or, alternatively, to be defensive, with something to hide, if he protests.

Akeem explains how important it is that he be perceived as "OK" by his peers, which presumably translates as "not a radical" or not a "Bad Muslim." Akeem is conscious that "everyone [was] talking" about his perceived Muslim identity, which was heightened in response to a prayer space solicited unknowingly for him by his employer (a narrative we take up further in Chapter 3). However, in his telling of the incident, he also reproduces and bolsters the Terrorist figure by noting that the joke might have made sense if he were religiously conservative. The effect of the Terrorist figure on relations between Muslims is thus alluded to in Akeem's offhand comment that he is not religious, as he both distances himself from highly observant Muslims and lends credence to the association of religious conservatives and terrorism. No matter what Akeem does or how he presents himself, he cannot escape the figure of the Terrorist. To add insult to injury, as he tells it, these "friends" positioned him so that he should be *grateful* to know he was the butt of this joke. They let him in on the joke "because we know that you are OK with it" and "that you are actually not a terrorist." In other words, they share their pejorative characterization with him only to continuously other him as another figure, the Peaceful Muslim who is OK. The Terrorist figure remains unquestioned. Akeem feels resigned to the association and to the cost in order to be considered OK: "They will always associate me with Islam just because I'm from the Middle East." Demonstrating the asymmetrical power relations within their interaction, Akeem does not confront his colleagues and remains silent, aiming to dismiss the bin Laden association as a joke. He focuses on successfully completing his studies and moving on.

Under the guise of humour, the Terrorist gains momentum. Our participants' responses to such situations differ. Lila, aged twenty-seven, who after growing up in Toronto moved to Montreal when she married, recognizes not only that the reference positions her as a Bad Muslim, but also that she is perceived as dull or humdrum if she pushes back against the Islamophobic characterization. She described how her boss and colleagues in the marketing company she works for regularly make racist jokes and at times have gone so far as to call her a terrorist:

> From time to time, colleagues and bosses, I've had instances where jokingly, very jokingly, I've been called a terrorist as a joke. And that's fine, and ha, ha, ha, it's funny. But after a while it gets old, and it's tiring, and it's a constant thing where you're constantly having to defend your own religion. You know, you're constantly having to try to defend or trying to break the ignorance, you know, towards certain things. You're trying to explain to them that "No, it's not like this, it's actually like this."

As with Akeem, attempts to deflect these "jokes" will likely result in her characterization as humourless. The power to define such comments as jokes resides with those who make them, rather than with Lila.[15]

The experiences of Akeem, Lila, and many others resonate with the work of scholars who have analyzed the role of humour in perpetuating racist ideologies in the everyday (Sheriff 2001; M. Hughes 2003; Park, Gabbadon, and Chernin 2006; Santa Ana 2009). Humour can act as a conduit in the perpetuation of inequalities. In fact, it is often mobilized as a "channel for covert communication on taboo topics in contexts where discussion of the topic would be unacceptable if conducted in a serious tone" (Sue and Golash-Boza 2013: 1587). Precisely because it is difficult to displace, humour reproduces power imbalances. Individuals like Lila who attempt to contest a joke are described as humourless; their objections are often framed as a "breech [sic] in etiquette" (Sheriff 2001). This explains why some individuals choose to go along with the joke and remain silent, despite the fact that they are harmed by it. Doing so, however, inevitably legitimizes the usage of racialized humour as a "harmless" discourse that "escap[es] charges of racism" (Sue and Golash-Boza 2013: 1589). Lila describes how the Terrorist figure forces her to intervene, but in a way that must be gently performed. She aims not to allow anger or irrationality to surface in her response. These limitations are unfair and exhausting. Served as a joke, the figure of the Terrorist does not disturb her workplace's image as having a colour-blind, inclusive and equal environment (see Bannerji 2000 and Kernerman 2005 for further evidence of these quotidian prejudices on the national level).

Mahmood, whom we met at the beginning of this section, describes more generally how the Terrorist affects his personal and professional lives. Mahmood wears tailored urban apparel he describes, with smiling eyes, as an "MTV style." In part, his sartorial choices reflect his desire to keep his religiosity private. At his place of work, for instance, his "vaguely Buddhist" doctoral supervisor once suggested that he take up yoga to deal with stress. Mahmood was pleased that she was "surprised" when he told her the practice fell outside his Muslim beliefs. From his perspective, her suggestion made clear that he had successfully kept his religious life private.

Despite this gesture to "conceal Islam" (cf. Beydoun, forthcoming) at his place of work, Mahmood notes that one of his mentors has repeatedly suggested he change his first name to Mamadou.[16] This more senior scholar believes the name change might reduce potential stigma and discrimination associated with an "Arab-sounding name" and facilitate securing future employment. Mahmood explains his reservations:

> Mamadou still has the "Mah," and you can always tell someone Mamadou, but you can use Mahmood in your writing [to maintain the name he has used in academic publications to date]. But then I thought Mamadou sounds very Italian! [laughs] These are just ... it's surprising but you need to connect, to just, you want to connect to who you are. You want to maintain that. I mean, I think it's a value

system most people, you'd be surprised, sometimes you leave home [Sierra Leone], you have this cradle of civilization that you, everybody's attached to. It doesn't matter what. And there are certain norms that your parents think, values, norms, principles that they have, that they give to you.

The Terrorist shapes Mahmood's life to the point where he considers changing his name, though he associates his name with his identity, his family, and its values. The power of the Terrorist is illustrated in this example, reminding us of Mamdani (2004) and Shryock's (2010) observations about the Good Muslim/Bad Muslim stereotypes and Amiraux's (2016) analysis of the circulation of these frameworks as gossip.

A number of scholars have theorized why young people in the West who are Muslim (or who are perceived to be Muslim) are particularly vulnerable to this figure. First, anthropologist Talal Asad (2003) has articulated the multiple assumptions and binaries invoked in the Terrorist's prevalent configuration, including the notion that Muslims are bound by Qur'anic text but Jews and Christians have interpretive liberty with the Bible:

> On the one hand, the religious text is held to be determinate, fixed in its sense, and having the power to bring about particular beliefs (that in turn give rise to particular behavior) among those exposed to it – rendering readers passive. On the other hand, the religious reader is taken to be actively engaged in constructing the meanings of texts in accordance with changing social circumstances – so the texts are passive. These contradictory assumptions about agency help to account for the positions taken up by orientalists and others in arguments about religion and politics in Islam. A magical quality is attributed to Islamic religious texts, for they are said to be both essentially univocal (their meaning cannot be subject to dispute, just as "fundamentalists" insist) and infectious (except in relation to the orientalist, who is, fortunately for him, immune to their dangerous power). (10)

This Orientalist-informed imagined binding quality is understood to diminish Muslims' agentic power free from the text. This collapse can be difficult to deconstruct, as our friend found when asked to "define Islam as peace" for a radio program. The Qur'anic reader is thus understood as overdetermined by this supposedly univocal text; non-Muslims are constructed as liberal in contrast. Asad (2007) also suggests that the Terrorist has become a necessary other for the modern liberal subject, making his/her invocation constant and desired, even if a trope and discriminating against Muslims.

The Terrorist has other central features along with this textual stereotype. In addition to often being imagined as male, Razack (2008) highlights his racial contours. Razack shows how "Arab origins, and the life history that mostly Arab Muslim men have had, operate to mark them as individuals likely to commit terrorist acts, people whose propensity for violence is indicated by their origins" (28). For Razack, for whom race is the primary site of investigation and critical attention, "the very concept of racial profiling seems inadequate to describe what actually happens to those whose race, read as origins, life histories, and religious practices, marks them as potential terrorists" (32). She astutely demonstrates how, in practice, "post-9/11 profiling used 'race as a proxy for risk, either in whole or in part' and accepted that brown skin, 'Middle Eastern looks,' beards, and Muslim or Arab names provided good reasons to detain" (32). These are the common features of this profiled figure. Related to our discussion of the Terrorist, we seek to emphasize the intersection of Asad's (2007) and Razack's (2008) observations: the role of the Terrorist in informing the script and his relational impact on our participants, especially but not always men, who live in a world of increased securitization and surveillance, fuelled by rigid notions of Islam.

The Terrorist's spectre is ubiquitous. As we mention in the Introduction, a 2004 Council on American-Islamic Relations–Canada study found that 43 percent of its 467 respondents knew of someone who had been questioned by the authorities on security-related matters.[17] A 2016 poll by the Environics Institute for Survey Research (2016: 38) found that 35 percent of Muslim participants had experienced some form of discrimination in the past five years, whether due to religious affiliation, ethnic or cultural background, language or gender. Another poll found Canadians to have perceptions that reveal discrimination.[18] Still other polling data suggested that 29 percent of Canadians would have been in favour of Motion 103, proposed by a Liberal member of parliament, Iqra Khalid, in the fall of 2016 to formally speak against Islamophobia ("M-103" 2017). The motion was tabled following a mass shooting at the Islamic Cultural Centre mosque in Quebec City's Sainte Foy neighbourhood, in which six men praying were shot.[19] In the same post-9/11 context, religious studies scholar Paul Bramadat (2014: 12) notes that this era of securitization in Canada has increased the profile of certain religious traditions "well out of proportion to their actual numbers in society." In surveying a sample of thirty-five second-generation Muslim males from the Religion and Immigrant Youth in Canada project, sociologist of religion Peter Beyer (2014: 141) similarly found "the data we have collected tell us that the factors shown by other research to be associated with radicalization thus far do not appear to be significantly present in the young Canadian Muslim male population and therefore that there is little evidence of a strong possibility for radicalization beyond the very isolated few." In other words, fears about the radicalization of Arab and perceived Arab Muslim men are misplaced. Despite this evidence, the figure of Terrorist retains a powerful presence as a defining figure in the public imaginary and in Muslim lives.

Several "incidents" wove together to support the Terrorist as a viable figure in the Canadian imaginary, informing the perceptions, beliefs, and performances of Muslims and non-Muslims alike. On June 18, 2015, Bill C-51 received royal assent to officially become Canada's *Anti-Terrorism Act*.[20] The *Anti-Terrorism Act* amends the Canadian *Criminal Code*[21] and broadens the mandate of the Canadian Security Intelligence Service in ways that some have argued curtail civil liberties.[22] Heated public debate surrounded the bill (and continues to surround the law). The bill was passed in the aftermath of the shooting of twenty-four-year-old Corporal Nathan Cirillo, on October 22, 2014, as he stood guard at the National War Memorial in Ottawa (the nation's capital); the gunman was in turn shot and killed on Parliament Hill.[23] Incidents like this enhance the political rhetoric about the need to protect Canadians from terrorism. Shortly after this incident, media coverage about Canadian youth who were leaving to join ISIS militants[24] further ramped up the terrorist discourse. According to a 2014 Public Safety Canada report (cited in Heyer 2014), approximately eighty Canadians – mostly young men – were said to have left the country to join ISIS.[25] Similar international incidents in countries such as the United Kingdom, France, and Australia have been well publicized.[26] These incidents – as they are told in the media, commented on by officials, and circulated in public discourse – combine to create evidence of an imminent threat by the Terrorist who is imagined to lurk everywhere and anywhere.

Reflecting on these constant discursive reminders of the presence of the Terrorist, our interviews show a pervasive presence of this figure, often in the company of the Peaceful Muslim, who is invoked both by Muslims themselves to counter the voice of the Terrorist and, sometimes, as we saw in the opening example of the radio interview, by others seeking to introduce a counternarrative. Since we did not ask participants explicitly about this figure and did not initially code for this point, the fact that its violence and omnipresence were referenced by several of our participants, especially, but not exclusively, by male interviewees no matter their age and ethnocultural background, is striking.[27]

The Imperilled Muslim Woman

An occasional companion of the Terrorist is the Imperilled Muslim Woman. Interplay between these figures is illustrated by Dalia, who is in her mid-thirties. During our interview at a coffee shop in downtown Montreal, she recounts her interaction with a stranger sitting next to her on a chairlift at a Laurentian Mountain ski hill. Dalia, who was born in Lebanon, explains how their conversation started after she hung up from a quick mobile phone call during which she spoke in Arabic:

> I was sitting with this random person 'cause, you know, sometime you go [up in the chairlift] with random people. And he's, like, "What language were you talking?" And I was like, "Oh, Arabic." So he's, like, "So, are you Christian or are you Muslim?" And I'm, like, "Oh no, I'm Muslim." And he's, like, "Oh! You can snowboard?" And I'm, like, "Yeah, why can't I? I have two legs!" I really said that in a very joking way, and he started ... and I'm like, "It's a joke OK?" And he's, like, "Well, do you if your brother or your father [are] here? And I'm, like, "No, I'm, I'm here alone." He's, like, "Really? You're allowed to go out alone?" And I'm, like, "Yeah, why? Why wouldn't I be able to?"

He's, like, well, "No, you hear on the TV and the radio." I'm, like, "Exactly. You know [what] you hear on the TV, on radio. You need to speak with people, you know?"

In this chairlift exchange, a mobile phone conversation in what for him was an unrecognizable language led Dalia's seatmate to assume the nature of her relationship with her father and brother and to question her agency. His sense of entitlement in posing such personal questions speaks to how he quickly and facilely positioned the male members of her family as oppressive and her as an Imperilled Woman embroiled in patriarchy.[28] His collapsing of her Muslimness with patriarchy allowed him to reproduce patriarchy by inserting himself into her life with judgment. Dalia attempted to jokingly disarm the situation by focusing on her ability to ski ("I have two legs!"), but the skier ignored her generous out and referenced popular media ("you hear on the TV and the radio") to rationalize his intrusion.[29]

This scenario is one in which the Patriarch is imposed by a stranger. In other moments in her interview, as for many of our other female participants, Dalia reacts to this othering of her Muslim male relatives as oppressive. She mentions twice that her father, who is an imam, "never imposed anything" on her or her siblings:

Growing up, my father was obviously an imam, but he never imposed anything on us. Like if it was prayer or fasting or the veil, he never imposed anything because he said that at the end of the day, if he was imposing and we were agreeing to that, it's as if he, we, considered that the woman is inferior to men. You know?

Nour, aged twenty-eight, similarly describes a colleague at her public high school, which complicates the question of choice:

I had somebody ask me when I first started wearing hijab [in high school], she knew that my dad played a big role and so she assumed that, she assumed that my dad forced me. And she said, "Why don't you just come to school and then take it off?" I was, like, because even though my dad sort of said to me, "I'd like you to wear it soon,"

I'm not going to disrespect myself, and I'm not going to disrespect my father by coming to school and taking it off. I've made this decision. I'm not going to take it off.

Nour's narrative demonstrates that these figures are not homogenous. Her father influenced her teenaged sartorial choices. She makes clear that although parental respect was significant, the decision was hers. Significantly, almost all our female interviewees felt compelled to dislodge the Imperilled and Patriarchal figures by activating a new set of figures: the Liberated Muslim Woman and the Enlightened Muslim Man, in sometimes overt and other times more subtle ways. Dalia's account, for one, parallels Shryock's (2010: 10) description of fathers, husbands, and brothers as "treat(ing) women as equals, and committed to choice," and women describing themselves as not being the subject of any type of imposition.

Though she sometimes is seen as the victim of the Terrorist, the Imperilled Muslim Woman is also often in the company of the Patriarch, a third figure who is a father, brother, or uncle. The figure of the Patriarch relates to the Imperilled Muslim Woman insofar as he is constructed as residing in Muslim families, with Western families being imagined as having been freed from his influence through the myth of women's equality (see McRobbie 2009; Fine 2010). The myth of women's equality tells a sanitized version of history, ensuring that "there is no trace whatsoever of the battles fought, of the power struggles embarked upon, or of the enduring inequities which still mark out the relations between men and women" (McRobbie 2009: 19).

As with the Terrorist, narratives circulate to construct the Imperilled Muslim Woman as a credible and real figure imagined to represent the majority of Muslim women. We mention three illustrative events briefly. One of the most dramatic and horrific stories in Canada is that of the Shafia "honour killings." On June 30, 2009, the bodies of four women were found in a car submerged in a lock on the Rideau Canal near Kingston, Ontario. They were three sisters: Zainab, aged nineteen; Sahar, aged seventeen; and Geeti, aged thirteen, and Rona Mohammad Amir, their father's first wife. On January 29, 2012, their father, Mohammad Shafia, mother, Tooba Yahya, and older brother, Hamed Shafia, were convicted of first-degree murder for the deaths. The trial judge (cited in Dalton 2012) invoked two figures – the Patriarch and the Imperilled Muslim Woman – in explaining that "the apparent reason behind these cold-blooded, shameful murders was that the four completely innocent victims offended your completely twisted concept of honour ... that has absolutely no place in any civilized society." The hue and cry that surrounded this case – which was widely imagined, including by the trial judge, as belonging to the uncivilized other – ignored the reality of family violence in Canada and the discourse of "desert," or deserving of punishment. This framework is often part of the repertoire of justification by many abusers. By displacing the Shafia murders as honour killings, the pervasiveness of violence against women in Canadian society was effectively ignored and the Imperilled Muslim Woman was highlighted as being uniquely vulnerable to such so-called uncivilized acts (see Beaman 2012b; Y. Jiwani and Hoodfar 2012). Muslim men are therein positioned as uniquely capable of this abuse (see Guénif-Souilamas 2006 and Ewing 2008 for similar characterizations of Muslim male figures in France and Germany).

The power of the Imperilled Muslim Woman figure is such that it dominates the characterization of Muslim women no matter what their comportment, or even their relationship with the Enlightened Muslim Man. Despite Zunera Ishaq's articulate objection to not wearing her niqab during her Canadian citizenship ceremony, which took place in September 2014, and despite her broad smile and twinkling eyes underneath the face-covering garment, Ishaq has been persistently imagined as this figure or, even if she herself is not imperilled, as representative of the dangers of the niqabi-clad woman. A year after the Ishaq case, in June 2015, the *Zero Tolerance for Barbaric Cultural Practices Act* received royal assent from Canada's governor general and included, among several amendments, denial of admission to Canada to permanent and temporary residents who are polygamous and "limiting the defence of provocation so that it would not apply in so-called 'honour' killings and many spousal homicides" (Citizenship and Immigration Canada 2015).[30] In defending this bill, the then immigration and citizenship minister directly tied this initiative to the figure of the Terrorist. The minister (cited in Sanders 2015) stated that Bill S-7 "strengthen[s] the value of citizenship. People take pride in that. They don't want their co-citizens to be terrorists."

Similarly, in this vein of protecting women, at one point during the 2015 federal election campaign the then prime minister promised that if he were re-elected he would create a "barbarian practices" hotline for citizens to report their sightings of such acts. In the midst of the 2015 election campaign, the same minister of citizenship and immigration said, "We need to stand up for *our values* ... We need to do that in citizenship ceremonies. We need to do that to protect women and girls from forced marriage and other barbaric practices" (cited in Powers 2015; emphasis added). Barbaric acts serve as foils for our values. For Ishaq, that she placed herself in dialogue with the Imperilled Muslim Woman was clear in some of her comments to the media in which she explicitly addressed, without prompting, her relationship with both her husband and her father: "I would only say that in my case, it was my personal choice. Nobody has ever forced me," and she has "never been forced to do anything" (CBC News 2015c). An abusive man shadows her and must be constantly disavowed.[31] She too must rely on the Enlightened Muslim Man to try to dislodge the Imperilled Muslim Woman figure.

Discussions of women's agency, particularly that of Muslim women, have been a core focus in the critical literature on Muslims in society.[32] Not only is this emphasis not new, but it also follows a broader pattern in the literature on religious women, which signals the tendency to call into question the ability of conservative religious women to exercise any agency.[33] This is further complicated by a strand of feminism that critiques religious women, who are imagined as both without agency and suffering from false consciousness.[34] Anthropologist Mayanthi L. Fernando (2010) argues that secular assumptions about freedom, authority, choice and obligation preclude public intelligibility of particular kinds of religiosity. Anthropologist Nadia Fadil (2011: 96) similarly highlights the complex agency of the nonveiled Muslim and makes an important observation that has implications beyond Muslim women: "The secular regulatory ideal is not gender neutral, but draws on a particular perspective on the (female) body, which views the disclosure of certain bodily parts (such as the hair and face, the figure) as essential for achieving 'womanhood.'" As we discuss in the next chapter, in these formulations the secular is associated with freedom and the religious with oppression and lack of agency and choice. The religiosity of the Imperilled Muslim Woman figure is similarly unintelligible.

A relational dimension between different figures becomes particularly visible when we pay attention to how women experience this figure. Indeed, in practice, many of our female participants find themselves in defensive positions, in which they end up mobilizing other figures, such as the Enlightened Muslim Man or/and the Liberated Muslim Woman, to dislodge the perception that they are imperilled. In other words, like Dalia, each has to insist that her father, husband, and/or brothers are emancipated, peace-loving Muslims who treat them as equals and do not force them into anything, particularly in their sartorial choices. We develop this point further in our discussion of the Englightened Man and suggest these figures are so entrenched in the everyday lives of our participants that they seem nearly impossible to displace.

The Enlightened Muslim Man

The Enlightened Muslim Man is often invoked to counter the Terrorist and the Patriarch, but also the Pious Muslim and the Foreigner. Our interview data reveal greater specificity, however, in that numerous female participants invoke the figure of the Enlightened Muslim Man in their interviews. He appears in more general discussions of marital and familial relations. He is a calm, measured, thoughtful, and considerate man who provides advice without imposing his point of view. He is invariably committed to ensuring that women in his immediate environment are agentic decision-makers. While his character traits are best understood in relation to and in contrast with these other figures, they are not necessarily explicitly visible in the narratives of our participants. They often act as shadows that help us understand the importance of the Enlightened Muslim Man. Let us turn to two participants to see common ways this figure materializes.

Sheila, a soft-spoken X-ray technician in her late thirties, converted to Islam five years before we met her, after meeting and later marrying Akbar, aged thirty-five. Akbar moved to St. John's sixteen years earlier from Bangladesh to complete a computer science degree. They met through a mutual friend and married quickly. In introducing herself and her background, Sheila carefully ascribes her conservative apparel

and demeanour to her preconversion Catholicism, not to her husband.
She explains:

> Inside my home, my life is pretty much ... I follow my husband when
> it comes to prayer, religion, practices. Outside, I try to follow a very
> conservative lifestyle. But I would, I have done that prior to changing
> [i.e., converting] too. I think the biggest shift would be the social side
> of, you know, being around people of my own community. I always
> cover my hair before entering the mosque or before prayer or, like,
> during fasting. Things like this. Um, or if I think it's appropriate. If I
> think I'm in front of people that I should be covered out of respect,
> I do that. But I haven't quite gotten so comfortable right yet to do it
> everyday. So that's in progress [...]
>
> You have people who are also very set in their minds that, uh,
> because they see a lady dressed very conservative or [wearing] the
> hijab, or if they see them follow their husband in the supermarket
> and they don't say a whole lot, automatically most people from here,
> especially older people, they will assume that this lady is not express-
> ing herself. Therefore she's not expressing herself with letting her hair
> out and undressing, taking off her coat, having short sleeves. People
> think that that's a control thing. For some reason, they get it in their
> minds from media, I guess, a lot of it, uh, that it's a control thing. So
> people get in their mind, like, "Well, uh, Sheila, what time are you
> gonna start covering your head? Is Akbar gonna make you cover your
> head?" That kind of thing. "Is your husband going to do that?" I was,
> like, "My husband has nothing to do with me covering my hair." That
> I told my coworkers, I said, "Don't be surprised if someday I come
> into work and I have my hair all covered!" That will come when I'm
> ready to do that [...] An educated Muslim would never enforce their
> wife. They can educate them.

Sheila does not wear hijab but dresses conservatively. She converted to
Islam after meeting Akbar. In these excerpts she outlines perceptions
about her conservatism that, she says, remain constant in private and
public scenarios, especially among her coworkers, and about her husband's involvement in whether or not she will later be veiled. She invokes

a "good husband" in this dialogue. Owing to her recent conversion, she says that she follows him "when it comes to prayer, religion practices" because he is more familiar with Islam and is a key source of knowledge for her. When they learn she has converted, the other nurses with whom she works wonder when, in addition to changes they note related to her diet and use of break times to pray, she might begin to cover her hair. They make assumptions about the power dynamics within her marriage. In response, Sheila signals Akbar's involvement in her conversion, but at the same time she makes clear that a good husband is not a man she must "follow in the supermarket" but is a spiritual leader. In this example, the Enlightened Muslim Man is not "controlling." He is not curtailing clothing choices or the way she wears her hair. He is educated and, for Sheila, willing to educate. In this way, as Shryock (2010: 10) describes, the Enlightened Muslim Man "treats women as equals, and is committed to choice in matters of hijab wearing (and never advocates the covering of a woman's face)" (see also Razack 2004). Explicit in Sheila's narrative is that she will decide if and when she begins to wear a veil, warning her colleagues, "Don't be surprised [if I come to work veiled]!"

For Samira, a woman in her fifties of Algerian descent, her father embodies the enlightened figure. In describing her life path and the ways she practises, she praises his wisdom that has helped her on several occasions to make important life choices. When we ask her about her religious journey, she explains how her father played a pivotal role in encouraging her to learn about Islam. Her father, she says, grounded her "gentle" understanding of Islam. She shares a particular moment in her life when, as a high school student in a Catholic institution in Algeria, she was faced with pressure from a nun to convert to Catholicism; her father's advice gave her the strength to explore her own religious path. She describes him as "extraordinary," "loving to read," and "always surrounded by books." With his knowledge of the tradition, her father responded by giving her a "lesson" in Islam. Samira says that after that, "I threw myself body and soul [*corps et âme*] into researching what Islam was about."

Samira elegantly points to how her father's advice was based on self-taught knowledge and significant education (akin to the Enlightened Muslim Man). He does not directly answer her question or force her to embrace Islam. Rather, he sends her on her own "independent" learning journey. On multiple occasions in our interview, Samira underscores her independence in choosing to embrace Islam: "There wasn't, there wasn't a wild force at home [forcing her to embrace Islam] [*Y'avait pas, y'avait pas un, force dingue à la maison*] [...] Everyone was free, everyone was free." Samira's portrait of her father is intimately related to the Enlightened Muslim Man figure: he is committed to knowledge, freedom, and self-development. She wanted to make clear that he did not impel her to practise or to be Muslim. In Samira's and Sheila's narratives, the activation of this enlightened masculine figure also serves to activate an equal and free feminine figure, which is how they see themselves. The traits of the Terrorist and Patriarch shadow the construction of this Enlightened Muslim Man. The latter is not irrational, does not resort to violence, and, most importantly, values women's sovereignty and independence.

A number of our female participants insist that their fathers, husbands and/or brothers are emancipated, peace-loving, enlightened Muslims, who treat them as equals and who do not force them into anything, particularly wearing the hijab, or deny them educational or professional opportunities. Again a trap is laid as this socially desired response serves to reify culture talk and, even if inadvertently, (re)produce the figures. Our point is not to dismiss or minimize the role of caring and loving men in our participants' lives, but rather to examine the ways in which women are compelled to present their independence in concert with the men in their lives as non-interfering or as promoting their independence. In other words, the pervasiveness of the Patriarch in public discourse forces the production of a counternarrative, which is symbolized by the Enlightened Muslim Man.

The Foreigner (and the Good Citizen)

Another figure – a racialized foreign other – is visible in our participants' discourses around citizenship. In some cases, this figure, as we saw in the radio show in this chapter's introduction, also takes shape in opposition and/or in relation to and interaction with another figure: the "good" citizen. Many of our participants describe how, despite efforts to participate in and contribute to the life of the polis, they are frequently constructed as others and/or often reminded of the fragility and partiality of their citizenship rights. The cues for this differentiation are often simplistic and visual. Namely, interviewees who wear headscarves and/ or are racialized are much more likely to be excluded from symbolic or political citizenship.

Sometimes, as Faizah describes below, exclusion is subtly reinforced. A thirty-six-year-old business school graduate student who settled alone in Newfoundland more than ten years earlier as a refugee from Iraq, Faizah has invested herself in adapting to Newfoundland culture to master the language and obtain full social membership. She is fun and gregarious and interjects local slang in our conversations. She laughingly shares a side-by-side photo she recently uploaded onto Facebook. On the left, in a photo taken on a trip to Iraq the year before, she wears a black niqab. In contrast, on the right, in a photo taken locally before a social event, she wears a short black dress, high heels, and a fashionable hairstyle. "This is me," she says, laughing at the sharp constrast in the two outfits and contexts.

Faizah describes how she is invariably reminded of her foreigner status by those in her surroundings, beginning with the ubiquitous question, "where are you from?":

> At the beginning it was nice because I knew people were trying to open up, to use this question as an icebreaker. But then, the more I connected to this community, sometimes I was wishing people could just bypass the fact that I was different and not ask me where I was from, because what if I stay here until I was eighty or ninety and die here? Would they still ask me where I was from? Even if I lived more years in Newfoundland than whatever the place I came from? So that was a hard one. And I even had discussions a few times on this question, and they were unpleasant conversations. You get the sense that you will never ever be considered a Newfoundlander. You'll always be an outsider. You have to be born and raised here, and it doesn't matter if a two-year-old passes you by and has no recollection or no actual memory or nothing about Newfoundland, but this person, because they were born and raised here, will be a Newfoundlander. And yet, after ten years of staying here, I will never be that. That was kind of tough, and I didn't like that this was not a possibility. And I

felt that even the people who would say, "Welcome to Newfoundland! We're glad to have you here!" It was nice, but it doesn't necessarily mean that you belong and that you're a true citizen.

As with the narrative of the radio host, there are politics underpinning hospitality. Faizah notes how even a seemingly inconspicuous question – "where are you from?" – is constant and thus activates the spectre of foreignness.

We found that the figures of the Good Citizen and the Foreigner, which emerge in the day-to-day interactions of our participants, are indirectly reinforced within the social imaginary through recent Canadian policy reports and bills (especially Bill 94, in 2010, and Bill 60, in 2013, in Quebec) and in the discussions surrounding these proposed laws. These policy debates influence how interviewees (especially Montreal participants) engage with the Foreigner and the Good Citizen figures and often lead to the activation of other figures such as the Terrorist. These figures are (re)imagined through high-profile news stories. The best known is likely that of Omar Khadr, a Canadian-born Muslim who, at age fifteen, in 2002 was accused and convicted of (among other charges) violating the laws of war for throwing a grenade that killed a US soldier in Afghanistan. Khadr spent ten years of his sentence in the Guantanamo Bay detention centre, during which multiple legal battles (including two Supreme Court of Canada decisions) took place concerning his case. There were questions regarding his confession, which his lawyers said was coerced. One publicly debated matter was whether the Canadian government should advocate for Khadr's repatriation. In 2012, he was transferred to prison in Canada to serve the remainder of his sentence. In May 2015, Khadr, at the age of twenty-eight, was released on bail and began living in Edmonton with his lawyer under court restrictions (CBC News 2015b).[35] The office of the minister of public safety released a statement upon news of Khadr being granted bail: "We are disappointed with today's decision, and regret that a convicted terrorist has been allowed back into Canadian society without having served his full sentence" (CBC News 2015b). Controversy escalated again when, in June 2017, Khadr received a $10.5 million dollar settlement from the Government of Canada, acknowledging the violation of his Charter rights in his wrongful imprisonment and abuse at Guantanamo. Throughout his imprisonment and repatriation, then escalating with the financial settlement, Khadr was constructed as Foreigner, Bad Citizen, and Terrorist.[36]

Among our participants, the Good Citizen and the Foreigner shape the presentation of self as well as frame the perceptions of others in constructing boundaries between "us" and "them." In what follows, we show how it is in the moment when these categories are voluntarily subsumed through interactional processes that culture talk is most powerfully reinforced, particularly in shaping the fields of possible actions of subjects.[37] Let us turn to some narratives to see how the Foreigner and Good Citizen operate.

Shama, a twenty-five-year-old of Iraqi origin, describes the impacts of civil membership exclusion in her life. Shama, who works as a lawyer in a Montreal-based private firm, prides herself on having volunteered with different groups through high school and university. Community engagement plays a central role in her life:

> Because for me, someone who stops me from working at X place [pauses and frowns with frustration]. First, I am not, I am not the type [*je suis pas du genre à*] ... If, for example, the Charter of Secularism goes ahead, I am not the type to [say], "OK, do that and I will move." No. I will fight until the end [...] I've probably paid more taxes than some Quebecers. I get involved. I have given so much of my time in volunteering. I've involved myself so much [*Je me suis tellement impliquée*], you are not going to suddenly tell me that I cannot work in this sector because I have a veil.

Despite her contributions through volunteerism and by paying taxes, Shama explains that wearing the headscarf constrains her ability to fully participate in civic life. In the quotation above, she speaks about how the proposed Quebec Charter of Secularism (under debate when we interviewed her) positioned her outside the realm of full citizenry.[38] While the Charter explicitly linked the wearing of the headscarf and limitations in participating in social life, Shama's employment experiences, including her difficulties in finding a job despite an excellent dossier, evidences how she is identified with the figure of the Foreigner. In one instance, in an interview with a well-known law firm, she was asked about her views on reasonable accommodation. While she remained calm and did rebuke the questioner, she found the question harmful and is convinced it was posed because she is visibly Muslim.

In contrast to the parameters of the Foreigner, Shama sees that publicly visible religiosity and full membership in Québécois public life go hand in hand. This is one of the reasons she encourages her Muslim peers to invest themselves fully in public life. For her, this engagement is central to dislodging this othering process. In her words, "Muslims should participate [in social life], work [more] [*les musulmans devraient s'impliquer, travailler puis*], and get positions because it is at that point that we will be able to have more ... have more arguments." Shama insinuates that to be accorded space in civic life one must participate twice as much as those in more privileged social positions. Like other participants, she has to constantly reiterate her commitment to citizenship to dislodge the Foreigner figure. She feels pressured to be an advocate. In other words, for her and for others, the script of the Good Citizen must be continuously reiterated in order to convincingly locate oneself within that figure, rather than within the Foreigner figure. Passivity means acceptance of this derogatory position.

While some of our participants question and/or unsettle these mechanisms of exclusion, at the same time, not unlike the radio show guests, others reappropriate and reproduce these figures in their own discourse, especially when they position themselves vis-à-vis current policy discussions, such as debates on reasonable accommodation and the allowance of headscarves/niqabs in public spaces. In this context, the figure of the Foreigner commonly takes shape in a distinction between "cultural"/"traditional" practices and "purely religious" practices. The Foreigner is described as following "cultural" practices, which are undesirable and/or non-normative religious practices. A number of our participants identified this figure as a still recent immigrant influenced by an "uncivilized" tradition. Thus, this character is not familiar and/or respectful of Canadian society and its norms, and as a result frequently makes too many unreasonable requests. In this formulation, acceptable "religious" practices, often opposed to "cultural" practices, capture observances that are followed by Canadian

Muslims, and that are compatible with "Canadian culture" (which itself is not readily defined).

The mobilization of the Foreigner and the Good Citizen is subtly evident in Aydin's discussion. Aydin, a twenty-nine-year-old post-doctoral student who emigrated with his parents from Saudi Arabia to the east coast of Canada when he was a child and who currently lives in Montreal, has opinions on this matter and wrote an op-ed on Islamophobia for a Montreal daily newspaper. A radio station subsequently invited him to be a guest on a call-in program, where he was asked by callers what he thought of "niqabis," women who wear face-covering hijabs:

> And so one of the people calls in and asks about the niqab. "What do you think about, what do you think about men who force their wives to wear niqab?" And then the radio host asked me, "Is it more, you know, women who wear the niqab are more pious than women who don't?" [...] It's totally optional for women, and so when those guys asked me that question on the radio, "Women who wear the niqab are more pious?" it's just BS. You can have a niqabi woman who actually, you know, has very low morals and ethics and who doesn't really practise her religion as much as, and as a non-hijabi woman does. It's just, you know, people perceive that niqabis are being so strict and religious. But when it's actually, again, you know, trying to enforce what they got back home, here. Because when she was eleven or twelve or thirteen she chose. And I really mean it, women do choose the niqab for whatever reason, friends or pressure. And she comes here [to Canada], and she wants to continue to wear it. But in doing so, I think she's creating a culture clash because religion doesn't ask you to do that or insists on doing something that culture doesn't really, that culture frowns upon, or Canadian culture at least frowns upon.

For Aydin, the niqab is a dress choice (not a religious obligation) that has more to do with culture and friends or pressure than with appropriate piety. By making this division, he reproduces two spaces: back home, where these practices are the cultural norm, and here, where modernity prevails and where appropriate piety is performed. This distinction is also a highly racialized construct insofar as niqabis, in his view, are necessarily new immigrants – "and she comes here" – despite data that suggest a significant percentage are converts.[39] Thus, the Foreigner is quite visible in his discussion. Aydin invokes a Huntingtonian "culture clash" that activates the Foreigner figure, who is undesirable and triggered in relation to the figure of the Good Citizen.

Distinguishing between reasonable and unreasonable accommodations also activates the Foreigner and Good Citizen figures in our participants' narratives. Here, the Foreigner emerges to frame a person who is dominated by his/her culture and who does not practise "true" Islam in the Canadian context. This person is unreasonable by making too many demands. The figure of the Good Citizen, however, knows how and when to make reasonable requests or refrain from making requests. These figures are thus not only imposed but also mobilized in Aydin's delimitation of proper Islamic practice. Aydin's distinction between what is cultural and what is properly religious also reflects Asad's (1986: 15) definition of orthodoxy through the prism of power and its changing constructive nature.

When we ask Dalia, whom we met earlier, what religious freedom in Quebec means for her, she similarly outlines its limits, but somewhat differently positions undesirable Islam. She draws on what we call a "discourse of demand"[40] to explain what she sees as "excessive" religious practices:

> Live and let live [*Vivre et laisser vivre*]. And so long as no one infringes on the freedom of someone else, it should be fine. Like, for instance, let's say someone wants to pray, but it's not the [right] time to pray because there's a conference. Well, this infringes on the freedom of the conference. So don't pray [*ben, prie pas*]. You can pray after. It's OK. It's allowed. But there are people [*Mais y'a du monde*] that are so egocentric, it's as if they only think about themselves and their religion, their faith, that they'll forget others. No, you have to coexist. There's giving and receiving [*Y a du donner et y a du recevoir*]; there is sharing. You cannot say to everyone, "Well, now, I cannot work this day because, I don't know, because I'm fasting, you know [*t'sais*]? Leave me alone, I am fasting, that's it." No, because even in our [Muslim

majority] countries they work during the day. It's possible, and it's not like it's impossible to reconcile both [...]

We cannot ask too much. You know? Like my sister. She worked in a hospital, and now she works in its administration. There's a patient who came with his wife who was about to give birth, and the resident was a man and even the OB/GYN was a man. And he was imposing, "I want a woman." But there was no woman [doctor]. What do you want? What do you want to do? We can't do anything about it. And it is these types of individuals that denigrate religion, that are responsible for the fact that we are labelled extremists. Because it's true; in a way we are extremists when we think like that.

In Dalia's conference and hospital examples, "coexistence" translates as maintaining workplace efficiency so that the greater good trumps individual religious-related requests. Dalia thus engages in an othering process, where individuals who she calls egocentrics and extremists are contrasted with respectful citizens. Dalia does not directly invoke the Foreigner, but the individual in her example asks too much and is unfamiliar with and unable to respect Canadian norms, which include capitalist productivity.[41] In this delimitation of the Good Citizen, she aims, like Aydin, to delineate proper Islam. Similar to other participants, Dalia describes how reasonable Muslims practise situationally with a *fiqh al-aqalliyyat al-muslima* ("Islamic jurisprudence for minorities") interpretation. For her, egocentric Muslims taint the tradition by being overly demanding; they denigrate true religious practice capably performed by the Good Citizen. Moreover, by using the term extremist, Dalia invokes and traces a linkage with the Terrorist. Both are excluded from the nation in her telling.

The Pious Muslim

Siddra, aged fifty, cares for her three daughters and two sons at home. She self-identifies as Muslim, is of Pakistani origin, and lived in Saudi Arabia and Dubai before relocating with her oil-industry-working husband and their children to St. John's. When we prompt her, in her bright living room, about her religious practices, she twice notes her lack of formal training in Islamic theology and voices concern that she is not providing the "right" answers. Siddra infers that the right answers would better reflect conservative interpretations of the traditions of Islam. Later in the interview, when we ask her our standard concluding question about how the state might address concerns or issues related to being a Muslim in Newfoundland, she becomes very animated: "I want my children to [be able to] walk to the [public] library. If they can walk to McDonald's, they can walk to the library!" While wearing a hijab and engaged in everyday prayer and dietary practices, Siddra's primary concerns are not with these facets of her identity. We begin our consideration of the Pious Muslim with this interview to also consider ways in which qualitative research on Muslims – in both majority and minority contexts – has tended to focus on the Islamic Revival movement and on the most pious.[42]

Indeed, in the course of our interviews, some of our participants acknowledge their lack of formal knowledge about Islam and voice concern that they were not giving the right answers. When asked about particular practices, others preface their comments with the caveat that their ways of practising deviate from the right way. Enthusiasm emerges in Siddra's voice when she speaks about her concerns around a lack of municipal services. If our interview schedule (or questionnaire) had only focused on the most politicized elements of her practice (namely her hijab), her more pressing concerns about getting her children active in the community, which she understands in Islamic terms, would have been missed.

Returning to the radio program with which we began this chapter, we note how the host also frames his question around a predefined normative and orthodox understanding of piety. When he requests a description of the key features of Islam for his listeners, he implicitly asks for elaboration of the five pillars. This framework is usually indexed in overviews of Islam and works well as a quick snapshot of primary forms of practice and belief. The notion of pillars has a theological basis said to stem from the Hadith (the sayings attributed to the Prophet) in which Muhammad describes the foundations of Islam as having been "built upon five."[43] The pillars aid in standardizing and categorizing Muslim knowledge, beliefs, and practices. As anthropologist Robert Hefner (1998: 92) argues, "World-religions-based [approaches are a response to] demands for a unitary profession of faith." We see two other central factors that explain the continued salience of the pillars: first, a scholarly privileging in the field of Islamic studies of the immutability of the text of the Qur'an, a textual emphasis that narrows the possibilities of difference and ignores the everyday and the mundane; and second, a scholarly emphasis on the visual and ritual components of religiosity, perhaps because there is little doubt they reflect "religion."

The circulation of the Pious Muslim figure has also been buttressed in the past decade in Canadian public imaginaries by what has become known as the "Sharia debate," so named because Islamic law became the site of a maelstrom regarding private family law arbitration. The debate took place from 2002 to 2005 in the province of Ontario, where most Muslim Canadians live. At the centre of this controversy was whether faith-based, legally binding private family law arbitration decided by a rabbi, imam, or priest and made available in that province in 1991 (by a Conservative government that sought to privatize a number of programs in a cost-reducing endeavour) should be abolished. As though Islamic law were a uniform instrument, this framing falsely raised a spectre of the stoning of women and capital punishment.[44] In this debate, the Pious Muslim dangerously invoked Sharia in matters of family law in ways that its opponents suggested constituted a Canadian sanction of patriarchal-motivated, religious, irrational punishment. The Islamic Institute of Civil Justice, a group that advocated for Islam-based, faith-based arbitration (as was its legal right), stated that so-called Good Muslims should use their services, which negatively cast piety in aggressive shades in the public eye.[45] We note this debate, which took place over several years, because a uniformly negative and religiously rigid Pious Muslim circulated in the media and in public policy discourse until the law changed and no longer legally sanctioned faith-based arbitration.

The Pious Muslim figure is pervasive. We too replicated this normative perspective on Islam in our reliance on stereotypical conceptions of religiosity as prompts on a handful of occasions. In a few cases, we inadvertently asked about monolithic five-pillar-focused practice when interviews lulled. When interviewees struggled to describe their Muslimness, we asked them about prayer, Ramadan, and charity, drawing simplistically on the pillars. On other occasions, we assumed a certain level of piety when we asked questions about negotiation in their everyday lives, like the example of Caroline to which we will turn next.

In another instance, we inquired about *how* an informant dealt with prayer and food restrictions in their workplace. In so doing, we assumed that these were important issues for that person. This reflex, to return to the pillars, has a number of noteworthy consequences, of which we take up two. First, flexibility and contradictions within practice are more easily obscured. By prompting participants with the pillars, we may have inadvertently encouraged our interviewees to describe religious practice statically, reflecting an Orientalist predisposition to view Islam solely by reference to texts and how they impel the believer. Second, this unintentional emphasis on five-pillars Islam in our interviews may have acted as a subtle form of shaming that served to underpin essentialized characterizations of the Good or Pious Muslim, exacerbating the tendency among participants to identity with more conservative versions (see Mamdani 2004; Jeldtoft 2011: 1144). Put differently, prompting participants with the pillars may have unintentionally constructed less pious versions as unrelated to real Islam.

Our affirmation of the Pious Muslim figure is more visible in our interview with Caroline, a thirty-five-year-old Montreal-based convert. When we asked whether she chose a daycare for her son that serves halal meals, we assumed that this dietary restriction is important to her. In her response, Caroline carefully explains why she and her husband finally opted for a non-halal daycare.[46] She says that halal daycares in her area of the city are rare, and that to place her son in one of these facilities would have involved a long commute, which she did not have the "courage" to do. She feels and expresses her discomfort with their choice, as it deviates from what she imagines she should be doing:

> INTERVIEWER: Your son, is he at daycare? And did you choose a daycare where they offer halal meals? Or how have you managed this? [...]
>
> CAROLINE: So [*Fait que*], we took – we decided to let him eat meat even if it's not halal ... while asking Allah to forgive us because we are lazy and [uneasy laughter] that's it.

In this case, the way in which we framed our question foregrounded religiosity in Caroline's daily life. Like Siddra, she apologetically explained her choices, framing her daycare choice in such a way that given the circumstances, she was unable to follow correct Islam.

Upon first glance, these points may appear negligible. Our interest in quotidian religiosity meant that we asked about and foregrounded religion. Yet, in this discussion we also have aimed to consider how our unscripted follow-up questions shifted our participants' presentation of self to some degree. In other words, despite seeking to adhere to a decidedly discursive approach, researchers, ourselves included, may inadvertently contribute to a pressure towards conservatism or orthodoxy in social scientific interviews and accounts of Muslims. Given our goal of capturing practice as lived – which we aimed to reinforce with our methodology in our interview schedule – this realization is embarrassing.[47] Albeit involuntarily, we too on occasion dramatically limited the parameters of lived Islam in ways that privileged a narrow version of piety.

In making these points, we are not saying that there is a proper object of study (i.e., that practice is necessarily more complex or more worthy of study than text). Rather, we want to consider the pillars' intellectual purchase. This consideration takes place in the midst of two trends we have noted: first, in Islamic studies, the aforementioned focus on the centrality of the Qur'an; and second, in social scientific scholarship after 9/11, the focus on and, therein, reaffirmation, of a pious Muslim archetype. For these reasons, difference and lived experience are flattened. As described in the Introduction, in order to better historicize and politicize individual interpretations, we crafted our interview questions so that they did not overtly accentuate the pillars. Yet, despite this methodological attention, when we began analyzing the transcripts, we were struck by how our own work inadvertently recalled those pillars and thus reproduced and mobilized the figure of the Pious Muslim.

***

As we undertook the interviews that undergird this book, we could not ignore the constant presence of the figures we describe in this chapter. We have therefore sought to consider what the figures produce and elide. The hegemonic power of the figures should be clear. Our participants are forced to engage with them, even if by ignoring them. Their constant presence means that they are continually produced and reproduced. Responding to one figure also inevitably mobilizes others. Thus, at least discursively, interviewees have little leeway to modify the terms of prevalent discourse and to locate themselves outside/beyond those characters. As we will show in Chapters 4 and 5, the figures become more complex and messier in participants' navigation and negotiation of religious factors in their day-to-day lives.

The figures are bolstered by the black-and-white binaries that Mamdani (2004) calls culture talk. We grant that his theory highlights the power dynamics in which all our participants find themselves. But, along with Shyrock's (2010) contribution, we have also critiqued Mamdani's work. The figures do not necessarily work in opposition; some work in tandem. At the same time, though we hold that the figures are produced and reproduced by multiple actors, Muslim and non-Muslim alike, it is important to acknowledge that the impact of the figures is rather different for Muslims, no matter how they adopt that identity (whether atheist or pious). It is in part this impact that we have sought to address.

A current Canadian climate of surveillance, securitization, and circumscription bolsters a constant call for Canadian Muslims to perform "goodness" and to show that they are peaceful and unthreatening in response. Despite often being well-intentioned, attempts to demonstrate that Muslims are peace-loving and benign – whether on a radio program or in a myriad of other circumstances – are damaging. They implicitly bolster the figures we identify here, which offer performative scripts that are difficult to improvise or contradict.

These archetypes and the stereotypes they convey fuel Islamophobia, discrimination, and violence and also beget more subtle damage. Not surprisingly, on this score, many of our interlocutors expressed fatigue, exhaustion, and dismay with the omnipresence and rigidity of the figures. As we saw with Sheila and Dalia, some interiorize the figures so they are activated without mention. Others try to resist them and hope to change the conversation. Sana, an Iraqi-born young woman who wears a hijab, responds to the verbal attack of a stranger in a Montreal convenience store who tells her she does not "deserve" to celebrate International Women's Day. About the incident, Sana says, "It took me by surprise, but it was almost like, like I almost got immune to it. So sometimes I just like laugh it off and shrug my shoulders and walk away. So you don't know what to say at the end." Sana's non-Muslim colleague who was with her at the store at the time of the incident became infuriated with both the mobilization of the figure and Sana's seeming nonresponse. There are clearly scripts attached to these figures that are difficult, as Sana attempted, to avoid.

For her part, Ouria, a thirty-one-year-old reporter, explicitly mentions that she does not want to speak about her hijab or her Muslim identity anymore when asked: "Today I don't feel like speaking about it, to be honest [...] I just don't feel like talking about it. There's been too much talk about it. It is like a subject – like a piece of gum that you're chewing, and there's no sugar left at the end. There's no taste [*Y'a plus de goût*]. It's like, OK, can we move on to something else? Quite simply [*Tout simplement*]." Ouria imagines another way to dislodge the figures. She wants to change the conversation, to discuss nonreligious matters in her daily life. This shift is difficult as she constantly finds herself in situations where the conversation zooms in on her religious identity. Ouria despairs that "no one accepts [*on n'acceptera pas*] that you speak about the economy or the environment or arts and culture. But you can speak about being a Muslim and you stop there." And yet she accepts the challenge and continues to try to displace overplayed conversations, even if her interlocutors do not listen.

In considering the politics of knowledge production, including on a radio talk show program in St. John's, we also see this fatigue as an invitation to shift our gaze as researchers. Indeed, this overemphasis on religious identity is reproduced by academics (see on this point, for instance, Gianni 2005; Kumar 2012; Dessing et al. 2013; Jeldtoft 2013; Turam 2015). We are not saying that there is a right or wrong object of study. Rather, as Ouria asks us to do, we can consider more than her hijab in our analyses. In other words, by attending to these expressions of fatigue and desire and by developing research questions more closely attuned to them, scholars might contribute to recasting the conversation and to displacing the pervasive framework created by the figures, which all reference imagined Muslim identities.

This shift in focus could displace the pervasive framework created by the figures that inhabits our own scholarship and is present in our quotidian lives, including on a local radio program. Perhaps this shift could impact everyday conversation and interaction that disproportionally shape opportunities for Muslim Canadians like Mahmood, Sheila, Dalia, and Ouria.

Knowledge Production and Muslim Canadians' Historical Trajectories   **2**

A Mosque on the Prairies

"Alberta Moslems Build First Canadian Mosque In Edmonton," reads an August 19, 1938, headline on page 10 in the *Globe and Mail* national daily newspaper (see Figure 2.1). The column described the construction of Canada's first mosque, for between 150 and 250 "Mohammedans," in Alberta's capital city. Other historical accounts about the first official mosque in Canada detail that building permits and permissions were initiated by Ms. Hilwie Hamdon,[1] the dynamic president of the city's Ladies' Muslim Society.[2] Hamdon and other members of the society were said to have gone from shop to shop down Jasper Avenue, Edmonton's busy main street, requesting business owners donate to the mosque's construction fund (Al Rashid Mosque n.d.; Hamdani 2007: 6; Dayrit and Milo 2015).[3] The Ladies' Muslim Society was successful. With donations in hand, the next challenge was to employ a local builder who likely would have never seen a mosque in person. As Figure 2.2 suggests, the original Edmonton mosque featured Orthodox Church–style domes, some say influenced by the Ukrainian heritage of the contractor.

Another article, dated December 9, 1938, from the *Edmonton Journal* (see Figure 2.3), announced the "City's Mosque Will Be Opened Sunday Night," attended by the mayors of Edmonton and Hanna (a town approximately three hundred kilometres south of the city) and Abdullah

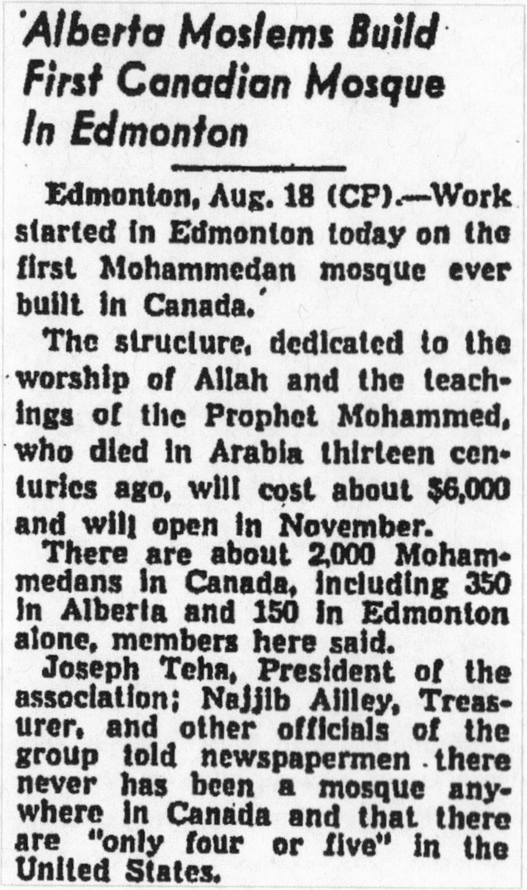

Alberta Moslems Build First Canadian Mosque In Edmonton

Edmonton, Aug. 18 (CP).—Work started in Edmonton today on the first Mohammedan mosque ever built in Canada.

The structure, dedicated to the worship of Allah and the teachings of the Prophet Mohammed, who died in Arabia thirteen centuries ago, will cost about $6,000 and will open in November.

There are about 2,000 Mohammedans in Canada, including 350 in Alberta and 150 in Edmonton alone, members here said.

Joseph Teha, President of the association; Najjib Ailley, Treasurer, and other officials of the group told newspapermen there never has been a mosque anywhere in Canada and that there are "only four or five" in the United States.

Figure 2.1 Newspaper article about the construction of Canada's first mosque in Edmonton, 1938 | *Globe and Mail,* August 19, 1938

Figure 2.2 Al Rashid Mosque, Edmonton, circa 1940. | City of Edmonton Archives A98–55

City's Mosque Will Be Opened Sunday Night

Indian Statesman Will Conduct Special Ceremony

250 TO PARTICIPATE

Edmonton's mosque—the only one in Canada—will be opened formally and officially Sunday by Abdullah Yusuf Ali, Moslem scholar and Indian statesman, with an address at 7:30 p.m., it was announced Friday.

Also participating in the inaugural service will be F. A. Shaker, mayor of Hanna.

Many of the 250 members of the Moslem community in the Edmonton district—most of them are Syrians—are expected to attend the service, and because it is anticipated that the capacity of the mosque will be taxed, invitations to only a few non-Moslems are being issued. The mosque is located at 108 ave. and 102 st.

Figure 2.3 Newspaper article about the opening of the Al Rashid Mosque in Edmonton, 1938 | *Edmonton Journal*, December 9, 1938

Yusuf Ali, a prominent British-Indian Muslim scholar and translator of the Qur'an. Yusuf Ali performed a dedication in "beautiful, precise, eloquent English," according to an account of the event in the same newspaper (cited in Hamdani 2015: 3). This article also noted that most of Al Rashid's members were of Syrian origin and mentions that a large number of non-members were expected to attend the opening. As it was the first mosque built and inaugurated in Canada, the city's officials, residents, and a Toronto-based national newspaper took notice.

These news items from the 1930s offer a glimpse into the initial institutionalization, in Western Canada, of Islam.[4] Our data from Montreal and St. John's include similar kinds of narratives, with the first centre officially opening in the former in the 1950s and in the latter in the 1990s. Today, 95 percent of Canada's Muslims live in urban centres, most in Toronto and Montreal, but also in smaller cities like St. John's, Winnipeg, and Kelowna. But beginning in the second half of the nineteenth century, the vast plains of northern Alberta were a significant arrival point for Arab pioneers. Even if, in comparison with the post-1990s period, few Muslims were settling in Canada in the 1930s, archival records and journalistic accounts evidence a long history of presence and cobuilding. This history, which has been the subject of little scholarly work and few early media accounts, is, in our view, important. For a number of reasons we outline in this chapter, the Muslimness of these nineteenth-century pioneers was neither as remarkable nor as remarked upon as by the turn of the twenty-first century.

One of the aims of this chapter is to introduce a story that differs from the figures lodged in (neo-)Orientalist, (neo)colonialist and Islamophobic representations we described in Chapter 1.[5] To do so, we draw on two stories of settlement. The first is the story of Larry Shaben, whose grandparents migrated in the 1920s to northern Alberta from the Baka'a Valley, in what is now Syria. The second story is a more recent account centring on the journey of Asmaa Ibnouzahir, who migrated from Casablanca, Morocco, to Quebec with her parents and siblings in the 1990s. As we will see, the stories of Shaben (1935–2008) and Ibnouzahir (born in 1980) shed light on the very different times and the social locations in which they were lived and told. They also reflect a constant and a changing story of the reception of Muslims to Canada, who to date have been mostly first-generation immigrants. The story of Shaben and his family unfolded in tandem with the Western settlement and expansion of Muslims in Canada at the beginning of the twentieth century, at a time when Canada grappled with early economic development and nation-building projects. The Ibnouzahir family's settlement seventy years later in Ottawa and then Montreal occurred in a different economic and political moment. In part, Shaben's and Ibnouzahir's stories reflect differing immigration and multicultural policies. Beginning in the 1990s, these policies gave priority to educated migrants without guaranteeing them employment in their field post-migration and accorded the province of Quebec the ability to favour francophone migrants. In addition to these realities, the Ibnouzahir family's experience was also coloured by world events that made their Muslimness the object of public scrutiny. And yet their journeys hold commonalities. Like all new immigrants to Canada, both Shaben's and Ibnouzahir's families navigated and negotiated in the midst of harsh and cold winters. They lived within families where Islam intersects with other political, social, and economical commitments and preoccupations. They both became active members of a variety of communities. They also both wrote and shared parts of their stories (L. Shaben n.d.; Ibnouzahir 2015b).

This chapter thus draws upon Shaben's and Ibnouzahir's narratives to consider the factors that have shaped and impacted the arrival (for those who immigrated) and growth of a heterogeneous religious community, which we then contrast with scholarly accounts of early Muslim immigration and with those Muslim immigrants that have followed post-9/11, before considering the most recent knowledge production on Islam and Muslims in Canada. While there is a pervasive idea in scholarly circles that there is little written on Muslim immigrants in Canada before the 1990s, we found the opposite to be the case, but only because their "Muslimness" was not the centre of inquiry. Moreover, scholarly knowledge production of Muslims in Canada has significantly shifted. Many of the studies about Muslims in Canada before the early 2000s that we uncovered focused on their ethnic backgrounds.[6] Starting in the early 2000s, the social scientific literature began focusing on these same individuals' Muslim identities, at times replicating the Good/Bad binary and other attendant figures we discussed in the previous chapter.[7] While 9/11 heightened these identities, scholarly participation in this reduction is worth noting. Thus, these families' stories also help us to critically assess the scholarship on Muslim Canadians. We suggest that the widely held belief that the literature on Muslims in Canada is scarce might be the result of disciplinary blindness and/or reflect how literature not specifically attending to religious identity is regularly overlooked. The third objective of this chapter is to highlight a notable gap in the literature of empirical research. We argue that research that focuses on the everyday is important as it often tells a different story than research focused on the law and on the media. We ask whether this gap is the result of a post-9/11 focus on demonstrated discrimination and prejudice that, even if inadvertently, contributes to a narrow view of Muslim life in Canada.

Muslims at Canadian Confederation

The Dominion of Canada was founded on July 1, 1867, establishing three British colonies as four provinces: Ontario, Quebec, Nova Scotia, and New Brunswick. Three years later, what is now Alberta was sold to the Dominion by the Hudson's Bay Company.[8] With the first national census in 1871, eleven Muslim men of Lebanese origin were counted in northern Alberta. These men likely worked in the farming industry (Haddad 1977; B. Abu-Laban 1983: 76; Waugh 1994). Records also show the arrival of a Muslim family of Scottish origin, James and Agnes Love and their baby James (the first of eight children), in 1854 (Hamdani 1997, 2007: 4; Zine 2012a: 4). The first known Muslim-born Canadian was their daughter Helen in 1858. A small number of migrants continued to settle on the Prairies so that, by the turn of the twentieth century, closer to 400 Muslims were counted in the national census, most of whom were of Lebanese, Turkish, and Syrian origin (B. Abu-Laban 1983: 76; J.I. Smith 1999).[9] The news story that covered the opening of the Edmonton mosque mentions that most of those in attendance were of Syrian origin.

These early immigrants to Alberta initially established themselves as merchants, bringing goods to fur traders and remote farms. Lac La Biche was particularly significant in linking the Athabaskan region to the Hudson Bay trade route in the north (B. Abu-Laban 1980; McDonough and Hoodfar 2005: 136). The migration motivations of these early settlers were multiple. Most were men with little formal education or English-language fluency who worked as labourers, shopkeepers, and peddlers (Waugh 1980; Eid 2007; Carter 2015). Some young men, of whom some were likely Christian, may also have been fleeing conscription into the Ottoman army (see Lorenz 1998). Ali Abu Shehadi, for one, arrived in Lac La Biche in 1906 with the Klondike as his destination, after having spent time in Paris, Montreal, and Winnipeg.[10] He was too late for the gold rush, so he worked as a travelling merchant. Abu Shehadi changed his name to Alexander Hamilton in 1909.[11] Whether he did so on his own volition or as the result of his encounter with a Canadian immigration officer who struggled to pronounce his name remains unclear (Waugh 1980: 125; Awid 2000: 33; Hamdani 2015: 3). Once in Edmonton, according to his eulogy written and read by his son Sine Chadi, "Ali peddled dry goods from his suitcase. Business was good and they [he and his uncle, Hussein Abouchadi] were able to buy one horse and a buckboard buggy." Alexander or "Ali" found success in Northern Alberta in his many and diverse businesses, which inspired him to found the area's board of trade. Coincidentally, we interviewed Alexander Hamilton's great-nephew, Nadir, a full-time doctoral candidate who works as a voluntary advocate for new immigrant students at Memorial University's campus in St. John's. In a post-interview conversation about the origins of Islam in Canada, Nadir mentioned his familial ties to Alexander Hamilton and shared his cousin's eulogy with us.[12]

Hilwie Hamdon (née Hilwie Taha Jomha), who was mentioned earlier in this chapter as a key fundraiser for the Ladies' Muslim Society that contributed to the construction of the first mosque in Edmonton, migrated to Alberta in 1922 as a sixteen-year-old from the Baka'a Valley in Syria (now Lebanon) with her husband, Ali Hamdon. Hilwie's husband initially traded furs at Fort Chipewyan, one of the province's oldest European settlements that began as a trading post for the North West Company in 1788, before the family relocated to Edmonton "so the children could attend school in the city" (Awid 2010: 42; see also A. Hussain and J.S. Scott 2012). The Hamdons' lives intersected with another family of Syrian-Lebanese origins, the Shabens. The Shabens' settlement in Alberta began with three brothers – Saleem (known as "Big Sam"), Hassan, and Abdul Karim – who journeyed by boat to Ellis

Island in 1903 to flee military service in El Marj Bakka, Syria (now Lebanon). The brothers' story of settlement, the first of four generations to settle, was chronicled by Big Sam's grandson, Larry R. Shaben (n.d.). We will return to Shaben in a moment. After spending four years in the United States, primarily in Cedar Rapids, Iowa, where the first American mosque was said to be built (S. Abu-Laban 1989: 50; historical records show the first mosque in Ross, North Dakota, in 1929), Big Sam returned to Lebanon in 1907 to marry Fatima. Following the birth of their son, Albert Mohamed, they returned to North America, accompanied by Fatima's brother, Mike Shaben.

Like numerous other migrants in this period, Big Sam, Fatima, Mike, and their families then migrated north to work as peddlers before farming in the Howie district north of Brooks, Alberta. In part, they were drawn there by a growing Lebanese community, which included Sam's brother Hassan, who had settled there with his wife and their five children, and his other brother, Abdul Karim. Historian Sarah Carter (2015) details that on Hassan's application for a homestead, the dominion lands agent noted Hassan's country of birth as "Seria," the "middle part." Andrea W. Lorenz (1998: 29) describes Fatima's train trip from Montreal to Edmonton where she encountered "one 1907 blizzard [that] drove the mercury down to 48 degrees below zero" and vast prairies that were still mostly inhabited by Indigenous peoples. Big Sam and Mike travelled north from Cedar Rapids. Despite the considerable distance between the Middle East and Northern Canada, transnational ties among the Shaben family were strong. Big Sam's widowed sister, Amina, and her five-year-old daughter, Rikia, left Lebanon in 1911 to join the brothers and their families on the farm. Signalling the danger of these long ocean crossings, Amina's ship was unexpectedly rerouted to Mexico where, due to the Mexican Civil War, mother and daughter were stranded for four years (Carter 2015). Big Sam and Adbul Karim travelled south and were eventually able to meet them in Laredo, Texas, in 1915. Amina and her daughter Rikia settled in Edmonton, where Rikia attended public school (and went on to marry and have children with Mahmoud Saddy; see Awid 2000: 63–65).[13]

By 1922, Big Sam and Mike left their farming business for the village of Endiang, Alberta, where Big Sam opened a general store and Mike a poolroom. Eventually Mike returned to Lebanon, where he married and had one daughter, who herself immigrated to Edmonton as an adult. Big Sam's son Albert joined the business and renamed the store the Endiang Trading Company. In 1930, Albert married Lila Kazeil, who had grown up on a farm north of Swift Current, Saskatchewan. Albert and Lila had five children, including Lawrence (Larry), born in 1935. Albert's parents, Big Sam and Fatima, later moved their business to Calgary and retired in Edmonton, where Fatima lived until her passing at age ninety-nine. Albert kept the store in Endiang and added a second store in the early 1940s, in Byemoor, Alberta. By 1945, Albert sold both businesses to also move to Edmonton, where he and Lila established two grocery stores. There, according to Albert's son, Larry Shaben (n.d.), they hoped to find "new opportunities including the chance to meet and mix with other Muslim families." In Edmonton, Albert and Lila had a vibrant social life and were active in the local Muslim community. Albert was also a Rotarian and a member of the Edmonton Chamber of Commerce (Awid 2000: 60).

Their son Larry married Alma Saddy of Edmonton, in 1960, and they too had five children. In 1967, the family moved northwest to High Prairie, Alberta, where they purchased a business. In 1975, Shaben was elected to the Alberta legislature as a Conservative member of the legislative assembly (MLA) for Lesser Slave Lake, initially under Peter Lougheed's majority Conservative government and later under Progressive Conservative premier Don Getty. Shaben served in three cabinet portfolios for a total of fifteen years. He was the first Canadian politician to take his oath of office with a Qur'an (Hamdani 2015: 4). Shaben left politics in 1989, and he and Alma returned to Edmonton. By all accounts, Shaben led a remarkable life. Not only the first known Muslim MLA, he was also known because he survived a plane crash in northern Alberta, in October 1984, on his commute home from the legislature when he worked as minister of housing. Shaben attributed his survival to a convict who was one of the four survivors of the crash.[14] After 9/11, Shaben helped create an umbrella organization, the Edmonton Council of Muslim Communities, which included the Al Rashid Mosque. Shaben was appointed as a citizenship judge in 2005 (which he declined) and worked until his death in 2008 (Gerein 2008).

The Hamdon and Shaben families' narratives from northern Alberta capture some of the early arrivals of many young men (rarely accompanied by women and children), likely fleeing military service in Syria. However, this small initial growth was disrupted by the First World War. The Royal Canadian Regiment suggests that twenty-two Muslim men served in the First World War. Private Hasan Amat was one who lost his life in France, in 1917 (at the Battle of Hill 70; see Ensing 2017). Amat was not honoured for this service until one hundred years after his death. In this wartime era, widespread suspicion of potentially disloyal immigrants from "enemy" countries – namely Germany, Austria-Hungary, Turkey, and Bulgaria – led to their classification as "enemy aliens." This governmental categorization signalled the first in a lengthier twentieth-century story of formal governmental exclusion. In 1914 and again in 1939, the Canadian federal government invoked the *War Measures Act*, which meant that these groups were closely monitored and stripped of civil liberties. More than eight thousand so-called enemy aliens were interned as prisoners of war in remote camps across the country.[15] There is some evidence that in this heightened climate of securitization and incarceration a number of Turkish Muslims returned to Turkey (B. Abu-Laban 1983: 76).[16]

The Hamdons' and Shabens' stories of settlement and perseverance in northern Canada reveal encounters with systemic discrimination, but their narratives of adaptation and engaged citizenship also evidence another kind of continuity that focuses on lives lived in the midst of challenging winter weather conditions[17] and trying to cultivate often barren and rock-filled land in the late nineteenth century without training or experience, difficulties shared by immigrants of a range of origins in the Canadian Prairies. While Islam and its institutionalization played a role in their lives, these roles intersected with various other political, social, and economic commitments and preoccupations. It is clear that there were fewer families settling in Canada at the turn of the twentieth century compared to the beginning of the twenty-first century. But chronicling the settlement of the Hamdons and Shabens gives us a glimpse into what life in northern Alberta might have been like for early settlers and illustrates how Muslims have been part of Canadian socioeconomic and political life since before Confederation.

Post–Second World War

A number of nation-building government policies developed alongside the country's geographical expansion and population growth. Some, particularly those related to immigration and legal protections for minority religious groups, significantly impacted the quotidian lives of Muslim Canadians and preceded the reasonable accommodation model we take up in Chapter 4. Namely, as Patricia Kelly (1998: 86) characterizes, federal immigration policy between 1891 and 1962 ensured a racist and discriminatory "White Canada." With evidence and growing awareness of its complicity in discriminatory policies following the Second World War, at a moment that also sought to encourage the presence of more skilled labourers, the Canadian government reoriented its immigration approach. Between 1947 and 1965, therefore, Muslim immigrants represented more diverse countries of origin.

In 1967, Canadian immigration policy focused on a merit-based points system, moving away from a stated preference for British Protestant subjects.[18] The new system thus shifted towards a more "chosen immigration" that was less overtly racialized and Protestant-focused in its stated preferences. It meant that the Muslim population diversified and included Lebanese and Syrians, as well as Indonesians, Moroccans, Palestinians, Egyptians, Iraqis, and Indo-Pakistanis (McDonough 2000: 173). Also, in contrast to early immigrants such as Hilwie Hamdon, who at age sixteen had not had any formal education prior to migrating from Lebanon, post-1967 Muslim immigrants were often highly educated professionals who came to large cities to improve their economic opportunities (J.I. Smith 1999: 52), even as many sought to escape political upheaval (Eliade 1987).

By 1971, the Canadian census counted over thirty-three thousand Muslim Canadians, a substantial growth from the initial eleven one hundred years earlier (see Figure 2.4). Still, this figure reflects only 0.0015 percent of the Canadian population at that time. And these numbers likely do not include individuals like our participant Nadir's great-uncle, "Alexander Hamilton," in Lac La Biche, who may have sought to assimilate on paper and may not have been counted in the census data. Scholars have charted the politics of counting Muslim minorities (Fleischmann and Phalet 2010; Johansen and Spielhaus 2012). Notably,

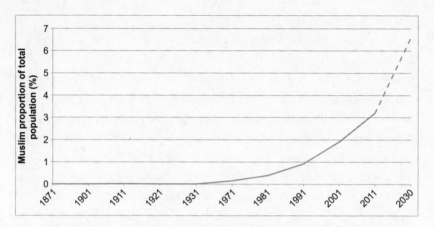

Figure 2.4 Muslims as a proportion of Canada's total population, by year

Source: Baseline national population data from Statistics Canada 2011a. Muslim population statistics from Hamdani 1999; 2001 Muslim population and total population statistics from Statistics Canada 2001; 2011 Muslim population and total population statistics from Statistics Canada 2011b; 2030 projection statistics from Pew Research Center 2011.

the category "Muslim" was listed with its own checkbox for the first time in the 1981 Canadian census,[19] when Muslims numbered approximately a hundred thousand (Bryant 2001: 7), again a substantial leap from a decade earlier, mostly centred in the provinces of Ontario, Quebec, and Alberta (B. Abu-Laban 1983: 79).

These demographics do not distinguish the different schools of Islamic law or different branches of the tradition. Historically and contemporarily, most of the Canadian population have been and remain Sunni. Shi'ias have also been present in Canada since the early part of the twentieth century; they are thought to account for about 15 percent of the national Muslim population.[20] The Canadian Shi'ia population grew, in particular, in the 1970s with migration from troubled areas (McDonough and Hoodfar 2005: 136; Mamodaly and Fakirani 2012).[21] A smaller number of Ahmadis also migrated as refugees in this period.[22] Ismai'ilis have garnered a reputation in Canada for their social activism[23] and involvement in politics.[24] The number of Canadian Sufis is more difficult to determine, largely because of the tendency of Sufi centres to attract "unmosqued" non-Muslims (those who are drawn to some orders' music, art, and spirituality) and because of Sufism's at-times contested location within Islam. Some Sufi centres are associated with Turkish, South Asian, and Iranian ethnic communities (Sharify-Funk and Dickson 2013: 192).

Increased immigration and greater diversity in the backgrounds of Canadian Muslims in these decades were also bolstered by a new federal government policy of "multiculturalism" that was followed by the *Multiculturalism Act*.[25] In theory, the 1971 policy and 1988 act were intended to foster commonality while nurturing cultural group differences. A number of scholars have critiqued these initiatives in practice, noting the policy's silence related to Canada's colonialist roots and Indigenous worldviews, so that, in fact, it promotes racism and exclusion (see Bissoondath 1994; Bannerji 2000; Yegenoglu 2003; Haque 2012: 250–51), a point that we turn to in our later discussion of reasonable accommodation.[26] As a more diverse group of immigrants settled in Canada and the notion of multiculturalism was enshrined, the first sociological analyses of these groups with attention to their religious identities were published. In the midst of this new language of multiculturalism in the 1970s and 1980s, Edmonton's Muslim population grew to almost sixteen thousand, necessitating a larger space than its original mosque. The first Al Rashid Mosque therefore closed and relocated to a municipal historical park in 1982, and a larger structure was built in a new location.[27] The community also financed the first Islamic school in North America, whose popularity encouraged a number of public schools in the city to offer Arabic language instruction (Waugh et al. 2015: 148).

Equally significant in setting a new tone towards immigration and religious minorities in this period was the introduction of the *Canadian Charter of Rights and Freedoms*, in 1982.[28] In theory, the Charter aimed to assure new directions in diversity and the protection of minorities, including religious groups. While some critique these policies, on a whole, as religious studies scholar Sheila McDonough and anthropologist Homa Hoodfar (2005: 133) argue, the sociopolitical climate in this period was largely indifferent to visible Muslimness: "Before the 1980s, Muslims in Canada lived in a society that was largely ignorant of Islam, but generally hospitable." This apathy changed with the Iranian Revolution in 1979. Scholarship and political attention accorded to Muslims also began shifting. Indeed, if in the 1960s and 1970s racialized immigrant communities in Canada were studied through the lenses of race and ethnicity,[29] then the Iranian Revolution (and, later, 9/11) accorded attention to these same individuals' expressions of religiosity.

The 1990s

Despite a recorded presence of Muslims in Canada since the 1870s and despite the social dynamism surrounding the construction of the Al Rashid Mosque in Edmonton in the 1930s, scholarly interest in Muslims in Canada began 120 years later, in the 1990s. This interest is statistically warranted as most Muslims immigrated to Canada in this decade. A 130 percent population increase between 1991 and 2001 (Statistics Canada 2001) is often cited in historical chronologies. In general, due to the previously mentioned changes to the country's immigration policies, arrivals in this decade held more diverse economic backgrounds and had attained higher levels of education.[30] In addition to refugee claims, in his study of Muslims in the early 1990s in Ottawa, religious studies scholar Ahmad F. Yousif (1993: 17) outlines five factors that drew Muslims to the area (in descending order): economic advantages; educational opportunities; political alienation from native countries; family sponsorship; and notions of freedom of faith and expression guaranteed in Canadian law, all of which we heard among our participants. Most of these migrants lived in nuclear families.[31] Also significant in this decade was the 1991 Canada-Quebec Accord that granted Quebec responsibility in its selection of immigrants (Hachimi Alaoui 1997, 2001; Labelle and Rocher 2009).[32] This accord meant that many more Muslims of francophone origin migrated specifically to Quebec (McAndrew 2010: 43).

In the 1990s, we turn to the second individual whose story frames this chapter. The Ibnouzahir family's migration to Canada reflects some of these changes in immigration policies that began in the 1970s. Asmaa Ibnouzahir's family first immigrated to Ottawa from Casablanca, Morocco, in 1983. Ibnouzahir and her older brother were toddlers then. Ibnouzahir's father was a computer scientist educated in France and England, so their immigration was facilitated by the aforementioned points system. This first Canadian experience lasted less than a year. Her father's inability to find employment in his field, her family's weak social network, and the icy winter convinced them to return to Morocco. This difficult first experience reflects, in part, some of the drawbacks of this immigration policy that favours qualified and highly educated immigrants but does not help them secure employment in their fields once in Canada.[33] The family's conundrums resonate with the experiences of a number of our participants when they immigrated to Canada. For example, Ouria, the young journalist, shares in Chapter 4 how her father, a university professor whose immigration was precisely facilitated because of his level of education (PhD) and his fluency in French, was never able to find a comparable job in Quebec.

Ibnouzahir's family gave Canadian migration a second try ten years later, as settling in Canada was a priority for Ibnouzahir's father. According to his daughter, he wanted his children, then teenagers, to have opportunities abroad like he had: "He wanted to offer us the quality of education he had received but without sending us to study alone abroad" (Ibnouzahir 2015b: 27). Montreal was their second point of arrival. Ibnouzahir's parents had hoped that a French-language environment would facilitate their transition.[34] This time, like Shaben's grandfather, Big Sam, after closing his successful business in Casablanca, Ibnouzahir's father set off in 1992 to complete immigration procedures and secure housing before his family joined him. Ibnouzahir, her mother, and now two siblings followed two years later. Settling in Montreal was equally difficult, however, because her father could not find work. Her mother took French language classes, where she made friends and volunteered at a lunchtime drop-in for disadvantaged children (Ibnouzahir 2015b: 38), but it was not easy. As with the Hamdons, the harsh winter vividly marked Ibnouzahir's memories of their first year: "The temperature fell below forty degrees [Celsius] [...] To top it all [le comble], the worst was when someone would say that the weather was beautiful in the middle of January or February [when it was freezing cold]" (2015b: 37). She recalls the difficulties and discriminations she faced attending public school, where she was one of the only visible minorities. Fortunately, she also encountered teachers and fellow students who introduced her to volunteer work and to different sports.

Despite his education, experience, and best efforts, it took Ibnouzahir's father five years to find employment in his field of information technology.

This situation created tension and affected his mental health, an issue for which, she says, he never sought medical intervention.[35] As soon as he began working as an information technology consultant at the CGI headquarters in Montreal (a Quebec-based IT company), the family purchased a home in the suburbs. Their happiness and prosperity were short-lived as her father died of cancer shortly thereafter, a tragedy that significantly punctuated the family's life in Montreal. Ibnouzahir (2015b: 38) explains how she found solace in her studies, in which she describes juggling "a series of acrobatics combining studies, swimming practices, rehearsals for the fashion show, and preparation, with other students, for a national mathematics competition." Ibnouzahir did not wear the hijab until she began university, but her teenage post-migration experience at school and later at CEGEP (Collège d'enseignement général et professionnel), a two-year pre-university general and vocational college that exists in the province of Quebec, echoes the findings of a number of sociological studies regarding the socio-academic experiences of Muslim girls in private Islamic schools in Canada.[36]

In a number of ways, the Ibnouzahirs' experience reflects that of many Muslims who migrated to Canada in the late 1990s. With the points system firmly in place, highly educated individuals from middle- and upper-middle social classes settled primarily in urban areas (McDonough and Hoodfar 2005: 136). By the 2000s, many Muslim Canadians – like most of Canada's immigrant population for that matter – lived in the Greater Toronto Area.[37] Today, there are also significant Muslim populations in the province of Quebec, notably in Montreal (6 percent of the city's population) and in the province of Alberta, in its larger cities of Calgary and Edmonton. There were 1,053,945 Muslims in Canada in 2011 (Statistics Canada 2013) – who made up a little bit more than 2 percent of the national population – and they represented the most ethnically diverse religious minority. The largest Muslim ethnic group was South Asian (Pakistani, Indian, Bangladeshi, Sri Lankan, and, through migration, East African), but there were also significant populations from the Middle East and North Africa and, more recently, from Somalia, the former Soviet Union, and Yugoslavia (Hussain 2004: 361). The Canadian Muslim population includes converts of various backgrounds (Mossière 2011b, 2013), who are difficult to count given how conversion is often private (i.e., not subject to the involvement of religious authorities) and due to the high numbers of Muslims who are "unmosqued" (Flower and Birkett 2014: 3).[38]

The number of Muslims in Canada is expected to triple, to nearly 2.7 million, by 2030, which would constitute 6.6 percent of Canada's total population (Pew Research Center 2011). This steady population growth has translated into greater institutionalization, with the establishment of several Muslim organizations in the 1990s.[39] In this decade, McDonough and Hoodfar (2005: 134) note a general shift from mosque construction to the creation of volunteer associations, which they see as reflecting the vitality and social commitments of Canadian Muslim groups. A. Hussain and J.S. Scott (2012) count more than 250 Islamic organizations in the Greater Toronto Area. One notable example is the volunteer-based Canadian Council of Muslim Women (CCMW),[40] inaugurated by Lila Fahlman (politician, PhD, and recipient of the Order of Canada) in Winnipeg, in 1982, and with whom a number of Canada-based scholars of Islam have collaborated.[41] Shaben and Ibnouzahir were themselves involved in establishing Muslim associations in their respective cities of Edmonton and Montreal (see Ibnouzahir 2015b: 106–13, 196–200), like a number of our participants in both mosque- and ethnic-based groups.

There are numerous studies that have documented the increased immigration of Muslims in the 1990s. We therefore disagree with Aaron Hughes's (2004: 346) observation that most published social scientific work on Muslim Canadians presents "either broad generalizations [about all Muslims] or a plethora of statistics." In fact, there are a significant number of French- and English-language studies on specific Muslim groups, even if initially through the prisms of their ethnic and national backgrounds. Muslim women of different origins have received the greatest amount of attention.[42] For a number of geopolitical reasons, their Muslimness was far more remarkable.

Post-9/11 Currents

A growing population and public presence of Muslims in Canada coupled with world events influenced a significant (and proven) rise in Islamophobia, as discussed in Chapter 1. Ibnouzahir's experience in Montreal relates some of these changes. She explains how after 9/11 her Muslim identity suddenly became the target of constant questions: it shifted from indifference to a gaze *sous les projecteurs* ("in the spotlight"). While her Muslimness up to that point was "shyly" (*de façon timide*) present in her life, she says that post-9/11 scrutiny pushed her to become more reflective about her religiosity and her spiritual path. This curiosity inspired engagement with Montreal Muslim associations, in which she hoped to demystify dominant pejorative images of Islam (Ibnouzahir 2015b: 112). Put simply, Ibnouzahir's Muslimness came under scrutiny, and she felt compelled to respond. Shaben was also involved in community organizations, in Grand Prairie and Edmonton, but in a very different sociopolitical climate, which surely explains why his writing on life growing up Muslim in northern Alberta transmits a different tone.

Not surprisingly, in the 2000s, in the wake of a heightened climate of fear and prejudice, scholars also focused their attention on the impacts of 9/11 for Muslim Canadians.[43] This research has been especially attentive to women's experiences[44] related to the meanings of religious signs and interpretations of Muslim family law. Jasmin Zine's (2001, 2006, 2007, 2008a, 2008b) attention to young hijabi women's experiences in private schools reflects this shift in the literature and is an important addition to scholarship on a group that had, until then, not been analyzed (see also Alvi, Hoodfar, and McDonough 2003, which also reflects this trend). A great deal of this scholarly work in the early 2000s focused on the meanings of the hijab and on "de-veiling," marriage and the *mahr* (dower), forced marriage, polygamy, and divorce in southern Ontario, Montreal, and, more generally, throughout Canada.[45] Following the murders of Aqsa Parvez in 2007 and of women in the Shafia family in 2009 (outlined in Chapter 1), scholars critiqued characterizations of "honour killing" in the media and in the Canadian courts.[46] A recurring Imperilled Muslim Woman narrative, which we addressed in the previous chapter and which is presented in media accounts (see Razack's 2008 critique), has similarly inspired a counter-scholarship discourse that examines rights (Saris and Seedat 2009) and female activists and "empowerment" among Canadian Muslim women (Bullock 2005, 2010, 2017; Hamdani 2007; Marcotte 2010), and has inspired the publication of more autobiographical perspectives.[47]

In addition to these foci on women's experiences, others have examined the impacts of a growing climate of securitization post-9/11 on Muslim men.[48] We introduced the case of Canadian Omar Khadr (born 1986), held at the Guantanamo Bay detention camp for ten years, in the previous chapter.[49] Dawson (2014) considers the radicalization of young Muslim men in the Greater Toronto Area who, following their 2006 anti-terrorism bust (the largest to date in Canada, and bolstered by legislation introduced post-9/11), became known as the "Toronto 18."[50] Beyer (2014) draws on thirty-five interviews with young Muslim men who grew up in Canada from his larger Religion among Immigrant Young Adults in Canada study to consider their experiences of securitization and how "none" is already "too many," and how, even if there is no evidence of wrongdoing, these young men cannot escape suspicion and surveillance. As a counterpoint to common pejorative depictions of young Muslim men, political scientists Katherine Bullock and Paul Nesbitt-Larking (2013; see also Karim 2004; Gova 2015) find that, in spite of the racism and misconceptions about youth in Islam in the media and general public discourse, the twenty Canadian Muslim youth they interviewed showed a strong commitment to Canada and were equally apathetic and highly engaged in Ontarian political processes. With the exception of Katelyn Cassin's (2014) qualitative study of Muslim men in the Canadian Armed Forces,[51] in contrast with the aforementioned work on women, little attention has been granted to Muslim men's lives in the scholarship.

Other public controversies have followed 9/11. In the Canadian context, these include controversies related to so-called Sharia courts in Ontario, from 2004 to 2006, and to a unanimously voted town charter against so-called barbaric cultural practices in Hérouxville, Quebec, in 2007. These cases – the Sharia debate[52] and the reasonable accommodation commission that followed the Hérouxville controversy[53] – spurred commissions and reports and produced formal policy recommendations. Interest in secularism in Quebec has also inspired comparison between the representations of Muslims and Islam in France and in Quebec.[54] In part, this comparison is also implicit in discussions of Quebec's proposed Bill 94, in 2010, restricting full-face veils[55] and the proposed Charter of Secularism, in 2013, and a similar project, Bill 62, introduced in 2016. Related to the full-face veil, other scholars have turned their attention to the precedent-setting *R v N.S.* Supreme Court decision regarding a woman's request to keep her niqab when testifying in a sexual assault trial.[56]

The media has followed and shaped the public consumption of all these controversies. Karim H. Karim (2003, 2009) chronicles discrimination in media portrayals of Muslim Canadians and has worked on a theoretical approach (2012, with Mahmoud Eid), which he calls the "Clash of Ignorance" (see also Arat-Koc 2006). Mohammed Zehiri (2009), Alan Wong (2011), and Rachad Antonius (2013) examine how Québécois daily newspapers misrepresent and sensationalize Muslims, whether through the language used, font size selected, or placement in the newspaper. With the exception of the Canadian Broadcast Corporation's widely syndicated, Zarqa Nawaz–written television series, *Little Mosque on the Prairie* (examined by Sheema Khan 2009; Dakroury 2012; A.B. Anderson and Greifenhagen 2013; A. Hussain 2015), few scholars have examined Islam and popular culture in Canada.[57] One notable response to pejorative media stories has been the recent counternarrative involvement of Canadian Muslim youth on Twitter and YouTube.[58]

In sum, the reader may notice that with the surge of writing post-9/11, much of the academic literature has focused on the negative implications of being a Muslim: wearing a hijab, promoting Sharia, seeking accommodations, enduring surveillance, and sourcing halal foods. Farhat Shahzad (2014: 467), for instance, shows the multitudinous ways the War on Terror and its discourse of fear – which she describes as "racism, Islamophobia, and social control" – affects Canadian university students no matter their religious background. This scholarship rejects an Islamophobic and racialized environment. A number of studies from Canadian Islamic community organizations have also demonstrated significant post-9/11 Islamophobia.[59] These reports also chart depictions in the mainstream media of Muslims as extremists, that hijabis have been especially targeted, and more anecdotal data regarding problems at airports and heightened securitization more generally.[60] The Canadian Islamic Congress, for one, conducted media research from 2000 to 2004 and found anti-Islamic content in the country's eight largest daily newspapers. They found a widespread use of terms like "Muslim extremist" and "Islamic militant" in reporting on conflicts in Muslim-majority countries (Canadian Islamic Congress 2004). In 2002, the Canadian Council of Muslim Women sponsored a research project that also clearly demonstrates the pejorative effects of September 11, 2001, on Muslim Canadian women.[61] There are, in sum, data to support the reality of Islamophobia. Our analysis of the literature, particularly in the first decade after 9/11, evidences how the current global political climate has influenced scholarly literature and policy discourse to prioritize almost exclusively the religious identity of Muslims and its problematic reception in scholars' analyses.[62]

The 2000s: A Scarcity of Studies on the Everyday
Chronicling the significant discrimination experienced by Muslim Canadians is necessary and important, as we have sought to do in the previous chapter. At the same time, however, this attention to proven Islamophobia has, we argue, led scholars to inadvertently focus on Islam and conflict. Policy-makers and the media have similarly produced a functional image of Canadian Muslims as defined by their religion, which is negatively construed.[63] This emphasis overlooks the diversity and complexities of the identities and lives of Canadian Muslims. For instance, note Shaben's active volunteer and political life; one local historian attributes his early success in winning a seat in the Alberta legislature, in 1975, to support from the Indigenous community near Kinuso, Alberta (likely the Swan River First Nation community; Awid 2000: 92). Or consider Ibnouzahir's successful professional and sporting life (which is evidenced in her autobiography), parts of her identity that are often ignored, especially in media accounts of their contributions to society. After finishing a master's degree in nutrition at the University of Montreal, Ibnouzahir became an international humanitarian aid worker and then completed a graduate degree in gender studies at York University in Ontario. Despite these achievements, Ibnouzahir cannot help but notice that when she is invited to speak publicly, conversation invariably centres on her religious identity. Media interviews, for example, often focus on when she wears and removes her hijab.[64] Similarly, a family physician interviewed for this study decided to remove her headscarf at work to avoid her patients'

questions, even if they were mostly innocuous (for further discussion of her case, see Barras, Selby, and Beaman 2016: 104).

In this context, there are a handful of quantitative studies that examine opinions regarding and contexts of Muslim Canadians (Leuprecht and Winn 2011;[65] Kazemipur 2014; Litchmore and Safdar 2016; Reitz, Simon, and Laxer 2017). Moghissi, Rahnema, and Goodman (2009) is the most comprehensive. Its findings are based on a comparison of four communities – Afghans, Iranians, Palestinans, and Pakistanis – in Canada and in their countries of origin.[66] A 2016 Environics poll followed a similar study conducted ten years earlier that examined public opinion and polled on Muslim beliefs and practices. The results, based on telephone interviews with six hundred Muslims, found that second-generation Muslims tended to be more adherent to religious practice than their parents were. Forty-eight percent of the Environic poll's respondents attended mosque weekly, up 7 percent from 2006 (Environics 2016: 17; see also Adams 2009). Other polling data suggest that compared to Muslims in the United Kingdom, Germany, France, and Spain, Canadian Muslims appear more content (CBC News 2007a). This last "good news" story based on quantitative data, however, was gathered prior to debates on the visibility of niqabs and to the new era of securitization that has increasingly problematized the visibility of Islam.

A greater number of qualitative research projects on Muslims in Canada complement this survey data. Here we briefly introduce six scholars who draw on qualitative data. Religious studies scholar Earle Waugh has written a great deal about Muslim practice in general and the lives of Muslims in northern Alberta in particular (e.g., 1994, 2008; Waugh et al. 2015; Waugh and Wannas 2003).[67] Waugh's (2012) work has been attentive to the history of institutionalization and to questions related to religiosity in health care settings. In one chapter, for instance, he examines how Muslims in Edmonton experienced hospice and end-of-life care and what challenges they faced. A second early pioneer in undertaking qualitative work, Jasmin Zine (2008a, 2008b), conducted fieldwork in Ontario Islamic schools. Zine has since expanded to look at Ontarian youth more generally in the post-9/11 era. Her work more generally has been significant in chronicalling Muslim youths' experiences with educational and social institutions.

A third scholar who has undertaken qualitative research is Julie Macfarlane (2012a, 2012b, 2015), whose work on the divorce experiences of Muslims in a number of North American cities, including in southern Ontario – where, the reader will recall, most Muslim Canadians live – has important findings related to Muslim life in Canada more generally. In addition to the hurdles faced by mostly foreign-born Canadian imams, she shows how Sunni schools of law are not points of reference in Muslim women's engagement with *fiqh* (Islamic jurisprudence) at the time of divorce (because of *talaq*, the common unilateral Islamic divorce by the husband, women are more likely to negotiate the terms of divorce). Instead, Macfarlane finds that at the time of religious divorce, Muslims in Ontario most often seek out the most expeditious religious ruling, a phenomenon she and other scholars on Islamic law in Canada have called "imam shopping" (Bunting and Mokhtari 2007; Saris and Potvin 2010; Macfarlane 2012b).[68] We make a similar point in our Introduction, insofar as our participants never emphasized these sectarian identifications in their accounts of daily life. Much like what Macfarlane's study illustrates, at the time of divorce, Muslim Canadians do not appear as concerned with the particularities of Sunni jurisprudence as with simply wanting to get on with it, in an Islamic way. This contextualization may also be evidence of a reliance on *fiqh* for minorities (*fiqh al-aqalliyyat al-muslima*) or the interpretation of jurisprudence with the Muslim minority context in mind.[69]

Religious studies scholar Rubina Ramji (2008a, 2008b, 2013, 2014) has published qualitative-based work on second-generation Muslim youth in Canada, drawing on data from a study of second-generation immigrant youths in three Canadian cities.[70] She categorizes fifty-eight female Muslim participants into (1) Salafists, (2) highly-involved Muslims, (3) moderately-involved Muslims, and (4) nonbelievers. She looks at parental influence, gender relations, dating, faith, role of religious institutions, drinking, smoking, dating, hijab, and the internet and concludes that all young women in the sample constructed their own religious identities and were highly aware of the beliefs of their parents (Ramji 2008a; see also 2008b). Ramji captures a pendulum effect among these youths in that many of the Salafist and highly involved participants are more conservative than their parents, and the moderately involved and nonbelieving participants are often more liberal than their parents. In part reflecting youth culture, her main point is that overall construction and maintenance of Islamic religious identities in Canada is an individual task that is not passively inherited.

Anthropologist of religion Géraldine Mossière (2008, 2011a, 2013) draws on interviews with forty-four Muslim female Québécoise converts to compare converts in contemporary Quebec and France.[71] More than half of her informants were born in Quebec to Québécois parents and could therefore be considered *Québécoises de souche*, or "old stock" francophone Quebeckers. Nearly all of her respondents came from Catholic family backgrounds and had married men who were born into Islam. Mossière (2013: 250) situates these women's conversion experiences within a renewed, alternative model of feminism, which rejects 1970s' feminism "that dominates the public square" in Quebec and is characterized by the prioritization of values upholding notions of community, family, and piety. Mossière astutely shows how Québécoise converts sought to reconcile what they saw as two worlds in the midst of public debates on reasonable accommodation: "Their process of conversion also offers Quebecois women the comfort of ethical and symbolic points of reference that the stigmatisations emerging in the debates on reasonable accommodations have paradoxically reinforced" (250). Mossière's work thus effectively demonstrates the range of challenges and negotiations encountered by Québécoise converts (see also R. Brown 2016b on food practices in Montreal).

A last example of field-based scholarship examining everyday Muslim life in Canada is anthropologist Parin Dossa's work, based in British Columbia. Her work includes a study of elderly Ismai'ili women in British Columbia (Dossa 1994, 2009) and an ethnography of disabled immigrant Muslim women in the Vancouver area (Dossa 2009). Dossa shows the multiple ways her participants are disenfranchised, and it is the only work to date on disabled Muslim Canadians' daily struggles. In her most recent monograph, Dossa (2014) pairs interview data on Muslim women in various locations in Afghanistan with data on Muslim women of Afghan origin in Burnaby, British Columbia. While describing the traumas of war and loss, Dossa presents their everyday experiences of racism in British Columbia and how cooking and food serve as cultural bridges and as coping mechanisms.

So in considering this scholarship on Islam and Muslims in Canada, what do we know about contemporary Canadian Muslim life? We know that Muslims like Alexander Hamilton and Hilwie Hamdon have been part of the Canadian population since before Confederation. We know that most, like Ibnouzahir, arrived in the 1990s. We know they are theologically, religiously, and ethnically diverse. We know that in comparison to non-Muslim Canadians, they are highly educated and underemployed.[72] Poverty rates remain high among both immigrant and non-immigrant Muslims, suggesting that this discrimination is more than just a temporary, recent immigration-related issue.[73] Data show that the global Islamophobic political contexts have seriously affected daily life in Canada, and the level of discrimination that Canadian Muslims face is rising. This climate, as Ibnouzahir explained, has emphasized religious identities. In this book, we interrogate the image of Canadian Muslims created by this focus, and our participants' narratives shed light on the dissonance that exists between these projections and the everyday lives of our participants.

***

This overview of the literature on Muslim Canadians has aimed to make evident the historical trends in their settlement (and, for a small number, their conversion), as well as to chart and analyze their quotidian lives and the different facets of these experiences. To be sure, we have focused on a certain kind of story, one that markedly differs from the stories we told in Chapter 1. Beginning with the construction of the Al Rashid Mosque, we have focused on the early Edmonton community that included Shaben, whose grandparents first migrated to northern Alberta. Shaben's idyllic childhood (and perhaps idealized memories) in Endiang, Alberta, is one example of a Muslim childhood in Canada:

> attending classes in the two room school; skating and playing hockey on the slough at the edge of town; milking Daisy, the family's gentle cow; racing to the community well for drinking water; playing tag at the stockyards near the railway station; having fist fights with the Charkas brothers; occasional trips to the big town of Hanna, and the excitement of rare visits from relatives. (Shaben n.d.)

These vivid pastoral images – of ice skating and a gentle cow – stand in sharp contrast with those of our participants in contemporary Montreal and St. John's, who live in urban centres and have likely never milked their family's "gentle" cow (although, to be fair, we did not ask them). These crystalized childhood scenes that Shaben described do not mention religious practice, perhaps because he wrote them for a generalized audience or because his family did not practise, although their involvement in mosque communities suggests that they did. Perhaps it simply did not cross his mind. We include these details of skating and playing hockey and of fistfights among kids to capture mundane elements we rarely hear about in the quotidian lives of Canadian Muslims. Younger, but equally cosmopolitan and well-spoken, Ibnouzahir shares a different narrative: one of frustration but with hope that she might contribute to shifting the conversation on minorities in Quebec. We excavate these everyday or more mundane narratives to contrast them with scholarship, especially current research that has focused on discrimination and conflict. One of our objectives in this book is to introduce, drawing from our interview data, a parallel narrative that captures both the heterogeneity of Muslim practice and belief and the moments that made up the days of our informants when we interviewed them between 2011 and 2013.

Secularism in Canada   3

The Contents of "Secular Canada"
> I never call it the "holiday party." People call it the holiday party because they want to accommodate everybody, but I'm, like, you know what, it's a Christmas party. We live in a predominantly Christian society. It's a Christmas party.

We met Nour on a December morning at a bustling teaching convention in downtown Montreal. Nour is a talkative and joyful twenty-eight-year-old high school teacher. She was born and grew up in Montreal. Her story, like many others we hear, offers insight into how the lives of our participants are affected by a context in which notions of the secular are contested, constructed, and shaped to frame religion in particular ways. The politics and contestability of how "secular Canada" is lived are exemplified by Nour's experiences of her annual office party and her refusal to call it a holiday party. This examination of the notion of secularism sets up our critique of the reasonable accommodation model in the next chapter.

In part, Nour's comments illustrate her imbrication in a broader reframing of the Christmas party as a holiday party. Some might argue that this transformation meets the pressures of a particular secular imperative, while others might link it more closely to a broader effort to be "inclusive" and "neutral" – echoing the reasonable accommodation discourse – and not necessarily connect it to a secular project. The disjuncture between this narrative of living in a secular society (in which Christmas becomes a holiday)[1] and Nour's observation about living in a predominantly Christian society lays bare our focus in this chapter: the refashioning of Christian practices and festivals as heritage, culture, or, in this instance, as an inclusive holiday. We also consider a comment later in her interview when she relies on a far more fixed meaning of the secular related to teaching her students about sex:

> I have to teach students about contraception. I have to teach them about safe sex. I don't believe in sex before marriage, but I don't let my beliefs ... I don't tell my kids, "Oh, you have to be celibate." I don't do that. So I have never, ever let that come in my ... So if someone were to say, "Just because I chose to cover my head I'm" ... because that's what the implication is. You know you're, *you have to be secular.* But why can't you teach in a secular setting and then have your own personal belief? (our emphasis)

We will return to the twinning of secular and sexual values that Nour describes here.

The exact contents of the secular are, of course, a matter of somewhat heated scholarly debate (e.g., Connolly 2000; Asad 2003; Jakobsen and Pellegrini 2004; Agrama 2012; Berlinerblau, Fainberg, and Nou 2014). Even those who position it as a socially constructed concept vacillate between a more fluid and a more fixed understanding. For our participants, the contents of the secular constitute much more than an academic debate. They are constrained, and occasionally enabled, by the various versions of the secular that circulate through public life. In this chapter, we attend to the ways that these constructions of the secular weave through their narratives as measures of their comportment, assumptions about their religiosity, and assessments of their ability to engage in and be full members of the social world. We see the secular as a container whose constitutive elements pivot in "cunning" ways (Fernando 2014a: 687). Above, Nour describes an equation of her headscarf with an inability to teach the entirety of the sex education curriculum. Her account relies on a fixed conceptualization of the secular, placing herself both within it and outside it simultaneously as she laments, "Why can't you teach in a secular setting and then have your own personal belief?" Her wearing of the hijab places her, in the view of some parents, students, and school administrators, outside the secular and the neutral. This placement constructs a divide between her as religious and them as secular. But, as we will see, this forced distinction between her so-called religious and secular selves does not map on to how she navigates these dual duties as teacher and religious believer.[2] She sees the secular basis of the high school as a protection from such presumptions related to her religious beliefs, where the secular and the religious are decoupled (cf. Knott 2013). Importantly, though, in Nour's employment situation and in her telling of it, the construction of "us" as secular remains unchallenged. But the holiday party, as Nour describes, is Christmas by another name.[3] Nour thus questions the unstated privilege accorded to mainstream Christianity in her secular workplace. She is not fooled by a name change to her employer's annual staff party that purports to reflect inclusiveness.

Nour's is one of many voices to identify the construction of particular practices as secular, most especially around the celebration of Christmas. The pervasiveness of the holiday party evidences the ways in which secularism is, in fact, imbued with a tradition of Christianity that is deeply embedded in Canadian society, even for those who do not experience the party as religious. This annual tradition subtly demarcates, locates, and shapes the lives of our participants. We begin this chapter with Nour's workplace experiences, as they open a window on the Christian normativity of the holiday party and offer an opportunity to explore the ordering mechanisms of the secular, which, as we discuss below, shape the everyday lives of our participants. Nour astutely exposes the positioning of certain forms of religiosity (i.e., her hijab) as visible and problematic, while others (i.e., religion in the Christmas party) remain invisible and normative.

In what follows, rather than approaching secularism as a fixed concept, we follow political scientist Elizabeth Shakman Hurd's (2012: 955) suggestion and understand it as "a contingent series of legal and political claims and projects that are deeply implicated in the definition and management of religion." We are interested in exploring how formulations of secularism in the Canadian context, and more particularly in the lives of our participants, work to dynamically delimit the place and shape of religiosity and affirm Christianity's embeddedness. In some ways this majoritarian religion is rendered invisible. Its rituals, sights, and sounds are part of "our" heritage. They are imagined as neutral, inclusive, universal, and, encompassing all of these features, as secular. Entangled in the secular are shifting notions about what is "private" and what is "public," and what is a concomitant normative stance about both. The power in this equation lies in determining where the line is drawn between what should be private and what should be permitted in the public sphere.[4] More broadly, key conceptual touchstones in descriptions of the contents of the secular include neutrality, values such as gender equality, and, always in the background, religion.

A number of scholars have called into question the secularization or extraction of religiosity from the public sphere.[5] Others have more explicitly explored the undergirding politics of such stories, particularly their impact on the governance of some religious practices and beliefs over others (e.g., Hurd 2012; Mahmood 2015). Others have pointed to the imbroglio between Christianity and secularism, including in the regulation of the interactions between religious practices and sexual behaviours (e.g., Jakobsen and Pellegrini 2004; J.W. Scott 2007, 2011; Fadil 2009, 2011; Cady and Fessenden 2013; Hurd 2013). The variability of the secular is nicely captured with the notion of "establishment," to use American language. Establishment is everywhere (Sullivan and Beaman 2013). The question is: What are its contours in any given context? Mapping the boundaries of these power structures helps us better see who and what are excluded.

The reader may wonder why we begin by mapping out these theoretical frameworks. We suggest that these theoretically driven analyses are important. They tell us a great deal about the political systems at work, the coconstructed relationships between secularism and religion, and the historical conditions that have shaped and promoted these articulations of the secular. In our examination of Canadian secular discourses, however, we are more interested in turning to how the secular maps on to how people live and how varieties of the secular order everyday life. How do Canadian Muslims navigate and negotiate this environment?

How do attempts to define and locate religions impact the lives of our participants? Most of our interviewees, like Nour, do not experience Canada as religiously neutral. Rather, they encounter and live within a country they recognize as intrinsically Christian. As we will see, the issue is not whether non-Muslims celebrate Christmas as Christians, but how many of our participants experience it as such.

Our interlocutors' stories reveal that it is the lack of acknowledgment of blurred boundaries and the related silent privileging of Christianity that are experienced as problematic. Indeed, their experiences show the prevalence of the idea that Christianity has been successfully privatized, while Islam, in contrast, is imagined as public, non-neutral, and, therefore, available for commentary, adjudication, and regulation. As we will see, our participants' narratives capture innumerable moments in which the remarkable stability of this story of the continued structuring power of Christianity is evidenced. Acknowledging this reality can help unravel not only what types of class, race, and gender power structure and political climates these delineations protect, but also under which circumstances these boundaries are made "dormant" or identified as non-issues (see Knott 2010a, 2010b). We therefore aim to look at the story of secularism in Canada from the vantage point of these narratives.

To consider how versions of the secular parable are deployed in particular circumstances and emerge in the lives of our participants, we have chosen to focus on three structuring elements we saw emerge in their narratives of everyday life: time, space, and norms of social interaction. More specifically, we explore how the interplay between the invisibility of Christianity and the visibility of Islam, often couched in terms of the language of public and private, emerges when participants negotiate Christmas, prayer, and social interactions. Again, these sites tell us something about the values and power structures laden in these arenas.

Time: The Holiday Party and the (In)visibility of Christianity

At Heritage Canada, the word "Christmas" is taboo. They use the expression "winter solstice" as if druid culture was part of Canadian "heritage"! [...] We'll remember the memorable decision by the Montreal administration in 2002 to rename [*rebaptisé*] the

> Christmas tree in Jacques-Cartier square the "tree of life" [*arbre de vie*].
>
> – Lysiane Gagnon, 2006 [our translation]

Christmas was not a theme that we had considered when developing our interview schedule, yet it arose in almost all of our conversations.[6] It was brought up in discussions around negotiations of religion in the workplace, in daycares and schools, at university, and/ or with society in general. This holiday is omnipresent in the month of December across Canada. Regardless of whether the holiday is publicly funded, it involves Christmas decorations, statutory holidays, parties, carols, and greetings. The holiday's presence stands in sharp contrast to attempts to downplay it in Canadian society, like the switch in language from Christmas tree to "tree of life" in downtown Montreal. The narratives that follow underscore paradoxes around Christmas, particularly the purported extraction of its Christian origins to reflect our culture. All our employed participants – within varied workplaces – had some experience with the ubiquitous Christmas party as a festive social gathering that typically takes place before the winter school break and statutory holiday. Christmas is thus a complex site of navigation and negotiation.

Like Nour, who asserted that it's a *Christmas* party (our emphasis), several of our participants considered Christmas to be an elephant in the room. Sara, aged forty, who is a researcher, mother of three, and a convert to Islam who immigrated to Canada in the late 1990s from Eastern Europe, chooses to address the elephant more formally. She describes how she responded to her university's holiday greeting sent to students, faculty, and staff:

> The distance-learning department, every year around Christmastime, they used to send a postcard, like, wishing "Happy Holidays." Many Canadians, they think that when they switch from "Merry Christmas" to "Happy Holidays," they embrace all cultures and everything. So I replied to them. I sent them an email. I replied to them that I really appreciate that, you know, they send me this nice postcard, but my religious holidays passed several months ago. And if they really want to be, like, accommodating, you know, and it's kind of easy to find

in the calendar when, you know, Sikhs have holidays and when Hindus have holidays and when Muslims have holidays. And then they can, they don't need to send postcards to people. They can just post, you know, on the university website that "Happy Holidays to all our Sikh students," you know, or "to all our Muslim students" or "to all our Muslim employees."

In her engagement with this university office, Sara seeks to make evident the underlying Christian normativity laden in the university's once-a-year greeting. She acknowledges the thoughtfulness of the distance-learning department and then tackles the illogicality of its gesture. For Sara, Christmas is first and foremost a religious holiday, a dimension that does not vanish by "switch[ing] from 'Merry Christmas' to 'Happy Holidays.'" By comparing Christmas with Sikh, Hindu, and Muslim holidays, Sara highlights the message's timing as explicitly Christian. Her unease with attempts to replace Christmas with Holiday is due to the department's (unsuccessful) attempt to evacuate its Christian dimensions to celebrate a cultural and commercial holiday. She suggests either a broadening to include other religious holiday reminders or eliminating the institutionally sponsored mailout altogether. For her, the holidays are not a part of Canadian or university cultures to which she belongs. Sara did not receive a reply to her email. Her experience resonates with another participant's efforts to push her university colleagues to recognize the Christianness of Christmas decorations and rituals in her supposedly secular workplace. Ifra, a forty-two-year-old woman of Pakistani descent born in Ontario, explains her approach with her non-Muslim work colleagues: "I don't do it in a way that's saying, you know, 'Thou shall not celebrate Christmas,' but, but I do, I do remind people [about the pervasiveness of Christian symbols at the secular office]."

The multifaceted and multisited nature of Christmas relays its cultural ubiquity. While our participants identify Christianity in the public realm through Christmas, they also emphasize that this presence is not problematic per se. Generally, appropriate food and drink options are of greater concern than the visibly Christian dimension of the celebrations. In other words, in many cases, Muslim identities and the celebration of Christmas, including its Christian dimensions, are not lived as mutually exclusive or as a source of conflict. Ramzi, aged twenty-three and an X-ray technician, reflects on his use of Christmas greetings, which he conveys to patients whom he sees in December. He explains that he does not see this gesture as being a contradiction with his identity as a Muslim:

> RAMZI: [Christmas] does come up [with my coworkers]. People expect you to go to dinners and stuff like that, but I'm not really involved in that kind of aspect. If they ask me, I'm not interested, and then we leave it at that. But certain people are really pushing it [alcohol]. I just say, "Listen, I'm a Muslim, and I don't practise that." But you be nice and you be kind. And we still see a lot of patients during December time. And people say [to me], "How can you tell people to have a Merry Christmas?" It's just a greeting, all right! I say that greeting at times and I say, "I hope you have a nice Christmas and that your family's together. I'm going to spend my holiday with my family." People have different perceptions, once again, and I don't find harm in conveying greetings.
>
> INTERVIEWER: You interpret Christmas as your own family gathering?
>
> RAMZI: Exactly. People can interpret that in many ways. So that's how I do it.

Ramzi's comments astutely capture how Christmas can be interpreted "in many ways," including spending time off work with family like he does.

Dalia, a thirty-two-year-old student who migrated to Montreal from Lebanon when she was an infant and grew up in the province, describes how Christmas has shaped her identity as a Québécois Muslim. Dalia finds recent attempts to extract Christianity from the holidays deeply frustrating:

> They want to take off the crucifix from the Assemblée Nationale [National Assembly]. Why do you wanna do that? Quebec is Catholic. We know that, and we're OK with that. And it's annoying when they say, "Oh, it's the Muslims that wanna take it [the crucifix] off." We don't wanna take anything off! Or, that they banned Christmas songs in school. It's not our fault they wanna ban them. We don't! I grew up learning *Joyeux Noël* [Merry Christmas] and all the songs. I still

remember them when they come on the radio. Like, I'm sorry, we can have both of those, the best of both worlds. Like, growing up my parents told me, "Well, this is, you shouldn't do this; it's not in our customs." Like we didn't choose to celebrate Christmas, but we knew what Christmas was. We didn't have a Christmas tree, but we knew what it was [...] Like, I'm sorry, I'm OK with singing *Joyeux Noël* [Merry Christmas]. I don't care, you know.

Like Dalia, several of our participants stress how Christmas, especially when they have been raised in Canada, has become part and parcel of who they are. Dalia's "best of both worlds" comment demonstrates a fluid, nonexclusive or nonparticularist approach that embraces "both/and" and that we frequently encountered among our participants. This fluidity is evidenced across modes of practice and belief. The singing of Christmas carols, for instance, carries an emotional dimension that for some reminds them of their childhood and of December festivities. Nour, the high school teacher we met earlier, describes her own nostalgia: "For me, and I know I can speak for my siblings as well, we love December. Montreal is a different place in December [with] Christmas. When you grow up in the West, Christmastime becomes a part of your identity [...] I knew all the Christmas carols growing up ... It's part of your identity as a Montrealer." Dalia appreciates the *arbre de Noël* (Christmas tree) in Jacques-Cartier Square at the head of the Old Port in Montreal. In fact, Dalia's descriptions, as well as Nour's and Ramzi's comments, seem to be constructed as responses to a preconceived image of Muslims, whereby they are imagined as being disturbed by the presence of Christianity in the public realm. Our ninety participants are not. But Christmas shapes and situates their identities as students, coworkers, neighbours, parents, and children living in Canada. This both/and approach also belies the overmobilized paradigms that reify a conflictual framework within which the everyday lives of Muslims seem to be understood (see Razack 2008; Jouili 2009, 2015; Göle 2015).[7]

Our interlocutors do negotiate aspects of the holidays. They do so often in ongoing ways. Ramzi, for one, explains the balance he crafted and is comfortable with. On the one hand, he does not attend Christmas parties hosted by coworkers because he does not "practise that [attending

Christmas parties and drinking alcohol]." On the other hand, he wishes his clients, "Merry Christmas." For him, it conveys his wish that his patients spend this holiday season with their family, like he will. He thus focuses on the shared dimension of this holiday, which for him is spending time with family rather than on theological differences.

Tobias, aged seventy-one, who first immigrated to Toronto with his wife in 1976, narrates how he organized his government office's holiday party. His description captures some of the tensions between the notion that we live in a secular society and then spend most of the month of December celebrating Christmas, even if the festivities are devoid of theology. Tobias, a now retired government manager, did not ask whether his employees celebrate Christmas and/or whether they are Christian. Rather, he identified Christmas as a moment when people greet each other and share a drink or two to celebrate. In other words, for him this period of the year has nothing to do with the birth of Christ. It is a festive party. Like Ramzi, he is not bothered by wishing others a Merry Christmas. These beliefs were enacted in how, before his retirement, he arranged his workplace's festivities:

> TOBIAS: Around Christmastime, I used to tell my secretary to buy it – rum, whiskey, wine – and put it in the boardroom. So anybody who comes to say "Merry Christmas" to me, I say, "OK, have a drink." Because my staff, at the end of the day around Christmastime, they'd [want to] have a drink.
>
> INTERVIEWER: So you were actually facilitating.
>
> TOBIAS: So I, instead of lecturing everybody, I'd say, "OK, instead of you guys hiding and not enjoying Christmas season, I will buy it on government expense." I have an entertainment allowance, so I said I would buy it [alcohol] from the department. So I told my secretary, one of my staff, one of the directory, "OK, I'm making you in charge of this. You order whatever you guys need. Anybody that comes from outside, from other departments, to greet us, offer them a drink."
>
> INTERVIEWER: So it sounds like you were able to kind of move between all of these ...
>
> TOBIAS: So I would be there and sit with them. And you can have a drink, and I'll have a Coke or something and that's fine.

For him, the Christmas party was a social moment. Tobias adds that he did not feel pressure to facilitate the drinking of alcohol in the workplace for acceptance or for promotion. But at the same time, he did not want to be perceived as uptight or unapproachable by his staff. He also seems amused by the situation when he tells us this story. Alcohol may not be theologically linked to the birth of Christ but is a part of office culture. "My staff, at the end of the day around Christmas time, they'd [want to] have a drink." He was careful not to purchase alcohol or partake in drinking it himself but facilitated what he imagines as a celebratory ambiance within the cultural traditions of his staff, including greeting each other and sharing a celebratory drink offered by his office.

Sabrina, aged twenty-seven, an outspoken and gregarious codirector of a provincial government–funded centre, takes a different approach. She also organized and attended her office Christmas party. Yet, she explains how she laboured to organize an appropriate gathering that mitigated her discomfort with alcohol and ensured her employees felt the annual party was celebrated. By organizing a family friendly laser tag event, she believes that she came up with an arrangement that offered everyone a relaxing and rewarding moment:

> Nobody needs to go and get loaded drunk at a staff party. It's better for us to go out and play laser tag for two hours and have a pizza. And then people can bring spouses and their kids, and it's more, it's fun! Who wants to look at just the people that they work with all day long? I don't like half of them [laughs]. And I'm, not that I don't like them, but I wouldn't choose to spend time with them. You know? So if I'm drunk, I mean, who knows what I'll [laughs] ... Can you imagine what I might say? So, I've been really lucky [to be able to organize it].

Sabrina appreciates that her managerial position allowed her to choose the location and the terms of the annual party, and she welcomed the end results.[8] She recognizes that her ability to do so would have been more limited if she were not in her position.[9] Sabrina's approach to the holiday party acknowledges the tangible presence of Christianity in the workplace calendar but also shows that some of the party's elements could be adjusted to ensure that it was open to a greater number of people.

This delimitation is visible, as well, in the line that Nour draws: she does not personally celebrate the holiday at home. She does not put up a Christmas tree with her family. She does, however, help organize the Christmas staff party for her school. The year before, she had suggested her uncle's restaurant, where there was, she makes sure to mention, a tree to accommodate its patrons: "And so it's a little bit ironic that they're having a Christmas party at a, at a Pakistani restaurant owned by a Muslim. But in that restaurant there's a Christmas tree because they're clients. They're accommodating to their clientele." Nour's description exemplifies a broader reappropriation among participants of a public/private binary to help them organize and navigate their participation. While they take part in the Christmas festivities in their public work lives, they do not celebrate it in their private family lives. They thus maintain these binaries while at the same time they question the neutral/irreligious characteristic often associated with the public realm.

We heard dozens of other Christmas narratives. Christmas occupies a significant amount of time and energy in the lives of the majority of our participants. It is a site of complex negotiations, even for those for whom it is a festive time of the year or for those who reject it. The holiday party moniker in particular frames and justifies the public presence of this event. Significantly, it also shields it from the secular's scrutiny of the religious, perhaps because images of Santa, not Jesus, decorate hallways and because the term is constructed as inclusive and neutral. Recall Hurd's (2012: 955) observation on the workings of secularism as legal and political projects implicated in defining religion. In this vein, we see Christmas as an example *par excellence* of how the secular influences the everyday lives of our participants: this holiday season is a highly charged site on which power dynamics over its meaning and symbols both play out and are enacted in changing and contingent ways.

Prayer Space and the Discourse of Request

In this passage, Aadil, a medical doctor, aged fifty-two, describes how he negotiated prayer space at work:

> I was looking [for] somewhere in the lab, and then I found a small area, which is just a store for slide microscopes. And I was praying.

It's less than five minutes when I want. And the people they, they said, "This guy is doing something!" [...] They [his colleagues] spoke to one Iraqi-originally doctor. They told her that, "We notice this guy going in this room for five minutes. We don't know what he is doing, but we are suspecting something wrong [in what] he is doing." And then one of the guys he came in, and I was prostrated on the ground. And he opened the door on my head, because the room is very small. It is one by two metres. It's very, very small. Just enough to, you know, to stand and to pray. And then they realized I was praying and not doing something wrong. Later, I went, I went to the lab director at that time, and I told them, "If you can give me access to the lunchroom, there is the downstairs, uh, the basement." And I told him that I am using it just to go for prayer. And there was a big argument over why he is needing this, why he's needing access. I said, "Come on, guys. I need it just to pray. Not more, not anything more." The same thing when I was resident in the health sciences. It was very difficult for me because there's no specific place to pray. Yeah. But when I became a staff now, with my room I can close the door and I can pray.

In our conversation, Aadil explains that when a fellow doctor opened the door and hit his head, the colleague "realized I was praying and not doing something wrong." Aadil's tone makes clear that he did not feel physically or emotionally comfortable using this "very, very small" space. The incident took place in Vancouver, where he completed his residency, before moving east, but is one that resonates with many of our participants. As we will see, Aadil's experience illustrates a web of social and power relations as well as what we see as a panoptic regulation of prayer, in this case, in a public hospital. We also locate Aadil's narrative in a broader discussion about prayer space whose dimensions are often circumscribed by controversial situations reported by the media.[10] Indeed, in what follows, we see these prayer-as-problem narratives as forming a part of a broader conversation that includes reports of religious freedom complaints with provincial human rights tribunals in which Muslims are described as asking institutions to accommodate their religious practices and make available, among other requests, rooms reserved for Islamic prayer.[11] And yet, as the reader will come to see from our discussion later in the chapter, some of our participants do ask for prayer spaces, while many others in their quotidian lives actually choose not to engage in a formal negotiation, but rather to work out informally questions around prayer spaces for themselves and with others.

In conceptualizing space, we draw on the work of a number of theorists who observe how space is socially constructed through social relations and interactions (Stringer 2013: 38, see also J.Z. Smith 1987; Massey 1993; Knott 2009, 2010a). Martin Stringer's (2013) observation has resonated for us in thinking about the centrality of space in discussions of everyday life. The social relations described by our participants are embedded in and contribute to the constitution of space and, more specifically, to religious spaces, and, even more particularly, to Muslim spaces (see also Metcalf 1996). Aadil's story reflects a negotiated and often flexible and pragmatic approach to prayer, which, we argue, remains largely absent from much academic literature and most public discussions about prayer. The second story, Hassan's, teases out our concern with what we call the *discourse of request*. The third story, of Akeem, is a bit different, though it also relies on the relational aspect of space. It is more firmly located in the organizing impulses of the secular in the spatial location of the religious. Once located and circumscribed, the religious is better monitored, regulated, and governed. Last, part and parcel of the constitution of the religious in this instance are shifting notions of the public and the private. Prayer spaces, whether in one's own office, a shared or common space, or in a mosque locate the religious and render it open to scrutiny through a panoptic-like gaze.

Scholars discussing *salat*, Islamic prayer, in particular in the European context, have also highlighted the public and visible dimensions accorded to the practice and have often approached prayer as a source of tension in the public realm and as an example of a transgression of secular rules, which imagine religion as private (Jouili 2009, 2015; Göle 2010).[12] Sociologist Nilüfer Göle (2015), for one, examines "everyday" European Muslims through controversies, which, perhaps inadvertently, reposition them in sites of conflict only. In a similar vein, in her work on Muslims in contemporary France and Germany, Jeanette Jouili (2009: 458) shows how prayer can oscillate from a visible to an invisible practice, attributing this oscillation to how a space is claimed. She explains that the act of claiming renders the practice visible in the public realm and can be, in some cases, avoided to prevent conflict.[13]

Jouili's (2009: 458) last point on "claim-making" is important, particularly in our discussion, for how it mirrors a common assumption laden in the reasonable accommodation model: it reflects a discourse of request that is increasingly associated with religious minorities and with Muslims in particular (see Barras 2016). Religious minorities are expected to request religious accommodations (including, as we see here, for prayer spaces), thereby making their religion public, visible, and, significantly, open to scrutiny. This discourse is powerful in the Canadian context given the emphasis on the legal notion of reasonable accommodation that carries the idea that someone asks for an accommodation or for an adjustment of the norm when she considers that she is being discriminated by this norm.

Let us turn to Hassan, a sociable young man who was born and raised in Montreal. His story of arbitrating a fellow employee's prayer request allows us to critique the Canadian reasonable accommodation discourse, which we see as rendering Muslimness visible and the object of ongoing scrutiny. In this passage, we focus on his unofficial designation as spokesperson for Islam at his job in the human resources (HR) department of a crown corporation:

> [At my job] they'll [my colleagues] come and ask me a question. And they know that I'm Muslim [...] I've become the spokesperson of religion [*le porte-parole de la religion*]! I assume that in the future, depending on case, they'll come to see me, and I won't have a problem in providing them answers. If I'm not sure of something, well, it can happen, if I'm not sure of something, I'll go ask. I'll have the answer from the imam the next day. You know [*t'sais*], I am still very connected in the mosque close to our house. I'm very close with the imam. And [*pis*], I don't hesitate to go ask questions. If I'm not sure, I'll definitely go ask questions to a second and third imam and ... three opinions, yeah, that's it. Just to see where I'm going.

In our interview, Hassan outlines how he was asked to determine whether an employee's request to not work on Fridays because of midday *jumu'ah* prayer was reasonable. Was the employee's congregational prayer practice similar to Christian Sunday community prayer, which is unencumbered by work duties? If yes, should he be granted the right to substitute working on Friday for working on Saturday or Sunday? These queries were posed to Hassan specifically because he is Muslim. Hassan takes this theological role seriously; paralleling a central form of Islamic jurisprudence, he consults with a number of imams to create consensus.

Hassan recounts how he began his role as an unofficial theological arbiter. We use this adjective because, in consultation with a handful of religious leaders, he interprets the traditions of Islam to determine what is appropriately Islamic in a Canadian crown corporation, an interpretation some might call *fiqh al-aqalliyat al-muslema*. To be clear, in his conversation with us, in no way does Hassan voice offence or doubt about this task. Rather, because he regularly attends mosque and knows his imam well, he expresses pleasure and considers himself qualified to assume this responsibility. Hassan's role as *porte-parole* (spokesperson) for Islam in this crown corporation is also facilitated by his work in a human resources department, where questions of dispensation and accommodation are regularly raised. His overt religious role appears to have emerged over time. He did not officially offer to make these determinations. His colleagues know that he is a Sunni Muslim, as he frequently discusses his beliefs with them at lunchtime – particularly during the month of Ramadan when he joins them while fasting – and at after-work events when he does not drink alcohol but chooses a Perrier (bottled water).

Despite his expressed enjoyment of these theological debates, we see this religious arbiter role as potentially conflicting with his appointed HR responsibility to chronicle and respond to grievances and requests. Hassan is specifically asked to make theologically normative decisions. Owing to his relationship with his mosque's imam, he consults with him (and, he says, with two other imams if necessary) if he is unsure of the "proper" response. In response to this case, Hassan determines that no, the employee in question should not have the right to an entire day to attend Friday prayers. Such participation calls for a one-hour absence, which could be compensated by moving the timing of the individual's lunch break. Hassan assumes that the employee will attend a mosque close to work.

Even though Hassan likes this role, other respondents in a similar position conveyed a range of ways the discourse of request affects them. Raja, aged fifty-two and a medical doctor whose hijab renders her visible, describes how one of the Muslim residents asked for her advice on where he could pray at the hospital. Raja says she took care to make clear that he should not pray openly in the resident room, as she felt to do so was "highly, highly inappropriate." Rather, he should pray in the hospital chapel to keep his religiosity less obvious to his colleagues. In this case, Raja mobilizes her authority to discourage the resident's religious visibility. Like Hassan and Raja, participants who held senior positions, even if they sought to keep their religious lives private, were often situated as resource persons on Islam by both Muslims and non-Muslims. Notably, in contrast to Hassan, even though Raja eschews the role of theological arbitrator, she nevertheless delimits the boundaries of acceptable Islam, demarcating private from public spaces, which remains a central axis upon which normative notions of the secular in Canada rest. Indeed, this prevalent paradigm of request requires employees to frame their religiosity as something public, thereby contributing to their hypervisibility and to rendering invisible the privileges afforded to majorities within the workplace.

Thus, the act of requesting, which requires that one makes one's faith public, is a process intimately involved in the "definition and management of religion" (Hurd 2012: 955). This request narrative shapes how Islam is imagined to work and how Muslims are imagined to act (on this discourse of request in contemporary Quebec, see Barras 2016). We are not saying here that individuals do not make or do not want to make requests. In some cases, as we see in the example that Hassan had to work out, they do. Rather, we want to flag the real and potential impacts that this "requesting" lens has on rigidifying how Muslims are perceived and, in particular, on isolating their religious identity. In this case, as if a homogenous entity, Muslims are often imagined as needing and wanting a dedicated (and, therefore, visible) prayer time or space and are expected to ask for it. And in some cases, this leads to asking other identified or self-identified "Muslims" to arbitrate these prayer requests. Thus, Muslimness becomes the central, if not the *only*, paradigm. This somewhat static and essentialized understanding of

Islam and Muslim prayer practices works to constitute our participants and the space around them in particular ways.[14] To be sure, some of our interlocutors need and want prayer space, but some do not. Many navigate and negotiate their needs by adapting to the situation in which they find themselves.

Let us now consider how our participants' stories reveal a confessional impetus, which supports a panoptic secular regime that renders prayer visible, under scrutiny, and governable. Akeem's university experience illustrates this point. Prior to Akeem's arrival as a laboratory assistant, his supervisor arranged to have a room available for him so that he could pray. This more senior faculty member assumed that because Akeem was of Middle Eastern origin, he was a Muslim. His supervisor associated Muslimness with the necessity for a private prayer room. Akeem depicts his work conditions and the social atmosphere when he began this research position:

[Before] I came to do my master's [degree], I contacted a supervisor and told them I was coming and everything. And then, um, before I came here – I learned this after coming here – my supervisor, he thought, like, he knew that I was coming from the Middle East, so he just assumed that I'm a Muslim. And then he went around [...] telling people that "Oh, I have a Muslim student coming," and he suggested, uh, like, I don't know if he did, actually, or if he said in front of people that he's going to suggest to the administration to provide a prayer room for me. And then people [in the lab] start being mad and then saying, like, "Why?" And he's, like, "'Cuz we know he's a Muslim, and they need a room to pray." And people are saying, like, "We're Catholic," or "We're Christians. No one asked us if we wanted a room. This is discrimination against us." And there was a big controversy about it. So when I came here and then, uh, the first day my supervisor asked me, he's, like ... and I said, "Oh, oh, I'm not, I'm not Muslim." And he's like, "But you're from the Middle East." [...] Then when I went to work, and then I started to know people. It's, like, "Oh, you are the student everyone's talking about." [...] They saw it like a discrimination against them, like, "How come no one asked us [if we needed prayer space]?"

This seemingly good-hearted gesture by a non-Muslim faculty member was most likely made to facilitate Akeem's integration into his new work environment. Yet Akeem is nonpractising and does not want Muslim to be part of his workplace identity. Conscious of his outsider foreigner status, Akeem does not seek any recognition – religious or otherwise – that would separate him from his labmates, wanting the focus to fall on his knowledge of science. His supervisor's actions thus caused him considerable personal discomfort. He says they initially alienated him from his non-Muslim labmates. Most pointedly, they commented that no one had asked them as Christians if they needed prayer space. These colleagues concluded that the omission constituted discrimination against *them*. Moreover, recall our discussion of Akeem's workplace in Chapter 1. Even once the request was cleared up, so-called humour in his workplace zeroed in on his purported religiosity and otherness, especially evident when his labmates "jokingly" nicknamed him Osama.

Akeem's supervisor did not consider that his student might not want to pray at work, might practise differently, or might not even be a Muslim. By approaching the university's administration about this potential prayer room, the supervisor projected a certain image of Akeem, which was purely from conjecture: an image where his religiousness was rendered visible and public, where a gesture of welcome might facilitate his anticipated demand. The variability of Islam was not part of the repertoire of his supervisor, who instead used a fixed notion of the Pious Muslim, pinning Akeem into a particular mode of being that does not at all represent him. One of the effects of this move is to force a particular mode of visibility on Akeem, as well as to draw a particular spatial boundary around him (the prayer room) that has come to represent who he is for his coworkers. In a sense, this spatial delineation imprisons him in a particular rigid identity, which is difficult to escape. The supervisor's efforts may also speak to an unintended ordering mechanism: seeking to ensure that Akeem's religiosity be contained to a prayer space and not to spill over into the lab.

Akeem's story resonates with Caroline's and Karim's experiences. They also do not see the need to make, or feel comfortable making, their practice visible in the public sphere. Caroline, who works for a nonprofit organization, explains how she got into an altercation with her former boss precisely because Caroline did not ask her boss if she could pray in her office. For Caroline, praying is something that "belongs to [her]. It's private." However, her employer expected that Caroline would inform her boss of her practice and its frequency. In order to avoid doing so, Caroline decided to pray outside her office, at a local mosque, during her lunch break. For her, differentiating her religious commitments from her workplace identity is a more comfortable arrangement, where she does not need to justify her practice or ask permission:

> I have my lunch break, no problem. It's a five minute walk. I go [*J'm'en va*] pray quietly, in peace. So [*Fait que*] this is the mechanism that I set up. I certainly could have told her [my boss] ... Listen, I would pray every day in my office and, you know [*tsé*], arrange something with her, but I didn't feel like it. Because at the same time, I tell myself, it belongs to me. It's private. I don't have to justify myself to anyone. I don't need to be accountable, to start saying, "Well [*ben là*], forgive me, I'm going to close the door for five minutes. Does it bother you?" [...] So [*Fait que*] I eliminate all tensions. I go out, *that's it* [said in English]. So this is how I manage this [prayer] at work.

In another example, Karim, aged thirty-one and an engineer, describes his satisfaction with the informal Friday prayer arrangements in his office, where a colleague books a conference room but does not advertise what it is for. While he thought of asking human resources to develop a specific company policy addressing prayer, he is reluctant to do so as the current arrangement works well: "I figure if it's not broken, let's not try to fix it, you know? So, it's working as it is."

While we find, similar to Jouili (2009), that prayer for our participants oscillates between visibility and invisibility, this oscillation is not necessarily related to the fact that they want to render their practice public by formally making a request for a prayer space or that they choose to ignore this aspect to avoid conflict. Rather, in a more socially constructed way, for many of our respondents, what is identified as central is navigating and/or negotiating an arrangement that allows them to locate a quiet and comfortable place during the time they need to pray.

The issue of finding a fixed space has often delineated the boundaries of prayer for Muslims in public discourse. In contrast, our research shows that this focus fails to capture the subtleties of practice. Nariman, a Canadian-born twenty-five year old, explains that when she was a university student, her prayer arrangements varied according to the circumstances within which she found herself. If the weather was nice, she might pray "on the field [of her university campus] because there was so much green space." But if she "was in a rush in between classes," she might pray "in an isolated [space] like stairs or [a] hallway or [a] classroom, something like that." Thus, in the first instance, Nariman prayed in a place where her practice would be made visible to the public eye. In other instances, she chose an isolated, private place. Whether or not her practice was made public was not essential to her. Nariman, a reserved woman who was born in Qatar and immigrated to Quebec when she was a child, sought places that allow her to have a comfortable moment with herself and, more practically, fit with her schedule, the weather conditions, and her mood on a particular day. Her flexibility offers a nuanced story of how prayer is practised and counters the more rigid ways prayer is imagined in scholarship and policy.

Nariman's account is also illustrative of the importance some participants give to exploring the layout of their environment – whether an office, a university, or a shopping centre – in order to find the right place where they will be comfortable praying. This search for a place implies that participants may choose to combine prayers, pray in a seated position, or skip prayers until they find a suitable place. The perceived attitude and openness of one's boss further shapes these interactions. For Maria, aged twenty-seven, who works in advertising, one needs to "judge the location of the place." She compares the spatial organization of her last job, in a bank, to her new place of employment. At her former job, she worked in an open-space layout. Because she felt it was not appropriate to pray in her cubicle, she asked her boss if she could use a "small conference room." Her new workplace is more relaxed, with fewer employees. In this environment, she does not feel the need to ask and just "go[es] in a conference room for a second" to pray. While Maria seems more comfortable *not* sharing her need to pray and not making an outright request, she stresses that her decision to make her practice visible is contingent on her work environment. That is, she would consider speaking to her employer if the layout of her office made it hard for her to find a space or if she thought her employer might have an objection.

Likewise, Khail, aged thirty-six, a provincial government employee, explains that he does not ask his boss about daily prayer because his boss "is very accommodating." In his case as well, the space where he prays changes. At break time, Khail sometimes prays in his cubicle but at other times seeks out a more private space, like the storage space because "a cubicle is open." While in some cases, such spaces can be/or are made visible to the public eye, this is not necessarily the case. Yet, conflict is rarely the reason, or the *only* reason that motivates our participants' decision to ask for a space and to share (or not share) their practice with others. What is most often identified as important is that these spaces – whether allocated to them or one they appropriated – allow them to be (or to put themselves) momentarily outside the busyness of a typical workday.

In navigating and negotiating prayer space, our participants encounter the secular distinction between the so-called public and private as neither fixed nor stable. For several interviewees, a public place can be invested in and constituted as private. Thus, time – in this discussion, a moment marked by the need to pray – is key to understanding how space is invested in and lived by participants. Like Caroline, who we met earlier in this chapter, many of our participants identify the act of praying as something private, personal, between them and God. We heard stories where closets, dark rooms, conference rooms, staircases, and other unexpected places are transformed for a few minutes into prayer rooms. Akako, a twenty-four-year-old student, explains how he uses a work storage space to pray. Another participant, Hanan, a twenty-eight-year-old computer scientist, discusses how she uses small rooms that are "big enough [...] to just pray":

> HANAN: At my workplace, I didn't have to ask for a prayer space. They didn't provide one, but I basically ... What they have are small rooms where you can have personal phone calls if you want, and they're big enough for me to just pray in them. So I assumed I can use it for other stuff, and I was able to, and nobody said, "No," so I just use it for that.

INTERVIEWER: Did you ask or you just used it?

HANAN: No, I just used it. Yeah, um, 'cuz, well, to be honest, the door's not, it doesn't have a window or anything or it doesn't ... So to me, like, it's as if I'm making a [private] phone call anyways. So I described it [...] like a wireless phone call to God. I was, like, this is funny!

Some interviewees, like Nadia and Samira, explain that they stopped looking for the "right place." They create a "bubble" around themselves and transform a busy place into a quiet one where they can briefly isolate themselves from their surroundings. For these women, missing the *asr* (afternoon) or *maghrib* (sunset) prayer when they commute is not ideal. A bus or metro seat and parts of their body are transformed into prayer spaces. Samira is matter of fact about this contextualizing: "So I sit in the subway, and I isolate myself. I go into my world [*je me mets dans mon monde*] and I do my prayer in my head." In a sense, the place in which they find themselves when it is time to pray becomes the right space, regardless of whether it is public or private. For them, time is thus central to comprehend how space is constituted.

These narratives tell us a number of things. Participants do not necessarily see a need to claim prayer space.[15] Some do request the allocation of a quiet space when they need to pray, but rarely do they express the need to be given a dedicated prayer room or a multifaith prayer space. In most cases, the decision to share or not share their need to pray with others follows self-reflection and a determination of the environment in which they find themselves (in our next chapter we elaborate on this process of self-reflection, which we label navigation). It is possible that conflict in some cases explains why interlocutors choose to keep their practice private. But in the majority of cases, participants choose not to share their arrangement precisely because it works for them, and they are comfortable with it.

Our participants' narratives also tell us something about how dominant public discourses and claims around the place and role of Islam tend to overlook everyday complexity. In this section, we have thus mapped two streams of experiences which sometimes overlap: first, those who see a discourse of demand framing their requests for space, which, like for Akeem, delimits the situation even when no request is made. The secular here shapes spatial conceptualizations of the private and the public spheres. Second, our participants recount everyday practices of prayer, which are navigated outside the panoptic regulation of prayer space.[16] In this stream, participants determine the secular frames protecting particular practices, activities, and beliefs as part of a shared Canadian culture while, at the same time, excluding others. Religion is sometimes framed as something that is and should be private and at other times should be part of public life. This constructed variance of public/private and of religion/culture plays through our participants' experiences of Canadian life and in the processes of regulation of their own religious practices. The flexibility of these categories, often not controlled by our interlocutors, speaks to the powerful malleability of the secular.

Norms of Social Interaction

Nariman, the young accounting student whom we met earlier in this chapter, describes her ambiguous relation to handshaking in her everyday life:

> NARIMAN: I don't shake hands. Unless it's something, somebody who's non-Muslim and they don't really, they don't really think that's an issue and they kind of stick out their hand, so I kind of feel bad for leaving them hanging, so I shake their hand. Um, but if it's a Muslim then I would just be, like, if I'm hesitant, then they'll understand why [...]
>
> At work, since I just started recently, during my interview I think I shook hands with my manager, like, five times just because he's very friendly. I don't know why. He tried to end the interview a couple times, but then he started saying something else. Then I'd have to shake his hand again, and then my coworkers, a couple of them are guys, so they wanted to give you high-fives or something like that. And I'm just, like, I try to make sure I do it nicely but not too awkwardly, um.
>
> INTERVIEWER: So you let them know? Or –
>
> NARIMAN: No, I just try to [hold back]. Either I have something in my hand or I try to say something that distracts them or something like that [...] I don't want them to feel like they're being disrespectful.

Nariman explains that despite her discomfort with shaking hands, she may nevertheless engage in this practice when her actions might put her non-Muslim acquaintances in a difficult position: "I kind of feel bad for leaving them hanging, so I shake their hand." Nariman explains how she negotiates not shaking hands, depending on the context. If she is interacting with Muslim acquaintances, they are better able to interpret her cues (e.g., her hesitancy); non-Muslims, on the other hand, may not be able. For example, Nariman describes how she felt obliged to shake her friendly manager's hand five times in a job interview for a popular fast-food restaurant chain. For her, not doing so would have appeared as disrespectful. In her day-to-day interactions with her colleagues, she chooses not to share her religiosity with them and developed tactics to avoid physical contact – in our interview, she mentions that she prefers high-fives – in an attempt to avoid upsetting others' sensibilities or the ambiance of the workplace. Her experience speaks to the malaise that is sometimes felt by interviewees with respect to scripted norms regarding social interactions and delimiting the appropriate place and form of religion.

Our participants' narratives on quotidian social interactions, like Nariman's account, highlight more subtle and latent ordering mechanisms than the ones around prayer spaces, but they are equally important to understand the power of the secular.[17] Earlier in the chapter, we noted scholars who examine the secular. Asad (2011: 661), for one, notes how these ordering mechanisms' normativity and invisibility are what grant them power here in relation to the "secular body":

> Unless you knew someone well you couldn't tell whether she was a believer or not merely from the way she spoke or behaved. What does this say about the secular body? One answer may be that [religious] belief, where it exists among liberal moderns, is so deeply repressed that it has at best a very tenuous connection with observable behavior.

Such social norms have a habitus-like quality insofar as values and dispositions are linked to ways we position and carry our bodies, what clothes we wear, and even our physicality in social relations. Connolly (2011: 272) includes "dress codes, regularized gestures, public vocabularies, strategies of justification, and styles of walking" among these secularized attributes. These, he says, have been "filtered so densely into secular, public life that they did not appear as affronts" (272). Anthropologist Charles Hirschkind (2011: 634) presents the ubiquity of these secular norms as "the water in which we swim." Yet, as the social moments illustrate, these waters can be invisibly choppy and challenging.

We see this version of the secular in contemporary Canada, as depicted by our interlocutors, as articulating universalizing norms around gender. These norms crystalize on two values: the putative equality of men and women as an established fact in Western democracies and the expectation that women should appear/behave a particular way that is presented as neutral. These universal norms include expectations around touching (handshakes, cheek kissing, and hugs) between men and women and the visibility of women's bodies. While for some of our participants the norms of touching and exposure are not problematic, for others they are. The linkage of the secular to gender equality means that rationales stemming from religion of all types, but especially Islam, are excluded from acceptability, essentially designated as the other or the stranger in the secular family. More tangibly, loosely defined notions of the secular serve to manage and sanction expressions of acceptable sexuality and proper social interactions between men and women in the public sphere. As Connolly (2011) notes, their normativity means that these expectations do not appear as affronts but, quite the contrary, as neutral and benign expectations that are immune from challenge. Our participants' experiences of navigating, being called to respond to these expectations, and their expression in social relationships (as with *le bec* [kissing on the cheek], as well as touching or hugging) as well as the monitoring of their clothing reveal some of the secular's expectations (or scripts) of bodily performance and presentation.[18]

In this section, we turn our attention to explore how secular-framed norms influence the ways our participants greet nonrelatives. Such greetings can be emotion filled, which ups their ante.[19] *Le bec* is a greeting commonly used in Quebec and, therefore, was identified as an area of negotiation for participants in the Montreal area; our St. John's interviewees also mentioned physical interaction, including handshaking and hugging. For some of our interlocutors, shaking hands and/or kissing practices do not require any form of negotiation; either they are incompatible with how they interact with others or such greetings are part and parcel of their everyday. For many, however, these practices are identified as an area of negotiation. Generally speaking, some will shake hands or kiss because they see these gestures as part of the culture in which they live and worry that failing to participate would be felt as an insult by the person who presents his hand or his cheek in a gesture of initiation. Yet, they might not necessarily be comfortable with such greeting practices and mention that they only do it if the other person offers his/her hand or cheek. Others will shake hands but not kiss. And still others try to avoid doing both but will consider the feelings of others, devising strategies to counteract the disruptive effect of their practice so as to not make others uncomfortable (see Fadil 2009: 448).

This adaptive attitude towards practice and social interactions is illustrated by a moment described by Farida. This twenty-nine-year-old participant, born and raised in Montreal, explains that since opening her own business she shakes people's hands on occasion. The alternative is not palatable because not doing so can "sometimes [...] really offend the other person." Yet, she is still not fully comfortable with the practice and never initiates the interaction, explaining, "If they don't show it [their hand], I won't offer." Her biggest worry, however, is how do deal with *le bec* in a Montreal-based setting:

> FARIDA: [Physical interaction] is tricky because that's something I'm really not comfortable doing. 'Cuz I'm, like, "OK, I'll shake your hand" but, you know? And sometimes I'm caught off guard. [...] I'll just go, "No," and they'll come, you know – *bec/bec* – and that's it. And for me it's a little bit, like, OK.
>
> INTERVIEWER: And how have you, how did you deal with that? Did you find a way?
>
> FARIDA: Umm, I'm still working on that one. Because I find that the people who will, the men who will go forward and do that [two kisses on the cheeks], they have no clue what is acceptable and what is not acceptable to me. And I don't want to go and crush them, right? So I'm still, I mean, if, if I can, like, for example, let's say my son's friend. So we went to their birthday party and the father, he

came [over and] was all, like, he had a beer in one hand, he came and was, like, *bec/bec*, you know, "Welcome to our home." And I was, like, "Oh, great." So when we were leaving, I kind of avoided him. I said, I waited until I was across the room and was, like, "OK, bye!" And I'll just, like ... but since then I mentioned it to his wife that, you know, we don't, we don't do that. You'll notice my husband doesn't do that. So then, now it's not an issue because I'll always hug and kiss the wife, and for him I'll say, "Bye, see you later," you know?

One can see here how Farida is uncomfortable with *le bec*, but also, like Nariman, with the idea of upsetting what Fadil (2009: 444) terms "dominant sensitivities" latent in liberal-secular regimes.[20] Farida is conscious of the emotionally charged nature of this physical interaction. She sometimes feels obliged to engage in the practice either to protect the feelings of her interlocutor or because she is simply "caught off guard." Farida's description of her non-Muslim masculine entourage suggests it is not always sensitized to the idea that she is uncomfortable and that touching nonrelatives counters religiously understood rules around propriety. She reflects that "the men who will go forward and do that, they have no clue what is acceptable and what is not acceptable to me." Though seemingly oblivious to her religious identity when it comes to physical touch, these same men will, however, question her on her Muslim identity because of her headscarf (we expand on this point further in the last section of this chapter).

Recent attention in Canada – particularly in Quebec – has focused on restricting full-face covering garments such as niqabs and burqas as undesired in the public sphere. Some of the rationale for these restrictions[21] exposes an idealized, modern neutral secular body (specifically, a naked face, which can nonetheless be augmented with makeup and surgery), of which we are rarely aware given its normativity. In this case, as Selby (2014) argues with reference to post-2011 legal projects on full-face veils in France and Quebec, the secular narrative locates a public sphere free of religious signs as emboldening women to freely express their sexuality, while concomitantly assuring gender equality. Our hijab-wearing participants experienced these expectations of the secular body most acutely, triggering a range of emotions from discomfort to anger; only two male participants described a negative response to their beards. At the beginning of this chapter we heard from Nour, whose ability to teach sex education had been challenged by parents, colleagues, and students because of her headscarf.[22] Nour is careful to respond to this assumption with kindness, emphasizing her professionalism to demonstrate that she can be both a practising Muslim and a skilled teacher. Still, Nour finds these regular assumptions offensive and her attempts to debunk them exhausting. To use the framework we introduced in Chapter 1, Nour is impelled to play the Liberated Muslim Woman figure.

Many of our hijab-wearing participants share a similar feeling of exhaustion as they feel a constant call to explain and to justify their hijabs, including answering questions that range from why they wear it, whether they are forced to do so, and if so by whom, to whether they are for or against gender equality.[23] Ouria, who we mentioned in Chapter 1, and who began wearing her hijab at age twenty-two, describes the questions as "exhausting": "It is like a subject – like a piece of gum you're chewing, and there's no sugar left at the end." She would like to stop having to explain herself. Another participant, a female family physician, stopped wearing her hijab in her practice. She says she loses too much time explaining the significance of the garment to curious patients. Another woman, Ifra, whom we met earlier, wears Pakistani-style dress to work on occasion but does not cover her hair. She notes, "Oh my God, that's work [wearing hijab] in this culture. It's a lot of work." In a sense, wearing the hijab frames these participants' external perceptions of their politics and beliefs and thus influences their interactions with their entourage.

The consequences of failing to meet normative gender expectations are real. Some female participants worry that their access to the job market or their ability to perform well in their jobs are compromised because of how their headscarves are perceived.[24] Shama, whom we met in Chapter 1, explains the difficulties she faced finding a job in the legal profession, which she attributes partly to the fear of potential employers that their clients will feel uncomfortable working with her because of her hijab. Shama discusses her articling experiences in a courthouse and in the legal department of a Quebec municipality. As far as she knows, she was the first hijabi "in the hallways of the courthouse." Shama explains that her overall experience as an intern was positive. In fact, she was surprised at how well she was received: "I'm really lucky. I was assigned to one of the most open judges!" Her veil appeared to pose a greater challenge when she interned with the municipality, in particular for those working in the administrative office: "You know, my internship supervisor: perfect. No problem. It was really the others, the others, the secretaries and all of them. They all lived in the, in the area [that's more suburban] [...] Those weren't the best six months of my life." Shama's supervisor told her she was an exceptional intern, so Shama wonders why her employment was not extended when the position she filled was subsequently advertised. She speculates that she was hired by the city on a temporary internship basis, thereby allowing the department to satisfy a desire to showcase religious diversity and to comply superficially with equity policies, without actually hiring her permanently. Like a few participants in our sample, Shama attributes this negative experience of low-level and insecure employment to the particularities of her homogenous and racist work environment and not to power structures more generally.

Even when she succeeds in securing a job in her field, her quotidian work life is influenced by colleagues' and clients' perception of her hijab. For Shama, the veil is not negotiable; other elements of her beliefs and practices – like praying during the workday or shaking hands with non-relatives of the opposite sex – are less pressing. The latter, she explains, might prove problematic in working with clients so she prefers not to push on this point. Shama, therefore, negotiates these other practices on a case-by-case basis.

A few of our interviewees describe being asked subtly and sometimes less subtly to modify their practices with reference to pervasive secular norms. Thus, not only are their practice and religiosity often constructed as hypervisible, but they also become the subject of repeated interference by their entourage. Many interlocutors in their entourages intervene to assure these secular norms. Sana, a twenty-five-year-old accountant of Iraqi origin who has been living in Montreal for more than fifteen years, explains that during her studies in management, a fellow student suggested she change her appearance when attending networking events: "I was asked, 'Well, is there any way where for the cocktails you could, I don't know, wear it more as a bandana than a veil? 'Cause it might help you get jobs.' So I got a bit of direct advice, if you want, from some very helpful people, but that's their advice." These examples speak to how dominant social norms – conceptualized as the parameters of the secular – govern the nature and shape of participants' religiosity, given their relation to gender norms, particularly but not exclusively for women wearing headscsarves. In their social greetings with others, participants often modify their religious practices. On the one hand, they are worried that not doing so would put those around them (who are often unaware that their way of greeting might not be the *only* way) in an uncomfortable position or, worse, offend them. On the other hand, when participants engage in embodied Islamic practices, or when those around them assume they are Muslim, even when, as Asad says, "You couldn't tell whether she was a believer or not" (for instance, through a name that they associate with Islam or through association with skin colour or a particular accent), their Muslim identity often becomes hypervisible and, consequently, *the* subject of inquiries, fears, unease, and suspicions.[25] Undesired religiosity thus comes to define the terms of social interactions, differentiating some interlocutors like Sana and inviting criticism, normalizing impulses, and discrimination.

***

In their accounts of the everyday, participants draw our attention to a number of ways the secular serves to shape and delimit acceptable religiosity, in turn shaping the parameters of the power structures in which our interlocutors navigate and negotiate their lives. We saw the rather superficial rebranding of Christmas under the premise of securing religious plurality and inclusivity. These narratives also point to the ways in which secularism is used to construct prayer as visible and governable. Finally, the equation of a particular formulation of the secular with gender equality produces a divide between women who are religious and those who are not, which comes to mean those who are emancipated and those who are not. More significantly, the stories in this chapter highlight how in contemporary Canada, articulations of secularity, cloaked under rhetoric of impartiality, structure time, space, and social relations. These narratives illuminate the shifting boundaries of the secular and some of the consequences of its invocation. The narratives of Canadian Muslims show how the imagined locations of religions – namely the invisibility of Christianity and the hypervisibility of Islam – are indexed and mobilized.

More broadly, these experiences remind us of how the religious and the secular are constructed in Canada. Though our participants' lived realities point to how they experience Christianity as public and present, the notion that Christianity is private dominates. This positioning has the consequence of rendering Islam particularly visible and masking the latent empowered position of Christian norms. When this secular is imagined to represent neutrality, inclusivity, and accessibility it becomes infallible.

The stories of Nour, Sara, Ramzi, Aadil, Hassan, Nariman, Farida, and others encourage us to revisit the supposed impartiality of the Canadian secular public sphere and how neutrality is articulated. Their descriptions of how Muslim identity is experienced as hypervisible, as a transgression, as often being *the* prism that defines them, not only question the notion of neutrality, but also call for reflection on the spaces produced by these constant othering processes. Policing and (re)producing such inequitable boundaries dangerously affirm and withhold non-neutral values. Nour's plain assertion that "We live in a predominantly Christian society" is a useful starting point. By insisting that Canada is secular, which invokes notions of neutrality and the notion that we are free from religious influence, we ignore the voices of those who experience it as Christian. This is not to advocate an erasure of Christianity from society and social life but to confront the consequences for those it does not privilege, whether religious or not. It also allows the recognition of how this way of seeing religion radically shapes the religious lives for minorities in the shared public sphere: rendering them more visible, positioning them as spokespeople, forcing them to make "requests."

Let us further consider Dalia's suggestion that "we can have both of those, the best of both worlds." This narrative tell us a different story – a story where celebrating Christmas and being Muslim are not self-exclusionary, where prayer can be about being comfortable with a space and not solely about requesting a space, and where gender equality and Muslim identity are not incompatible. These everyday narratives invite us to change the terms of the dominant conversation that focus on Muslim identity to engage with creative and lived ways of being. With this in mind, we now turn to the myriad of ways of being among the hundreds of everyday stories we heard.

Narratives of Navigation and Negotiation

4

At a Montreal Breakfast Diner

On an overcast February morning at an advertisement agency in downtown Montreal, Maria faces a conundrum when two non-Muslim technicians from the United States complete work on a server. She is alone in the office as they finish their work. The job is well done and completed early, so she seeks a gesture to thank them. She explains:

> I come in early, and I open the office. And they were there, and then I'm, like, um, "Did you have coffee?" And they're, like, "Yeah, we will later." And I'm, like, you know, "Let me get you breakfast," right? And, you know, when someone says, "No, no. It's OK," and then, kind of like, they're saying, "Yes"? So [...] they were stepping out and I'm, like, "Where are you guys going?" "We're just gonna go grab a coffee." I'm, like, "Really? Please let me, um, let me gift you this." And they were, like, "Nooooo," but it was yes all over their faces!
>
> So I went down, I went walking to the, to the, it's on St. Laurent [Boulevard]. It's called the Vieux St-Laurent. It's a breakfast place. And I'm like, "What do you guys eat?" And he's, like, "Oh, you know, I like my eggs and my bacon and my potatoes ..." and all of that. I'm, like, "Sure, no problem." But the problem is that I cannot offer bacon to someone. I cannot pay for it. You know what I mean? [...] The eggs, the potatoes, and all, that's fine. I felt, I had an internal struggle.

In her description of this early morning interaction, Maria, a recent Bachelor of Commerce graduate who quickly found work in her field, finds herself in a delicate position. Arriving at a nearby breakfast café of her choosing, following her insistence to treat them to breakfast, the workers order meals with bacon, a choice that oversteps her understanding of Islamic rules around pork consumption. Maria must decide in the span of a few moments whether or not to revoke her generous offer. As we will see, in the end, she does treat them to breakfast. But she is still working through this "internal struggle" when we meet her later that evening at a downtown café.

As she recounts this scenario from earlier in the day, Maria notes that key for her is that she did not have anything to gain from the situation in bringing the out-of-town workers to the diner: "So I think that it would be kind of acceptable [from an Islamic perspective]. You're doing a good action by offering them and not getting anything out of it. It's not [as] if it is an exec and, 'Hey, you know, I'm gonna buy you coffee. I'm gonna buy you lunch.' I had absolutely no interest in this." Still, the morning's events present a socially and morally challenging situation for her. The workers initially declined her invitation. But because Maria saw that "it was yes all over their faces," she insists on a gesture of thanks. When she hears their order, Maria also does not escape the boundaries of Canadian sociability, which might make retracting a breakfast offer complicated. We began this chapter with this story to consider, more broadly, the ways that self-defined Muslims in Montreal, Quebec, and in St. John's, Newfoundland and Labrador, *navigate* and *negotiate* – two terms we explore more deeply here – their religious identities in their daily lives.

How do navigation and negotiation take place? We see the former primarily as an internal dialogue about how to act or react in a particular situation. Maria quickly navigates and considers the pros and cons of rescinding her twice-made breakfast offer. The latter reflects how she interacts with and attends to power dynamics with those around her, in this case with the technicians, the diner employees, and her absent employer, as the invitation could also impact these relationships. Of course, the navigation/negotiation distinction does not mean that they are necessarily discrete categories or completely separate exercises. For many of our participants, navigation and negotiation go hand in hand. Navigation often acts as a first and important step in an external negotiation. Ideally, it gives participants time to figure out the arrangements with which they feel comfortable with respect to their religion in a particular setting. It is only then that, in some cases, they choose to approach their colleagues and friends to share their religious needs with them. Our interest in recovering moments like these is to consider these internal thought processes and external negotiations. Particularly when the resolutions are positive, these moments often go without saying. Moments in which religiosity is worked out are rarely documented and theorized.

In considering navigation and negotiation, we do not assume that any of these are neutral moments. Maria's need to navigate and negotiate reflects skewed power relations. Her interlocutors appear to lack sensitivity to her potential religious beliefs related to food. She does not wear a hijab and says she does not want to share her beliefs about Islam, let alone about pork, with these men. In this scenario we see how navigation and negotiation are contingent on many factors that, for many, are not fixed. On the one hand, some of our other participants may have faced no dilemma in a similar situation; they would have had no problem with paying for breakfast bacon. Others would have likely said – whether plainly, apologetically, or jokingly – that bacon was off limits. Still others fall somewhere in between. In the discussion that follows, we consider numerous ways in which our participants respond to these moments. At the same time, despite this range, there are overarching commonalities. Almost invariably, as for Maria, for all of those we interviewed respect is paramount in these decision-making processes. These processes appear to be part of being a good roommate, host, coworker, or friend, in addition to being Muslim. Most negotiations take place with consideration for those with whom they interact, with a minimum of fuss and in a pragmatic and practical manner. Again, as we saw in our discussion of Islamophobic and Islamophilic figures in Chapter 1, this does not mean that there were no incidents of prejudice, misunderstanding, and disappointment in what we heard. However, in general, in contrast to what we perceive to be a dominant narrative of conflict, dissatisfaction, and demands for accommodations with the reasonable accommodation model, the stories that participants shared with us were generally thoughtful and conciliatory.

In this analysis, we hope to highlight these narratives' ambidexterity, no matter our participants' commitment to the traditions of Islam. Some theorists describe this vantage point with the language of lived religion (de Certeau 1984; Orsi 2003, 2005; Heelas and Woodhead 2005; Knott 2005, 2009; McGuire 2008; Woodhead 2011, 2014). Religion, including Islam, as *lived* is richer and more varied than is commonly imagined, particularly in textually based analyses. Religiosity is one among many moral registers that can be "cobbled together" (James 1998).

We also want to attend to the fragility of these moments. One can easily imagine alternate resolutions under other circumstances or for different individuals. Maria herself acknowledges that she would have acted or justified her actions differently if the technicians had been executives, women, or visible minorities, or if they had not been so pleasant. That they had travelled to Montreal from the United States and were not familiar with the city also encouraged her to take them to a popular local breakfast spot. Maria's thought process illustrates how her religious identity is one element among others that she is trying to balance. She is a worker, a racialized minority, a woman, and a host. Her "theological arithmetic" in the moments after the breakfast order is placed reflects the flexibility and heterogeneity of her experience with Islam. She determines she can pay for the pork given that she does not prepare or consume it. Greater harm would come from revoking the offer. Still, even if we focus on the contingency of these situations, this does not mean that participants see their religious worldviews as fragile. Maria's faith and sense of self are not being questioned. Rather, our point is that religiosity is one element in the decision-making process of our participants. A score of other interests were articulated as important to our interlocutors in these moments: usually pragmatic concerns (the weather, costs), hospitality, neighbourliness, and respect.

In this chapter, we turn to stories like Maria's with two objectives. First, we seek to capture the processual dimensions of daily navigations and negotiations. In this way, with consideration for the structures of power that shape opportunities and life options – whether under the auspices of secularism or within the figure stereotypes that overdetermine social relations – we aim to document moments in the lives of Muslims in Canada, with attention to how Islam is lived and practised. Second, this empirical objective has theoretical implications in displacing how Islam is commonly described and conceptualized as monolithic or unchanging. Paying attention to the arithmetic of these daily moments deliberately moves us away from the stratified, non-neutral, and colonial-influenced language of accommodation and the discourse of request to a language of navigation and negotiation. We argue that the navigation/negotiation framework is better equipped to grapple with the fragility and complexity of these moments. The shift in language we propose aims to draw the reader's attention to how negotiations require participants to balance multiple elements of their lives – including but not exclusively their religiosity. Lastly, there is often give and take when situations are worked out (itself a determination we aim to leave to our participants). Prior to examining everyday narratives, we begin with some of the conceptual and theoretical ramifications of the terms we employ. We then turn to the experiences of our participants by exploring three locations we found to be replete with navigation and negotiation: daycares, schools, and sports facilities.

From Accommodation to Navigation/Negotiation
In making sense of our participants' narratives, we grappled with terminologies that capture their creativity, exchange, and mutuality. To be clear, these moments of navigation and negotiation occur in interactions with non-Muslims and other Muslims in order to make decisions about the best course of action. In some cases, working it out involves adapting one's religious practice. In others, it is about finding a way to practise one's religion in a particular environment. In others still, it may mean holding strongly to one's convictions.

The Language of Accommodation
Over the last decade, the term *accommodation* has increasingly been used in connection with religion in Canada and elsewhere (Dhamoon 2009; Beaman 2012a; Bielefeldt 2013; Wong 2011). Like we saw in Chapter 3 with Hassan's response to requests at his workplace, it refers to the

idea that someone "asks" for or "requests" an accommodation – an adjustment of the norm – when she considers that she is being unfairly differentiated or discriminated by the norm. As already briefly discussed in the Introduction, usage of the term accommodation in Canada is related to the legal notion of reasonable accommodation that was, until recently, limited to employment law. With the *Multani v Commission scolaire Marguerite-Bourgeoys* decision in 2006, the Supreme Court of Canada used the notion of reasonable accommodation for the first time outside of employment law. The court ruled that the request of a twelve-year-old student from Montreal to wear his kirpan, a Sikh ceremonial dagger,[1] in a public school should be accommodated to respect his religious freedom.[2] This decision triggered vivid debates about the rights of religious minorities, the parameters of multiculturalism, the potential for harm (symbolic and, with a dagger, real), and the nature of Canadian secularism. Beaman (2012b) notes that much of the public reaction to the court's decision in Quebec, but also across Canada, was negative. The backlash "focused on the idea that there was simply 'too much' accommodation happening" (Beaman 2012a: 13). With this case and with discussion in government commissions and legal projects following it, reasonable accommodation acquired a life of its own outside the legal arena and became part of common parlance in how Canadians consider religious diversity.

Despite its prevalence, we deliberately do not use the term accommodation to refer to how our participants work out aspects of their daily lives. A central goal undergirding this project is to problematize previously popular approaches that utilize the language of accommodation, demand, and tolerance. Alongside others (e.g., Berger 2010; Klassen 2015), we worry that this language reflects and produces unequal power relationships. Not unlike the term *tolerance* (on the limits of the notion of tolerance, see, for instance, Jakobsen and Pellegrini 2008; Povinelli 2002; W. Brown 2008), these unequal relationships come out of the concept's structuring of an "us" and a "them." That is, an "us" (the body or individual deciding whether a request should be accommodated) is put in a position of authority to evaluate or accept that a religious request (by "them") is reasonable or, alternatively, to look for and to strike a compromise. The norms that undergird accommodations are left unquestioned. Those making the requests, who are often conflated with religious minorities, are inevitably put in a vulnerable position in this dichotomy. The "them" are rendered passive in the process, as though hanging on to rigid religious requirements. In other words, the use of accommodation locates the "us" and the "them" on different ends of a power spectrum. The "us" are never asked to question or shift their frameworks or practices.[3] While power relationships still structure the navigation and negotiation processes, we hope that these terms convey a sense of mutual exchange and dialogue. Together, they offer a discursive lens that, at least from the start, does not assume an intrinsic difference between actors involved, insofar as one party does not accommodate the request of the other.

The distinction between navigation and negotiation emerges from our interlocutors' description of varying moments in their everyday interactions. We noted how numerous participants worked out religious practices and commitments on two levels: with themselves and/ or with others. An accommodation lens structured around the idea that individuals necessarily make verbal or explicit requests misses this recurring point. Again, our participants expressed a range of ways in which navigation occurs. Several interviewees expressed satisfaction; they may have not wanted to outwardly express and render their religion visible, like Maria at the breakfast diner. Others, as we will see, are uncomfortable making verbalized requests due to shyness, a wariness of making others uncomfortable, or simply a need to keep their faith private.

This conceptual shift from accommodation to navigation and negotiation comes with its share of methodological conundrums. Blanchot (1962: 355) tellingly reminds us how "the everyday: it's the most difficult thing to discover" [*le quotidien: c'est ce qu'il y a de plus difficile à découvrir*]. Demands for accommodations are easier to recover and locate, as they require that someone make a formal request for an adjustment. Negotiations and navigations are more unpredictable than demands and requests and thus are harder to capture in qualitative interviews. In addition, not all everyday negotiations are overt or create longer-lasting resolutions or tensions. They are not necessarily memorable. There is a spectrum of discomfort in these moments often folded into the negotiation process, a point to which we turn in the next chapter. Despite these challenges, we see capturing these processes as important, as they are constitutive of how Islam is commonly lived in Canada.

Although we focus on their experiences, Muslim Canadians are not alone in negotiating and navigating their religiousness and other aspects of their selves. Everyone's quotidian life is replete with navigations and negotiations, whether religiously motivated or not. These moments are ubiquitous: the person next to you on the bus wears a potent (and putrid) perfume. More alarmingly, a stranger standing in line behind you makes a hateful comment under her breath. Your host serves you food that you find unpalatable or, worse, a dish that causes allergies or counters religious or ethical beliefs. Your neighbour's barking dog wakes you from sleep. Your boss is inflexible on a holiday request. You do not agree with the decisions supported by your political representative. Someone close to you inflicts harm in a way you find worrisome or even dangerous. Even the most antisocial individual cannot avoid these encounters, in person, by phone, and even by text message, email, and social media. We all navigate and negotiate, even if, depending on one's privilege,[4] some of us are compelled more than others into these situations. Christmas, described in Chapter 3, is a case in point. For many of our participants, because of their intersecting positionalities, this holiday is an arena of complex navigation and negotiation. Those in managerial roles or positions of power, for instance, have more leeway in shaping these interactions (see Barras, Selby, and Beaman 2016, where we discuss this power vis-à-vis our participants who work as public servants).

These moments are largely unavoidable, and – with the exception of those times when they escalate into full-blown confrontations or disputes – are not easily recognizable, remembered, or narrated. They often go undetected. Their unarticulated norms are unexamined, which is one of our tasks here.[5] Methodologically, attention to these moments means that we asked participants about their beliefs and practices by pointing to contexts and situations, hoping this specificity would allow them to tailor their accounts of religiosity. We therefore directed our interviewees to share and reflect on their social interactions not only in major life events but also in their everyday lives (i.e., at work, school, in restaurants, at supermarkets, in hardware stores), in an attempt to capture these subtleties.

Elements of Negotiation: Multiple Registers of Being and Working Consensus

Another challenge that comes with using a language of accommodation is that it tends to carry two assumptions. In the first place, this perspective focuses upon religious minority practices. Requests for days off at Christmas, for instance, neither occur nor emerge in the framework of accommodation as they are statuatory holidays embedded in the Canadian calendar and cultural fabric. In the second place, the accommodation framework tends to focus on rigid and conservative expressions of these practices. An "accommodation reflex" reflects what we see as a broader policy and scholarly trend, where religious differences, and in particular Islamic differences, are isolated and made visible, and where Muslims especially are often reduced to their religious identity (on this tendency for reduction, see Hefner 1998; Gianni 2005; Kumar 2012; Dessing et al. 2013; Jeldtoft 2013; Selby 2016a). Therefore, our invitation to adopt a language of navigation and negotiation should also be understood as an effort to move away from this flattened and partial understanding of religiosity that privileges specific expressions.

We focus on everyday interactions. To be clear, we do not have a stake in advancing any one interpretation of Islam over another; we are not interested in delimiting a proper object of study. Fadil and Fernando (2015: 75) raise concerns related to what they see as normative assumptions laden in many employments of the "everyday" framework within anthropological analyses of Muslims. They usefully question what is *not* the everyday (i.e., the exceptional or the impossible) and call attention to "reductionist account[s] that privilege religion at the expense of political, economic, and other structures" (60). On this we agree. Our use is not, as Fadil and Fernando allege of other scholars employing this language, a "recuperative site of humanist possibility" (74) or a triumphalism of liberal Muslims. For us, synonyms for "everyday/every night" include mundane, ordinary, usual, quotidian, and the unexceptional. These moments can take place in public and private spaces. Lara Deeb's (2015: 94) definition of "everyday Islam" has resonated with our project, particularly her last point that eschews grand theory and stresses the necessary importance of context in considering religiosity. Deeb writes:

> I have always taken "everyday Islam" to mean attention to the ways in which people draw on ideas that they understand to be rooted to varying extents in Islam in order to figure out how to handle everything from handshaking to prayer, from dress to which cafes to hang out in and what social invitations to accept. Rather than debate whether or not Muslims are guided by religion, my approach has been to ask how various understandings of morality (including but not only religious ones) come together in relation to everything ranging from fasting to flirting. How does one then define what constitutes the realm of piety in the first place? That in itself should be an ethnographic question, situated and contextual.

Indeed, in thinking about representations of Islam, our use of the everyday aims to steer away from the exceptional. We have been struck by how scholarship, media, and government-informed analyses tend to rely on versions that are before the courts or are related to the most conservative versions of Islamic traditions, especially through embodied practices (e.g., Göle 2005, 2015; Mahmood 2005; Jouili 2009, 2015). Several of these studies are important and innovative for rather than focusing, as studies on Islam did a decade ago, on Islamist movements as political threats, they seek to capture how religiosity is lived and experienced on a day-to-day basis. Moreover, because a great deal of this scholarship focuses on Muslim women, this scholarship has also worked towards debunking liberal precepts that assume, among other things, that feminist agency and religious commitments are self-exclusive. Yet, as others argue (i.e., Schielke 2009a, 2009b; Deeb and Harb 2013; Dessing et al. 2013; Jeldtoft 2014), this focus on conservative practice and belief through the prism of Islam carries the risk of overlooking the complexity and incoherencies that mark day-to-day life, including among the most conservative.

These studies tend to concentrate, to cite Jeldtoft (2013: 23) on "highly selective forms and shapes of Islam and Muslim life [e.g., public expression of religion] [...] even though the implication is that it is Islam and Muslim life in general that is being discussed and studied."[6] They also overlook "forms of Islam and Muslim life which are often less visible and less easily identifiable" (Jeldtoft 2013: 23; see also Schielke 2009a: 36). Focusing on the hypervisible carries the danger of giving a particular authority to Islamic conservative positions and gatekeepers, which are frequently the most visible and referenced (cf. Dustin and Phillips 2008). In other words, some scholarly discourses tend to produce a narrow range of images of Muslims and Islam. We also note this constricted depiction in public policy discourses in Canada, notably in policy reports, government commissions, and bills.[7] The reasonable accommodation model's promotion of visible, unchanging religiosity parallels this impulse. Policy documents are significant because they can be translated into legal projects that have a great impact on the daily lives of Muslim Canadians.[8]

We contend that a framework drawing on navigation and negotiation is better equipped to capture how participants balance multiple registers of being, including, but not solely, religiously understood beliefs and practices. Lara Deeb and Mona Harb (2013), in their study of Islam and leisure in Lebanon, and Samuli Schielke (2009a, 2009b), in his work on moral ambiguities in Egypt, use the language of "moral registers" (Schielke 2009a: 169) or "rubrics" (Deeb and Harb 2013: 18–19) that can (un)easily coexist, overlap, shift, or compete with each other. In this vein, subjectivities are dialogical processes influenced by the balancing of these different registers. In their ethnographic studies based in Lebanon and Egypt, these anthropologists acknowledge that the (co)existence of these different registers or rubrics can shed light on the formation of moral subjects.[9] While our research is less interested in the modalities of moral constructions and more on practices and the pragmatic ways of being, we find that this emphasis on the balancing of individuals' multiple registers resonates with the processes we heard in our interviews.

This emphasis on balancing echoes religious studies scholar William Closson James's (1999: 286) metaphor of "cobbling" religion, which contrasts with the tendency, including in academia, to (re)produce an image of monotheistic religions that requires exclusivity and consistency. Cobbling highlights a tendency to alternate between and draw on different traditions depending on circumstances, emphasizing diverse ways of being religious so that individuals' beliefs and practices are "cobbled together from various sources rather than [being] a monolithic and unitary superordinating system of belief" (289). Notions of cobbling or patching are helpful because they capture the dynamism involved in processes of navigation and negotiation. Different parts of the self do not merge but rather are cobbled together "without [losing] their distinctiveness" (279).

Balancing and cobbling also remind us of the delicate nature of the processes. Maria navigates her workplace-related dilemma by piecing together various bits of reasoning that include theological, social, and personal considerations. She might have found the end result unsatisfactory if the individuals for whom she bought breakfast were regular local employees, or if she found herself in a different work environment or at another point in her life course. Other circumstances could change so that she would need to think and craft another arrangement. The cobbling depends on with whom you are working it out. The personalities and values of neighbours, classmates, teachers, and employers influenced the shape of the assemblage of our participants and the feasibility of balancing registers.

For us, this instability or fragility resonates with Goffman's (1956) notion of "working consensus."[10] To forge a common ground, working consensus necessitates a dual engagement and underlying respect from those involved. Goffman argues that an unstated shared sense of a situation is what gives social interactions coherency. The adjectival "working" captures the precariousness and ad hoc nature of how consensus takes shape and "consensus" captures the mutuality of the interaction (Goffman 1956: 10). Goffman explains that "the impression of reality fostered by such a performance is a delicate, fragile thing that can be shattered by very minor mishaps" (56). Indeed, knowing the rules requires a subtle and ever changing social sophistication on the part of all those involved.

Alina, aged forty-three, reminds us of the fragility of consensus. Here she describes a mundane interaction with her apartment block neighbour that shows the unequal burden she carries in ensuring consensus and mutuality in their interaction when the terms of their interaction shift:

> I was leaving the [apartment] building with my family to attend an event, a religious event at the mosque. So I was wearing my [hijab], you know, I was following the dress code. And then she [an elderly

woman neighbour] saw me. I saw her, and we greeted each other. And then all of a sudden she said, "You know what? I miss your dark curly hair." I was, like, I did not know what to say because uh, I mean, I knew that she did not mean, that she did not mean to be unrespectful or anything, but she was just trying to gently convey a message that, you know, she's not that comfortable seeing me go through such [a] transition. And I tried to explain to her that I'm going to a place of worship right now, and I have to, you know, follow the dress code. And she said, "Oh yes, I know. I don't mean anything bad," and she started to become apologetic. And then I felt for, I felt bad for her, not for myself but for her because she kind of regretted having made such a comment in the first place. So I tried to conclude with some humour and I said, "You know what? I mean, my hair is, most of my hair is gone now, and I'm getting old, and they are grey, they are less, so there's nothing really worth being missed anyway." And she laughed and then we, you know, said goodbye in a friendly atmosphere. But [...] it [Alina's newly worn hijab] kind of changes the terms of, you know, friendship, the terms of friendship or communication between the parties.

Alina recognizes that the hijab she wears to attend an event at the mosque shifts their usual interaction, at least in the eyes of this non-Muslim neighbour. Aware that the woman appeared to regret having commented on it, Alina generously reframes the neighbour's comment as a shared concern with greying hair. Alina's encounter is a good illustration of how a small but displaced comment or a change in dress can affect the "terms of friendship" or the stability of the consensus and reveal deep-seated power imbalances.

A last significant concept in the academic literature that considers how individuals think through their everyday negotiations examines "tactics" and "strategies," terms originally proposed by Michel de Certeau (1984). Linda Woodhead (2014) builds on this initial distinction that seeks to show how power influences how people act and cope in everyday interactions. Mobilizing a strategy is the prerogative of the powerful because it demands time and space. As Woodhead (2014: 17) notes, "Generally speaking, the privileges of masculinity, dominant ethnicity, heterosexuality, able-bodiedness, class and 'whiteness' reinforce and are reinforced by strategic religion." In other words, so-called strategic responses in everyday moments typically involve setting the parameters of a working consensus or of a situation. A tactic, however, is typically a response to this engagement. Tactics reference negotiation tools used by those in weaker positions who occupy spaces and respond to dynamics set by the powerful, like Alina's tactic of laughing at her greying hair. Those using tactics do not set the terms of engagement; they "react rather than command, and machinate rather than strategize" (15). Possessing the power to shape interactions is thus significant in working things out. Similarly, in a narrative we saw in Chapter 3, Sabrina was able to slightly alter the nature of her office Christmas gathering because of her more senior position, even if not calling into question its Christian origins. Her relative power in setting the terms of engagement within a larger framework of Christmas enabled a different kind of gathering.

The distinction between strategies and tactics shows the power relations always present in these interactions. Still, despite de Certeau's (1984) influence on our thinking, we do not distinguish between tactics and strategies. We see his distinction as further entrenching (at times, arbitrarily) an "us" (using strategies) versus "them" (using tactics) divide that we aim to displace, following our participants' stories, with the navigation/negotiation model. Moreover, the distinction overlooks the flexibility with and overlaps how individuals work out difference. For instance, the solution that Sabrina describes at her workplace – changing a previous dinner-and-drinks office Christmas party to a more family-friendly afternoon laser tag event – contains power and politics but the tactic/strategy dichotomy is limiting in analyzing her story.

Instead, the notions of balancing multiple registers, cobbling, and working consensus have helped us conceptualize our navigation/negotiation rubric. These frameworks shed light on the complex ways people work out their (religious) differences in their quotidian lives with themselves and with others. Humour, kindness, educative roles, and/or the mobilization of nonreligious mainstream discourses facilitate them. We have also seen other participants who choose more direct activism or mobilized a discourse of request to ensure that their religious practice is formally acknowledged to gain some change. In some cases our interlocutors might resort to both formal and informal ways of negotiating differences, while in other situations, even participants in positions of authority might rebuff these approaches. Our interviewees' navigation and negotiation occur in innumerable locations.

With these aforementioned theoretical tools in mind (critiquing the language of accommodation, multiple registers, and working consensus), we now turn more concretely to some of the intricacies of these processes in daycares, public schools, and sports facilities. We first look at how parents balance (or cobble) different priorities in their selection of daycare for their child/ren. We then consider some of the techniques developed by participants to carve a place for their children's religiosity in public school settings.[11] Lastly, we focus on the working consensus in the arrangements crafted by participants in sports facilities.

Daycares: Balancing Different Registers

Canada does not have a national childcare program. For many parents, securing daycare space(s) can be a complex endeavour and a source of anxiety. Most provinces have a number of registered and unregistered institutions and home daycares available. For those who need it, parents typically factor in with whom they are most comfortable leaving their child(ren) and in what environment. Social class and financial accessibility are perhaps the most relevant considerations in these determinations.[12] In addition to logistical questions around location, availability, and cost, assessing childcare might also include whether the provider shares parents' values around discipline, sleep training, and diet. In what follows, some working parents in our study describe the thought processes and considerations (religious and otherwise) that preceded their childcare choices.

Nora is a Canadian-born twenty-nine-year-old of Egyptian descent. She lives in Montreal with her husband and son. For her, language is a priority. She speaks Arabic with her parents but says her fluency is "not that great." She wants her son to speak Arabic fluently, along with French and English. For Nora, this linguistic priority is tied to her Muslimness. She explains: "I'm not sure if it was religious concerns as much as linguistic concerns, but I guess they're sort of tied together."

Encouraging Arabic maintains a connection with her family's Egyptian heritage and facilitates access to the language of the Qur'an for her son. As she says, "Arabic is, like, the religion of most scholarly texts, like the Qur'an, Islamically. So, it's just much easier to learn the Qur'an and then to study stuff if you have access to Arabic." She has given this language concern a great deal of consideration and sees childcare as a place to develop these skills. To improve her odds in locating a daycare spot in Arabic, she deliberately moved to an area in Montreal where there is "a large Arab population." Nora opted for a private home daycare for this reason as well, even if it is further from her house and more expensive than a larger public facility:

> I didn't even think of asking [for] a CPE [*Centre de la petite enfance*, or subsidized public daycare], because I thought it would be a waste of time to even ask that [Arabic language] from a CPE. And even if I had someone agree, well, the caregiver will change and I'll be, you know, out of it [...] There's a daycare literally half a block up the street, but I didn't even consider it because it was a public daycare, and I knew they weren't going to be able to accommodate [Arabic].

Nora thus selected a daycare run by a woman of Algerian descent, who speaks Arabic to her son and French to the other children. Before making her decision, she engaged in informal negotiations with different providers and says she chose the one that took her concerns seriously. This ability to listen was important in establishing trust: "You're leaving your kid with this person every day for five days a week. You want them to take your concerns seriously even if they don't think it's a big deal."

She says that other registers important to her were negotiated with relative ease. Nora draws certain lines. She says she is not concerned, for instance, that her son does Christmas crafts, so long as the childcare provider does not give him a cross to colour, which for her is an overtly Christian symbol: "We don't celebrate Christmas, but it doesn't mean he can't colour a Christmas tree, you know, like in a picture book. I mean, she's not gonna give him the one that has a cross on it, but, but she can give him a Christmas tree [to colour]." When it comes to food, the priority for Nora is that "she [the caregiver] feeds them healthy home-cooked meals." That the daycare provider prepares halal-appropriate meals is a "bonus" but not central to her decision to send her son there. She explains that she has a flexible approach towards halal food outside of her home:

> I kind of more go along with, like, if you're eating at someone else's place or out, then we're not too picky about that [halal] [...] You know, it's funny, because I asked about food, but I asked more from the perspective of, you know, does she feed them healthy home-cooked meals? It [dietary restrictions] didn't even cross my mind. Mind you, I knew she was Muslim, so I knew she wasn't gonna be feeding them pork. I like to think I would have remembered to make sure they weren't going to be feeding them pork if I wasn't going to a Muslim. But with her, it didn't even come to mind [to negotiate].

Nora deduces that because the provider speaks Arabic and is of Algerian origin, she would be aware of Islam-related requests. This scenario and the working consensus they share reassures Nora about the menu, even without knowing the daycare's specifics beyond healthy and home-cooked meals.

From a methodological perspective, let us consider Nora's narrative in relation to the notion of multiple registers of being. Significantly, her Muslimness emerges in her explanation of her daycare decision because *we* ask her about it. She herself does not explicitly qualify religious-related concerns as a priority when she sought out childcare. For her, language is important because it values her Egyptian culture and gives her son linguistic access to read the Qur'an in Arabic. If language is non-negotiable, other elements like food and potential Christmas crafts are. Still, because the daycare provider is of Algerian descent, Nora assumes she will not need to explicitly negotiate pork consumption or the colouring of a Christian cross, concerns that may have arisen in another context and which for her are non-negotiable. In sum, Nora's daycare choice also captures how negotiations are pragmatic and thus variable. In many cases, negotiations are geographically contingent.[13] As we shall see in two other narratives, life events, financial considerations, and personalities also shape this contingency.

Farida, who described her navigation of *le bec* in Chapter 3, is also a young mother of two. She explains the mental arithmetic she undertook to locate childcare. For her, finding a full-time facility that would be able to cater to the dietary needs of her children (in their case, eating halal) was a priority. She decided to only contact private facilities (not the subsidized option available in Quebec) because of "the level of attentiveness to service" that she felt was absent in Québécois public facilities. In other words, she thought that negotiations would be easier outside a formal daycare institution. Farida enthusiastically explains how her circumstances allowed her to find a provider that would be attentive to her needs. At the time of her search, she was not working full-time and could take the time to call and visit different places, inquiring whether they would be ready to meet her needs. Navigation and negotiation can be time consuming. Farida acknowledges that under other circumstances things might have been quite different:

> Here I was very blessed, but when I was making the phone calls, it was hard. There was a lot of places. I can understand that if there's a family where both husband and wife are working, and they absolutely have to find somewhere, and that's the only place they come across, I can understand people who say, "OK, I just have no choice. I have to send my kid."

Nora's and Farida's financial situations allow them to consider a private option, which is not the case for all our participants, reminding us how social class shapes the possibilities and terms of negotiation.

Caroline, a thirty-five-year-old convert who, in Chapter 3, described her prayer arrangements at work, did not have the same financial flexibility available to Nora and Farida when sorting out daycare arrangements for her child. She lives in a suburb of Montreal, where there is less religious and cultural diversity. Caroline explains that in her area, "It's not very developed when it comes to Islam [*c'est pas tellement développé, côté Islam*]. And there's no Islamic daycare." She considered sending her son to a daycare that would serve halal food, but it required too great of a commute:

> Listen, I work five days per week. I have to be here at eight thirty in the morning. So [*Fait que*] I don't have time to add [*me taper*] forty-five minutes in transportation time to go to Montreal to bring him to a halal daycare. And also the fact that he's so small. I tell myself, it's not problematic. He's not aware yet. But when he'll be maybe three or four years old ... I'm not telling you that I won't re-evaluate the situation [...] Maybe then, I'll tell myself, "OK, it's worth it, Caroline, that you drive half an hour every day," when he'll be old enough to understand. Now, he's not aware [*Là, y'est pas conscient*].

Given his young age and the extra commute it would necessitate, Caroline decides to enrol her son in a non-halal daycare and does not engage, to the same extent as Farida, in direct negotiations with the daycare provider. She inquires whether the daycare serves pork and is reassured by the fact that it does not. She also asks whether they could accommodate her halal needs. The provider does not mind as long as she supplies a substitute. Caroline explains that she considered packing her son's lunches, but after consulting with her husband, they decided that this option was too cumbersome: "So [*Fait que*] we took, we decided that we would let him eat meat even if it's not halal ... while asking forgiveness to Allah because we're lazy and [*pis*] [uneasy laugh] that's it [*c'est ça*]." One clearly sees how Caroline navigates different registers. For her, being Muslim involves "countless small adjustments, shifts, and pragmatic considerations" (Schielke and Debevec 2012: 9). Still, this arrangement is not without moral conundrums. She is not fully satisfied with it, but it is the best balance she has found at this particular point in her life. Additional commuting time and preparing a separate halal-appropriate meal for her toddler every day are not feasible right now. She says that she might revisit the situation later, when her son is a bit older and more conscious of religious requirements.

For these women, childcare arrangements demonstrate internal thought processes that consider the appropriate registers of being at particular points in time and in specific contexts. In some cases, the modalities of these assemblages are shared and negotiated with others, but not always. These assemblages can change as a function of context, class, age, priorities, and so on. Negotiations can also be triggered by unforeseen events, which require participants to be creative in their (re)assemblage. Farida explains how the only time she had to alter her arrangement with her children's daycare was when the daycare decided to give them tofu as a substitute for non-halal meat. While Farida acknowledges the efforts of the childcare providers, she asked them to keep it simple, telling them, "You can just make them a grilled cheese sandwich." While religious difference is the initial reason for this arrangement, Farida aims to keep the arrangement as straightforward as possible. In this case, she intervenes not because of religious convictions but because her children do not like tofu.

Public Schools: Mapping Out Strategies

Like daycares, public schools are spaces conducive to multiple navigations and negotiations for students, parents, and teachers. They similarly raise questions around the types of education participants want their children to receive. Questions around dietary requirements are less frequent than in some Western European countries, as public schools in Canada typically do not provide set meals.[14] Our participants with school-age children described numerous scenarios. In what follows we examine negotiations regarding taking holidays outside the school calendar (e.g., to celebrate Eid), finding prayer spaces, and participating (or not participating) in sexual and physical education classes. The reader will note the employment of a number of negotiating strategies ranging from acceptance, acts of kindness, and educating others, to drawing parallels (i.e., kindling sameness), making formal requests, and lodging complaints.

The most common negotiation strategy related to public school among our participants was to familiarize teachers, parents, and other children with the traditions of Islam, typically referencing the five pillars. For some, this education means teaching others about their faith.[15] Others draw parallels with more "mainstream" practices to displace the sense of foreignness that their practices might trigger. Farida, the mother of two we heard describe how she chose a daycare, explains that her dietary concerns have shifted now that her children are in school and she prepares their lunches. Even if their meals are not negotiated, she wants to lessen stigma around their food needs, and takes time to visit her children's classrooms to speak about Islam. She says she usually brings dates or samosas for the children, although one year she catered to her daughter's request for cheese and grapes. She describes this short lesson as a special occasion for her children, which she hopes will ease their integration at lunchtime if they eat items, like samosas, that were unfamiliar to other children.

Similarly, Raji, aged thirty-seven and a thoughtful father of three, explains that his children bring candies to school the day before Eid to share and mark the celebration of the holiday. The gesture also serves to gently remind teachers that his children will be absent the next day:

> Eid day [...] was Friday, so she [his eldest school-going daughter] didn't go to school. We explained to the teacher on the phone [that] we had this Islamic celebration. The previous day was actually Thursday. We, just to show that, you know, we Muslims may be different in the way, how we practise, than majority of the public here who celebrate Christmas, Halloween, and things like that. So we sent candies with the school kids, and we wrote a note that, you know, my daughter was celebrating Eid, which is an Islamic occasion, and for this she wanted to share these candies with you. So we, we're the same but different. Like you celebrate something, we celebrate something.

Raji makes sure to call the teacher to explain the celebration beforehand. He sees sharing sweets with the class as a way to position Eid as a holiday that involves similar festivities and familiar acts of sharing, like Christmas or Halloween. In this way, Raji emphasizes, "you celebrate something, we celebrate something," focusing on shared expressions of celebration and on treats that kids rarely refuse.

While Raji and Farida bring lessons and food to the classroom to ease their children's terrain of negotiations, other participants educate more directly to ward off misperceptions around Islam, of which they are targets.[16] Anna, an amiable thirty-two-year-old participant of Iraqi descent who immigrated to Montreal in her early teens and who wears a headscarf, recalls that as a young girl she was hurt by some of her teachers' comments, which worked to homogenize Islam in culturally and socially exclusionary ways. Anna describes how she gave a book on women in Islam to one of her teachers, who had previously openly voiced her dislike of headscarves in her classroom: "She really doesn't know what she's talking about [*de quoi elle parle*], this teacher. So I brought her a book [laughs] on the rights of women in Islam. So, it [the book] explains things and I gave her the book. I said, 'Madame, this is for you.' What can I say to her?"[17] Rather than engaging directly with her in a debate, Anna hoped that the book's explanation of the theological origins related to veiling might help bring nuance to her teacher's opinions.

Hijab-wearing women are most often compelled to embrace this education strategy in their everyday interactions. As we discussed in Chapter 3, the visibility of their garments attract curiosity, indifference, and, more commonly, discrimination. A number of our participants describe this educative role as tiring. This burden of representation is rarely discussed in the scholarly literature, but impacts young people, like Wafa, in immeasurable ways.[18] Sitting in a university community office, Wafa, aged twenty-two, sits up straighter as she speaks to these pressures. She describes being the only veiled person in her high school when she first moved to St. John's eight years earlier: "It was a lot of pressure, of course. Because you, every one Muslim woman, you are representing your religion. And to me, your behaviours and the way you talk and through your communication ... It's hard initially. You felt really like everything [you did], you were under the microscope that whole time, you know?" Like Anna's recollection of the experience with her teacher at school, Wafa remembers that some teachers put her on the spot, asking her to explain and, in one instance, justify her religious dress. At the same time, she also recalls an English teacher who stepped into this education strategy. Without any fanfare, the teacher assigned all the students a fictional short story about a young girl's empowerment by wearing a hijab. Wafa recalls, "I know she did it for me because she saw I was someone different, and everyone was really nervous to talk to me." Wafa clearly appreciates the subtlety of the teacher's indirect gesture, which opened up conversation among her peers as to why she wore a headscarf without forcing her to educate her classmates. Her experience points to how these moments of mutual respect, as explored further in Chapter 5, are dialogical, involving participants and their entourage. Though her teacher's involvement in her navigation and negotiation of dress may seem to be a minor matter, by acknowleging power asymmetries in her classroom, she recognized Wafa's hypervisibility as the sole hijabi in her high school.[19] The working consensus here is fragile: Wafa's overall experience could have ended quite differently depending on her teacher, her classmates, and the dynamics they all fostered around religious difference. Like Anna's story of sharing a book with her teacher, Wafa's narrative highlights how stories are useful tools in imagining a shared space.

While several participants rely on education, kindness, or drawing parallels with dominant non-Muslim discourses, a minority of our interviewees make formal requests to aim to have their needs heard and their differences accepted. In many cases, this appeal comes after several attempts at informal navigations and negotiations. Not unlike Raji, Aadil, a physician and father of five, notes how he first tried to carefully negotiate with his children's teachers about the possibility of them opting out of gym class. In our interview in his suburban living room, Aadil details some of the approaches he took. He explains how his family understands the prescriptions of Islam, such that gender mixing in physical education classes is inappropriate for his four daughters and son. Drawing on his experience in British Columbia and on some informal fact-gathering among local friends who are Muslims, he first outlined solutions developed by schools in other provinces to deal with similar religious requirements. He also proposed an analogy: just as physicians are required in their profession to respect the religious practices of their patients, so too should school teachers. These two discursive strategies were unsuccessful. He therefore, reluctantly he said, sent a letter to the school district, which overruled the school's administrator and granted his request to exclude his children from gym class. Aadil explains that in the end the administrator was sympathetic to his request because in his letter he enumerated ways in which his children could still participate in school activities without attending gym class. His children were well liked and not "demanding." Here we cite a lengthy excerpt from his interview, which we see as illustrating

his process-focused reasoning with his children's high school principal
and the administration:

> One of my daughters, when she started in [high school – name re-
> moved] they insisted that she has to go to the gym with the children,
> with the boys. And I went very nicely with the lady. I told her. I sent
> first a letter. I said, "From our religion, we are not allowed to allow
> her to do so. We are more than happy that she can go for gym if it is
> with the girls only. And this is practised in Ontario. I am one hundred
> percent sure about this. I have definite information about this. It is
> practised in Vancouver, in British Columbia, as well. So you'll not be
> the only province to do such a kind of thing for the children." And
> she was arguing with me for almost forty-five minutes. She is the
> vice-principal at that time and the lady responsible for this [decision].
>   Then I told her, "Look, I am [a] physician. Let us take it from this
> point of view. We respected the patient's wishes. Even, even if the
> patient would like to die, we have sometimes, according to Canadian
> law of ethics we are not to interfere." I told her, "Look, if there is a
> Jehovah's Witness who had a very severe car accident he is going to
> die, but according to their beliefs they are not going to receive a blood
> transfusion because this is not allowed by their religion. As a physician
> and according to the Canadian code of ethics, I am, as a physician,
> not allowed to force that patient to get a blood transfusion, although
> I know that he is going to die." So I told her, "Is it that a decision to
> participate in a gym activity is equal to one who is going to die? As
> [a] physician, we respected him even if he is doing, choosing a wrong
> decision, but still we respect his religion. But now you are telling me
> that you will not allow my daughter to be away from that?"
>   Anyways, I have to wait. And we raised a letter to the school district
> and finally they accepted. The point [is] that we gave them alternatives.
> I told her that if she's going to gym with the girls, we are more than
> happy to do so. But, too, I told her, "If she can take other class not
> only gym, like she can go to help [other students] with math, for
> English, for history, anything if you like. Third, she can help in [the]
> library, for example. If [the] librarian wants someone to do some stuff
> for her, she can help." So we gave choices.

For Aadil, maintaining positive relationships with the school and the vice-principal is important even if he does not accept their reluctance to allow his children to skip physical education class.[20] This desire to avoid conflict is why he considers going to the school district "unfortunate." He would have preferred a more informal, positively spun solution, like substituting the period with tutoring or library assistance. While he wants to be able to remove the children from these classes, as with many of our participants, his children's inclusion in school activities is equally important in his negotiation. In other words, in different ways, Aadil aims to craft a working consensus that emphasizes his children's participation in other school activities rather than their exclusion from gym classes.

Sports: Working towards a Delicate Consensus

Right now, I'm playing volleyball, badminton, swimming, karate, and yoga! And tonight I have a volleyball practice. Tomorrow, it's karate. Wednesday, badminton. Thursday, I rest. But really, everyday I have an activity.

Physical activities are imbricated into Ouria's everyday life, as they are for many of our participants. This means that gyms, sport facilities, and sports' clubs are sites replete with everyday navigations and negotiations, particularly for women. Our participants grapple with questions from what type of gym they should join, to what type of sports to practise, to how to dress appropriately. In the majority of cases, as for Sabah, in the Introduction, with the apartment building pool, the balancing of these elements requires a careful evaluation of the requirements of a specific activity, the physical and mental health benefits that it provides them, and their religious beliefs around modesty and mixing with nonrelatives of the opposite sex. For the three participants described in this section, expressions of Islam are important and influence their choice of facility or sport, but regular exercise is equally part of the equation.

The effort required to maintain or reimagine the terms of a working consensus was visible in many of our participants' accounts. In some cases, participants themselves comment on the fragility of the balance that they craft at a particular moment. Siham, a soft-spoken twenty-one-year-old physiotherapy student, wears a hijab and considers herself a practising Muslim. Here she reflects on her choice of a career path in physiotherapy, a profession that requires physical contact with men:

> It was, it was quite a struggle for me to actually think about going into physiotherapy. I'm, like, "This is quite a hands-on field that I'm thinking about going into. Am I ready for this?" But then, like, at some point I think in myself, I had to heighten my level of professionalism. Like, up until, maybe up until CEGEP, if I, like, touched another man, it meant something to me. Like, it, like, I would be very aware of it and be, like, "Oh!" Or I would be very shocked by it [...] Like, this is not something that I wanna do. But then, as soon as I got to university and I realized that I'm, I realized the kind of career path that I was inclined towards, I was, like, "Hmmm, either I have to decide now if it's something that I can't go over. If I can get over [it], not to go there." Don't go into a line of career that you feel that you're gonna be uncomfortable with or you need to heighten your level of professionalism. You need to get past it and realize why you're doing this. Ultimately, I want to work with geriatrics. I want to work with older people, the older clientele. So touching and that stuff, that's not an issue. It wouldn't be an issue. But in order to get there, I realized that I'm gonna have to do certain things. And I already do those certain things. Like, I'd, I'm gonna have to, like, tape a male athlete or maybe massage a male athlete. And I've done that now, and it just comes to a time where, like, you're doing this for your career.

Siham describes an ongoing internal debate. She explains that her reconciliation of seemingly competing ways of being would not have been possible when she was a teenager. At that point in her life, touching someone of the opposite sex was not open to negotiation; she was too uncomfortable. This kind of close physicality countered her beliefs. However, the circumstances of her life changed. Her choice of profession, and especially the training qualifications, require that she be comfortable touching bodies. Rather than give up this career path, she chooses to "heighten [her] level of professionalism." As part of her training she is required to work with male athletes on her university's cross-country running team. She says that she is able to cope with what she feels is a kind of moral dissonance in her current assemblage because her long-term goal is to work in geriatrics. With time and with a focus on the elderly, she expects that this discomfort will dissolve. This equilibrium, which required considerable navigation to figure out, remains fragile. Siham might, for instance, reassess her decision when she finishes her training, especially if she does not find a position working with the elderly. Other circumstances might change so that she would need to think of how to craft a new balance. Her narrative captures the dynamism within many of these engagements.

In other cases, participants see the consensus they have reached becoming more precarious and complicated by public debates, which Samuli Schielke and Liza Debevec (2012) describe as "grand schemes," that affect the everyday lives of our participants and the arrangements they craft. Several of our participants who modified the "traditional" sports uniform by wearing a hijab and/or by replacing shorts with longer pants had to renegotiate these ad hoc arrangements following recurring public controversies in Quebec on the wearing of visible religious garments when playing soccer.[21] Mada, a twenty-one-year-old university student who was raised in the United States, expresses her frustrations with these polemics. She makes a point to remind her team members that she can be a practising Muslim, a skilful and motivated soccer player, and a good teammate:

> So when I go play soccer, for example, yes, you may identify me as a Muslim. Yeah. Big deal. I'm still playing soccer, just like you. I'm still trying to win just like you. I'm still trying to be a good team player, like you. You know? [...] For me, if I play soccer with my scarf, it's not a religious thing. It's like I'm just playing soccer. [...] I'm just dressed this way. Literally. That's the way I see it. Just like she's wearing a jersey, I'm wearing a jersey too, but [also] a scarf. Um I don't, I don't understand that [the controversy].

Mada relativizes her hijab. For her it was part of her dress, covering her body like her jersey. In this discussion she emphasizes sport, her love of the game, and her desire to win, not her religious self.

In other cases, changes in the regulations of gyms or the availability of facilities upset a balance and require participants to craft a new arrangement. Many of our Montreal participants who are avid swimmers had to revisit their working consensus when the sole women's-only public swimming pool closed.[22] We met twenty-one year-old Wafa earlier, when she described how her high school English teacher introduced a reading assignment that included practising Muslim women. In our interview, in the busy student centre between her classes, Wafa explains that she has taken it upon herself to organize sporting spaces for the women's branch of her university's Muslim Students' Association. Negotiation of women's-only access times is stressful because the sports facilities she relies upon do not have firm policies.[23] She is never sure what to expect: "It doesn't seem like there's clear guidelines, and it seems like every supervisor does his own thing. Every manager has their own thing. So it's kind of annoying when that happens, 'cuz you don't really, don't know who to go to, and you don't know the rules about that." Not everyone finds a satisfactory solution like Sabah was able to work out in the arrangement with her building manager.

To avoid relying on the graces of a particular manager, thirty-year-old Nayla tried to locate private women's-only gyms or public swimming pools with women's-only hours, which she describes as a tedious and time-consuming process:[24]

> Swimming! I loooove swimming. I have tried to find a lot of, ah, centres for swimming, and there was one here: the Women's Y, the YWCA. That was the best [arrangement] [*Ça c'était le meilleur*]. That was the perfect centre because it was only for women, and they had a perfect swimming pool, and even they closed the, the windows because they knew. Even the trainers, they were all women. It was perfect, but then they closed it for, I don't know why they closed it down, and then I have constantly tried to find other centres [...] there's only one place and it is in a, anyways, it's somewhere in Montreal, and it's, honestly the only reason they do it one hour on two days a week, and the only reason is because this place was established by Jewish people, and we have the same, [a] similar belief [...] But because

of the hours, I can't always go. But I'm trying to find a centre, a proper-like gym centre, where they can offer more hours or maybe training courses for just women.

Other women in our sample find the schedules of women's-only facilities too limiting and opt to not exercise or to use coed facilities. To be comfortable doing so, they explain how they carefully choose their clothing and sporting activities. Ouria discusses how she opts for karate specifically because of the dress regulations: "I chose karate specifically because of the outfit [*l'accoutrement*]. The only thing I have to add is a headscarf on my head. Exactly. This is perfect. I have no problem. And this, this works well for me." Ouria swims regularly with a bodysuit, sometimes called a burkini when it includes a headcovering, which she bought on a trip to Syria:

> I have, I have my [bathing] suit, but for me it's ... Listen, I'm not very, very orthodox. In my head, during my time in the pool, there is no one that looks at me, and then you get out. That's it. You know? I don't walk [around] in a bikini. I am still covered from head to toe. Yes, it's tight, but I am in a swimming pool. In any case, I am at the point where I have to justify something which I shouldn't [...] I love swimming [...]
>
> If someone says something to me, I say, "Look, this is Spandex. I mean, this guy there has body hair from head to toe. And he has a lot of hair. OK? Go bother him. Don't bug me [*Achale moi pas*]." [laughs] So there are people who jump in with their diapers, with their hygienic pads. I want to say, "This is Speedo. No." So in any case I prepare myself. So that's it [*Ben c'est ça!*]! I always prepare myself in advance. Mentally ... So if someone comes to tell me something, I know what to answer. But it has to be logical. It can't be emotional. It can't be insulting for the other person, you know? [*T'sais?*] Don't try to insult the other person but simply [try] to open his eyes, you know. And, you know, think outside of the box, you know? That's it [*Tout simplement*].

Ouria loves swimming. She found a suit in Syria that covers her from "head to toe" and is tight enough to swim laps comfortably. As with the clothes she wears when she plays other sports, she considers comfort and practicality. She considers the quality of the material: "C'est du Spandex là" and "C'est du Speedo." For Ouria, crafting these sports-related arrangements is further complicated by the limited sportswear options available for women seeking to cover their bodies. To find appropriate clothing for the other sports she plays, she laments having to shop in the men's clothing section:

> I don't want to show my body [*montrer mes atous*]! And at the same time, I, I end up [*j'me ramasse*] buying men's clothing [*du linge pour gars*], which is super big and that doesn't fit me, simply because there's nothing for girls! [...] Because, I mean, because Islam is flexible. Islam is part of my life. Yes, yes, it's part of my life. And [*pis*] at the same time, I love sports. I don't want to do ballet. For sure, I don't want to do pole dancing! [...]
>
> For me, OK, karate with a headscarf is fine, you know [*t'sais*]? It's loose enough, and it's a modest outfit. At this point in time, as I say, finding clothes in shops that I can wear, nice clothes, and clothes that cover, you know, for sports, is very, very, very complicated.

Ouria's time at the pool reveals lengthy navigation and negotiation. She has found a bathing suit that covers her body in a way that feels comfortable, even if she is bothered by the efforts it required. On this navigation she concludes, "I am at the point where I have to justify something which I shouldn't." The verbal negotiations that accompany her suit at the public swimming pool require physical and emotional effort in ways that the far less hygienic practices of other swimmers do not. On occasion, Ouria has to negotiate her body-covering swimsuit with the staff at public swimming pools.[25] She explains how she prepares her arguments beforehand, using humour and creativity to highlight the suit's high-quality material. At all times, she takes the feelings of the person with whom she interacts into consideration. She says, "I always prepare myself in advance." In other words, she thinks beforehand about the inevitable glances and concerns with her non-mainstream bathing suit. She finds these particular navigations and negotiations related to sports clothing to be "very, very, very complicated."

In this section we have focused on sports and leisure activities, but we would be remiss to not add a few examples from other female participants who attach similar negotiations to the garments they wear. Recall Ifra, who, in Chapter 3, acknowledges the work that constitutes wearing a hijab on a daily basis in a minority context. She does not wear visible religious signs regularly, but she says that she feels politically obligated to push the imaginative possibilities of her coworkers with her clothing. She explains, "I do wear a Pakistani outfit, [a] Pakistani outfit at work. I do intentionally once a month or so. I mean, I don't really have a schedule, but, you know." Ifra likes the colours and style but mentally prepares herself for the additional questions and comments the outfit engenders. She is assertive and well spoken, but these conversations are not easy. Ifra assumes this work, to use her term, on a monthly basis.

In responding to questions at a municipal pool about her bathing suit, Ouria aims to keep her tone logical and unemotional. In general, she acknowledges the fragility of the working consensus that has been arrived at in relation to her swimsuit. Its acceptability varies as a function of the staff and fellow swimmers at a particular pool. In fact, other participants, like twenty-nine-year-old Asma, have not been as successful when faced with prohibitive regulations: "One day in the same pool, I was allowed to put my burkini, the other day I wasn't." Asma explains that at this particular pool, "They have a clerk at the desk who checks your swimming suit before you enter. Yeah. They wanna make sure." While some of these restrictions may reflect pressure for a secular body, as described in the previous chapter, this sport facility has officially determined that certain body-covering suits are unhygienic, a sanitation argument that moves away from common rationales for the secular body.

Ouria's experiences of navigating and negotiating appropriate dress at the pool summarises the thoughtfulness of her approach. For her, Islam plays a role in the arrangements she makes. Her sense of modesty means that she will not do ballet or pole dancing. But important too is her love for sports and her need to feel that she is appropriately dressed, that she can wear "nice clothes *and* clothes that cover [my body]" (our emphasis). Islam, as Ouria put it, is "flexible" and pragmatic. Her religiosity adapts to her daily life and to her dreams, passions, style (she wants to wear "nice clothes"), and priorities. The stories shared by Asma, Ouria, Nayla,

Wafa, and Mada depict how they navigate and negotiate their sporting lives, balancing what they see as appropriate clothing and comportment with the rules and expectations of different facilities and organizations. At times, they feel they are successful at crafting solutions that work, and at times they do not feel that way. Our navigation and negotiation framework allows us to document and reflect on the power relations, intricacies, and fragility of this balancing work. In contrast with an accommodation framework, this lens captures how our participants seek to cobble together multiple registers, which include but are not limited to their religious practices. It also captures the dynamism and creativity in these moments that an accommodation framework focused on requests would miss.

***

Since the early 2000s, the notions of cultural and religious accommodation – notions introduced by the Supreme Court in 2006 and concretized by government policy and the media's attention to exceptional cases – have become part of common parlance in Canada. Our participants' descriptions of their quotidian navigations and negotiations challenge the utility of this framework, however. Their stories – far more common than legal cases – suggest something else is going on. More often than not, differences are worked out informally. Internal navigations and external negotiations are overlooked when we focus on a language of accommodation, for it documents formally expressed demands. In addition, the navigation/negotiation prism sheds light on power dynamics, moral conundrums, and more common everyday moments that Muslim Canadians encounter.

To think about the complexity, creativity, and fragility of these moments – as for Maria when two technicians take up her invitation for breakfast and order bacon with their eggs and hashbrowns – in this chapter we have focused on three everyday locations: daycares, schools, sport facilities.[26] The stories we have recounted show the multiple ways our participants are welcomed, engaged, disengaged, and, at times, ousted through these encounters. The power dynamics involved in these moments are significant. As we have sought to underscore, even if everyone is bound to navigate and negotiate everyday, some individuals are compelled into these situations more than others. This unfairness or asymmetry can be attributed to a number of overlapping factors, including living as racialized minorities within the Christianness of the Canadian public sphere (as we described in Chapter 3) that can, at times, be traced to Islamophobia (discussed in Chapter 1). Furthermore, all the examples in this chapter relate to women's dress and/or to social comportment, which speaks to the importance of gender in thinking about these inbalances.

By way of conclusion, we want to return to some specific aspects of these processes of navigation and negotiation. As discussed, we chose these terms intending that they convey the complexity of how our participants work out their religious needs. For many of our interviewees this working out happens first and foremost within themselves. In fact, internal navigation is present in all the accounts we heard, regardless of whether participants choose to embark on a negotiation with others or not. Most often, individuals figure out with what they are comfortable at a particular moment. They then try to come up with arrangements to best cobble the multiple registers that make up their lives.

It should be clear that these processes require considerable mental energy and thoughtfulness. Ouria, who shared her preparations before entering a public pool, nicely summarizes this mental arithmetic with an example of navigation from her Christmas staff party. She humorously remembers her stream of consciousness when a colleague gave her a bottle of alcohol:

> There's a work colleague in Vancouver, and we don't know him. He didn't know me; he never saw me, but we work remotely [*on travaille à distance*]. He ... he sent everyone in the team a bottle of wine [laughs] for Christmas. And listen, I didn't take that as an insult because he's never seen me. And [*pis*] he gave a bottle of wine to everyone, including me. But [laughs] it was a funny moment because, honestly, I had no idea what do with it!
>
> Technically when you receive a bottle of alcohol ... our relationship with alcohol is not only do you not drink it, but you don't sit at tables [where there is alcohol]. You don't give it as a present. You don't touch it; you don't take it. Really you have nothing to do with it [*t'as rien à*

voir avec ça]. So, I didn't know what to do with it! So, I saw that my work colleague was like, "Yeah, well, what are you going to do with this?" And I told her, "I don't know yet."

I thought about all kinds of scenarios: Should I bring it back to my place and throw it away at home? But here as well, if someone saw me with a bottle, it would be a scandal. A scandal. So I can always empty it in the bathroom [at the office]. Oh, but no, this is not something that is done. Because I was scared to have a drop on me. It can seem crazy but, really, you know [*t'sais*], it's really considered very, very dirty. Not dirty, but impure, really. I can't refuse a gift either. So what I did is I gave it, quite simply, to my boss. So she was very happy, and that's it. I simply told her, "Look, I don't drink, you know [*je bois pas, t'sais*]?" [laughs]

What should she do with the gift? Ouria thoughtfully considers different scenarios and the parameters that limit her possibilities. She makes clear that she wants nothing to do with this bottle. Drinking alcohol goes against her religious beliefs and the possibility of physical contact is inconceivable. And yet she also does not want to refuse a gift from a colleague. In her decision, she balances her unease with alcohol, her physical aversion for its substance, her desire to not be seen with the bottle ("C'est scandale"), the feelings of her colleagues, and the potential reactions of her family at home. This mundane example is illustrative of the complexity in Ouria's internal navigation and, at the same time, of the simplicity (a term she herself uses) of how she ultimately negotiates the situation. She decides to give the bottle to her boss, who, not unlike the employees Maria invites to breakfast, appreciates the gift and appears oblivious to the mental energy put into the decision.

As discussed, it is often after this internal calculation that some participants choose to negotiate arrangements with their entourage. These decisions are contextual and tempered by social relations. The geographical location of participants (in some cases, whether they are in urban or suburban areas), as well as a multitude of other factors such as their age, gender, and socioeconomic standing, influence their decision-making processes. For many, a comfortable and safe atmosphere is also an essential prerequisite to negotiation. For Nour, the secondary teacher we met in

Chapter 3, a kindhearted secretary and consideration for her own health were important factors that led her to ask for a dietary adjustment in a meal made available by the school board during parent-teacher meetings:

INTERVIEWER: So at Christmas parties and things like that you were, in a sense, you were able to find options that were available to you [vegetarian options]?

NOUR: Yeah. And if it's going to happen that it isn't the case, then I just won't go. I'm not going to demand it.

INTERVIEWER: Why not demand it?

NOUR: Because it's not just about me. Like next week we have parent-teacher interviews. And in every school in the school board, there's a break in the middle where the school provides the meal for the teachers. And at my school, every year they order Dagwoods [a catering company]. And Dagwoods will send over a platter of sandwiches, and they will send over their vegetarian option, [which] will be a cheese sandwich, but then they will cut the cheese on the same machine as the meat so I won't be able to eat it. Only this year do I feel comfortable enough to say to the person organizing, "Can you just have them prepare a tuna sandwich for me?" It's a question of being, feeling comfortable, as well. You know?

INTERVIEWER: Comfortable with the people? I guess after a while with the people you are [...]

NOUR: Comfortable for both. I mean, if someone doesn't know me, and I ask them for something, they're going to feel put out. They're going to feel as if I'm forcing them to do it. You know? So, yeah, this is the first year, I know, and partly because, also it's going to be a long day for me. I'm pregnant. I have to think about whether I'm eating properly. And I feel comfortable with that school secretary who's in charge to say, "Can you do this?"

Nour's decision to approach the person organizing the food order that year and not in previous years is mediated by different factors. She has worked at the school for a couple of years. She knows and is comfortable with her colleagues, and with this secretary in particular. She is also pregnant. While she might have chosen to simply navigate her way through this situation as in previous years, by abstaining from eating the sandwiches, it is the combination of all these elements that incite her to initiate a negotiation this time. Put differently, her negotiation, like all negotiations, resembles a working consensus. It requires work. It feels delicate. Even a small change in her environment (a different secretary, for instance), or a bigger one, what Schielke and Debevec (2012) coin a grand scheme (e.g., debates on a possible Charter of Secularism to be implemented at the school), could affect her decision and/or the result of the negotiation. It is relevant to note that Nour also clearly differentiates the way she works out her situation from the act of making demands. For Nour, making demands too forcefully disregards the emotions of others and her membership among the staff. She prefers to deal with her situation more informally and flexibly, knowing that she can count on the secretary to respect her dietary needs.

Together these narratives illustrate how the language of reasonable accommodation that permeates current public discourse fails to capture the everyday navigation and negotiation of most of our participants. To capture these seemingly unremarkable moments, we have been attentive to how people figure out life as religious minorities in daycares, at public schools, and in gyms. These anecdotes relate mundane moments that academics rarely consider. Such moments tell us, in our opinion, more about how a minority religion in Canada is lived, navigated, and negotiated than the sensational accounts and legal cases to which we grant a great deal of attention.

Mutual Respect and Working Out Difference   **5**

We met Farida, the mother of two small children, in a suburb of Montreal on a cold November morning at a coffee shop. In the midst of recounting her daily life, recently focused on children's birthday parties and playdates, Farida mentioned the importance of what she called "mutual respect" in enabling her and her family to take part and feel fully included in these events. From her perspective, with mutual respect "you'll find a way past the small differences," but without it, "even small differences will be really big." In this chapter, we consider and take seriously this notion of mutual respect, language that was invoked by a number of our participants.[1] Mutual respect was designated especially when recounting moments in their quotidian lives in which difference is worked out with no fuss. In many cases, working towards a consensus enables a shared experience. Farida illustrates her understanding with a concrete example, a neighbourhood street party:

> We had the most wonderful neighbourhood. We had a really small
> street [...] So we had maybe twelve houses on our immediate street.
> We had, um, and all our neighbours were really diverse, from Jamaica,
> Trinidad, Guyanese, Pakistan. We did a street party. We said, "We're
> just going to do a full-day street party. Everybody's going to cook."
> Without me knowing, one of the neighbours had just asked me

casually, "Where do you buy your meat from?" And I said, I told them where I bought my meat. That neighbour had taken it upon themselves – they were Haitian – they took it upon themselves to tell all the other neighbours, except one decided not to, and that was fully within their right. They asked, "OK, how do you cook your meat? If it's cooked with pork, is that OK?" We said, "No. [And] we, we're really particular if something's fried." You know, we just explained our details. And I had no expectations. But the day of the party, everybody on the street had made halal food. And I was so humbled by that. I thanked them. I'm, like, that was so considerate of them. They went out of their way to pick up the meat and even, like, I mean, it was a street party. There's alcohol. But my husband and I had to go out for a couple hours, and we were going to come back and join the party. The few hours we were gone, they all drank, and they didn't pick up the alcohol when we were there. And I was so moved by that. I told them, we came back, and I said, "Look, we really appreciated it, [what] you guys are doing, but we don't want to ruin your party. If this is how you're enjoying yourself, we're OK with that. You know, if you feel like, if you guys want to drink, it's an open street party. By all means go ahead. I don't want to infringe on your customs." So then it was fine. We ate halal meat, and there was booze.

Farida sees the street party as a success – "I was so moved by that" – due to the ability of her neighbours to both recognize difference (i.e., be considerate of everyone's needs) and, more importantly, translate this recognition into practice. Yet, while the recognition of difference is important, she does not emphasize difference. Rather, mutual respect allows for the establishment of relationships and for sharing a meal together. In this instance, the neighbours found a comfortable arrangement, and almost everyone made an effort. One of them asked about where to purchase and how to prepare the shared meat in an Islamically permissible, or halal, manner. Farida and her husband acknowledged their neighbours' sensitivity around alcohol but encouraged them to "go ahead." Both gestures aimed to strike a balance between multiple identities and commitments. Farida says they all had a good time.

The block party is a success precisely because of the generosity and empathy that participants express for each other. At the same time, this achievement is fragile. It pushes participants out of their comfort zone and require that they, as another participant put it, ask "awkward questions" to ensure that differences and power-relations are acknowledged. In fact, Farida's neighbour asked several questions, giving her the possibility to explain her family's dietary "details." Sharing the meal also requires that Farida and her neighbours suspend their sense of rightness to care without judging. As Farida sensibly put it, a less desirable outcome is imaginable where difference would have been focused upon and mutual respect would have been absent.

In this chapter, we consider moments of mutual respect as narrated by our participants. These stories continue to counter a prevalent discourse that locates Muslims, focusing on hypervisible forms of Islam, in a "problem-space" (Agrama 2012: 28) of conflict, difference, and disagreement (and discrimination; see D. Scott 2004). As we saw in Chapter 4, our participants are called to and seek to balance, combine, and assemble different values, responsibilities, and registers of importance for themselves in their everyday lives. While power asymmetries require that certain people – in our sample, many of the self-identified Muslims – balance and negotiate more than others, a number of our participants expressed, at the same time, a sense of contentment with their negotiations and the consensus (or moments of mutual respect) they were able to craft. This chapter chronicles and analyzes these positively experienced narratives.

Moments of mutual respect require flexibility and speak to the porousness of boundaries between identities and to the idea that practices (including religious practices) are not fixed but often transform as a function of context and time. As Schielke (2009a) highlights, while identities and theologies can be characterized by a certain discursive coherence, this coherence becomes more difficult to sustain when it is translated into practice and confronted with the ambivalence and contradictions of the everyday. Schielke (2009b: S37) asks, "What happens when claims and ideals [...] come to be practised as guidelines in a life that has other, competing orientations and is characterized not by the primary purpose of perfection but rather by a struggle to find one's place in life?"[2] One way to consider the "struggle to find one's place in life" is to view everyday interactions as snapshots of daily interactions. As for Farida and her neighbours, these daily encounters often require improvisation. Farida describes one neighbour who creatively revisited the boundaries of his identity – asking her about the nature of halal meat and where to buy it – to engage and cultivate a relationship with her family. These interactions are often unremarkable. Still, following Connolly (2005: 124), we see them as fruitful spaces in which "new possibilities of being and acting" emerge. In what follows, we purposely shift our attention away from cases in which difference is rigidified, identified, and experienced as a problem, or described solely as a source of tension. Of course, this shift in attention does not mean that our participants do not experience these hurdles or moments where respect was absent, as discussed in other parts of this book.

Our focus on these interactions resonates with the methodological shift proposed by Amiraux and Araya-Moreno (2014: 93) in their discussion of religious radicalism and with others (e.g., Turam 2015)[3] who invite researchers interested in pluralism to take "mundane" interactions as their point of departure, rather than "abstract principles" or "individual trajectories" (Amiraux and Araya-Moreno 2014: 93). Indeed, as the reader will come to realize, this shift accords special attention to the dialogical and emotional dimensions of exchanges that, as these scholars show, are central to how pluralism and coexistence are worked out in mundane sites. This alternative focus may better illustrate how identities and lives shape and are shaped by these everyday interactions.

We are particularly attentive to what Farida and other participants call "moments of respect." These interactions are relational in that they require mutual recognition of difference. Recognition goes beyond tolerance. James Tully's work (e.g., 1995, 2000, 2004) has helped us think through the experiences of our interviewees (as has that of Skerrett 2004; Van Quaquebeke, Henrich, and Eckloff 2007; Elver 2012). While Tully's work on recognition focuses on more formal demands and struggles for recognition, his understanding of the *process* of recognition is useful to think about moments of respect. Four elements that structure this process (and that come back in the work of Connolly [e.g., 2005], discussed at greater length in this chapter) are particularly noteworthy (Tully 2000, 2004):

1. That acknowledgment of asymmetries of power is central to struggles for recognition. These struggles are precisely about changing the rules of recognition to address these asymmetries (Tully 2000: 476). Some individuals are more vulnerable in these exchanges than others.

2. That recognition is a mutual and relational process, in which participants' identities are modified through interactions with each other and in which participants become aware of the mutable character of their identities (Tully 2004: 99).

3. That this recognition of difference has to be nonjudgmental. In other words, recognition entails encountering the practice(s) of others as they are, in their "own traditions" (Tully 1995: 128). It has to be devoid of imperial/patriarchal mindsets to change the other.

4. That misrecognition "undermines the basic self-respect and self-esteem that are necessary to empower a person" (Tully 2000: 470). When recognition is privileged, participants in the exchange can make efforts to understand each other's practices to protect each other from harm (see also Beaman 2014a, 2017), which requires refraining from judging or seeking to transform others' beliefs and/or practices. For interviewees in our study, this empowerment more specifically includes protecting one another from discomfort, embarrassment, or exclusion.[4]

These moments are not always easy. They can call into question the boundedness of identities. They can necessitate the suspension of a sense of truth. We also use the adjectives awkward and uncomfortable to describe them. As we note at the beginning of this chapter, on this point, we draw on Connolly's (2005: 124) notion of an agonistic relationship, where one "absorbs the agony of having elements of [her] own faith called into question by others, and fold[s] agonistic contestation of others into the respect that [she] convey[s] toward them." Lastly, and significantly, successful interactions are most often process oriented rather than outcome based (Van Quaquebeke, Henrich, and Eckloff 2007). This distinction comes out clearly in the interviews we conducted, in which the emphasis is put on the process that allowed participants to share a moment with others rather than on the outcome or the recognition of their difference. As mentioned, these moments are woven through many of the stories participants shared with us. They shape daily social life.[5]

Similar methodological conundrums to those we describe in trying to capture processes of navigation and negotiations discussed in Chapter 4 undergird our efforts to document these moments. To reiterate, everyday practices and interactions are not as easily recovered as the belief-based, institution-located practices that have made up the bulk of the academic study of religion. We recognize the risks of such scrutiny of the everyday. As French studies scholar Michael Sheringham (2006: 360) points out, when the everyday is rendered an "object of scrutiny," it dissolves into something else because it becomes something that is treated as an event (which it may or may not be in practice). These challenges have marked our attempts to recover moments experienced as mutual respect for our participants. Moments of respect are often fleeting and mentioned in passing and, therefore, necessitate particular attention on the part of the interviewer, or what Jonathan Z. Smith (1982: 54) calls a "focusing lens." Finally, we are aware that relying on second-hand narrated description of these moments provides us with a different picture than if we were to study them with an ethnographic lens (on this methodological point, see Amiraux and Araya-Moreno 2014). Yet, their fleeting character would make using such an approach difficult.

In the remaining sections of this chapter, we draw on vignettes that convey these moments of respect. In so doing, our aim is to capture how our participants experience these moments and to reflect on what these tell us about how people work out differences.

Mutual Respect as Dialogical, Shared, and Agonistic

Quotidian moments of mutual and agonistic respect often centre around food and diet. Sharing meals are fertile moments of community creation, whereby the *act of sharing* requires a certain sensitivity about the needs of the different people involved in the meal.[6] As with Farida and the neighbourhood celebration, these moments of respect are identified as possible precisely because difference is recognized. The mutual nature of this process is also significant. One must not solely accommodate or tolerate religious differences among one's entourage. Mutual respect is a dialogical process, which indicates a sense of empathy for the other, or a *délicatesse*, as Samira, a lawyer in her mid-fifties, elegantly puts it. At the heart of this *délicatesse* is the idea that those exchanging should not feel judged or feel that others want to transform their practices. This form of recognition, as Tully (1995: 128) explains, is about accepting the other and her practices as they are, on their "own terms." Samira explains this process when she recounts an exchange with a friend, where they discussed her prayer needs that coincided with her friend's dinner invitation:

> When I went to their house [to have dinner], I said, well [*ben*], [...] "Listen, I cannot come at this time because it's a prayer time, but I will come a bit later." And the person told me, "Well, no, you can come to my home. It doesn't bother me. You can do your prayer at home." I said, "OK! If I can do the prayer in the house, there's no problem." So I brought my mat, my compass for orientation, and I did it. And the person was very comfortable. I didn't feel that she was pretending. There was no pretence. It was really sincere. *She accepted me the way I was.* And, and so for her, whether I did my prayer at her place or mine had no importance! (our emphasis)

What Samira retains from this exchange is the sincerity of her friend's invitation. Her host was not simply tolerating her practice, but genuinely "accepted [her] the way [she] was." Her invitation was devoid of judgment. Samira also made an effort in bringing her prayer rug and a compass to orient herself. This *délicatesse* requires a sense of caring and empathy for the other. In this exchange, similar to others, power asymmetries are subtly acknowledged. Practically, this recognition can translate into asking questions that mitigate some of these asymmetries. This can entail opening oneself to being vulnerable.

Farida's experience with her neighbours is a case in point. There is a clear asymmetry in that it appears that on her street only her family eats halal. Her neighbours are careful not to make Farida and her family feel excluded or uncomfortable during the party. Had the neighbour not expressly asked about their diet and then communicated their preferences to the others, a different outcome might have transpired. It is possible that Farida's family would have participated or might have negotiated their presence by perhaps eating their own food or avoiding non-halal dishes. But they would not have felt the same sense of validation and mutuality in these last two scenarios. They would not have been able to share the moment with their neighbours. To be clear, we are not advocating a blanket solution of serving halal products to create inclusivity. Rather, we note that what Farida finds most validating is the process: the informality, sincerity, and specificity of the question and the subsequent course of action.

Posing these types of questions is not necessarily comfortable. One can erroneously overstep bounds by inquiring about intimate areas of life. Recall the medical doctor we describe in Chapter 3, who says that she stopped wearing her hijab to work. As a medical doctor seeking to efficiently treat patients, at times their awkward, even if kind, questions might have engendered mutual respect. But she felt that such dialogue came at the cost of her efficiency and effectiveness as a physician. Such questions also carry the risk of making incorrect assumptions about the other, therein potentially damaging relationships. Rabi, aged fifty-three, who works in an executive position, describes a different scenario in which a "difficult" conversation is better avoided. He dines out a lot for his job and describes how some restaurant servers may not be aware that scrunchions (fried pork fat popular in St. John's) and bacon bits are pork products. He explains how this menu avoidance has been positive: "I let them know that I would only have vegetarian or fish [at a restaurant]. In fact, I am trying to lose weight. I've lost twenty ... eighteen pounds in the last two months!" And yet, for many of our participants it is this particular attention to their practices that is constitutive of what makes these exchanged moments of respect possible. Moreover, this attention does not necessarily have to take the form of a question. When participants are more familiar with each others' worlds, this exchange can also manifest through nonverbalized gestures. Samira notes later in her interview that she felt touched by the efforts of her friends, who knew that she ate halal, to cook food that she could eat when they invited her:

"Because they were aware that I'm Muslim [*Sachant que j'étais musulmane*], there was never red or white wine. And pork was not even an option, of course. Because they knew that for me it was prohibited. They would always find a way to make sure that there was fish, and or that it [the meal] was vegetarian." Her friends' particular attention to her religious practice protected her from both discomfort and feeling excluded. Their tone and approach celebrated Samira's sense of belonging and effectively shifted their mode of being from living alongside one another to living well together (Beaman 2016).

The shared dimension of moments of respect is also conveyed by Hassan, the thirty-two-year-old human resource officer born in Montreal whom we met in Chapter 3, who describes the *Petit-Noël* [Little Christmas] party organized at his colleague Géraldine's house:

When we have Christmas parties, well, we normally, every year, go to the house of someone. [We] go to a colleague's house, and, well, we do a small Christmas [party]. So, they know I don't eat pork, OK? And what is interesting is that they will respect the fact that I don't eat pork. So they say, "Well, since you don't eat pork, I will do this and that." For sure, there will be pork, but, you know, this doesn't bother me. I respect the religions and customs of others, you know. There is no problem. But they will also adapt themselves to me. This is what I like in customs, well, that I have a colleague called Géraldine. [She will say] "Well, you know, I will do this. Normally I do it with pork, but for you I will do it without pork, OK?" There I said, "Well, Géraldine, you're not obliged to do that." "No, no, no! You know, I really want you to taste this dish" [*T'sais, j'veux vraiment que tu goûtes à cette affaire là!*]. I don't remember what it was, but in any case, "I really want you to taste this dish! You know, normally I do it with bacon and with –" I don't really remember what, so she adapted it. So I found that, for me I found that it really touched me. I felt, you know, I felt that it was, I, I was someone important in the team.

Like many of our participants, Hassan chooses to attend his department's annual Christmas dinner. For him, even though he does not celebrate Christmas, the party is important, not only because it is a work-related event, but also because he enjoys spending time with his colleagues. In his case, the fact that Géraldine organizes a *Christmas* dinner – seen from Hassan's perspective as a traditionally Christian celebration – is not identified as a concern. Rather, Hassan sees her invitation as a welcomed opportunity to share a convivial meal with his colleagues. That he does not eat pork is negotiated with relative ease. He describes avoiding these dishes, and his colleagues make sure that there are alternative options available. Thus, he and his colleagues are aware and considerate of the differences in their lifestyles and dietary practices, and these are dealt with without fuss. What Hassan finds important to underline is Géraldine's *délicatesse* in her effort to modify a traditional dish because she wants him to taste it. He is touched by this gesture of care, which makes him feel like "someone important in the team." Géraldine's action allows him to try her traditional dish with his colleagues. In other words, while difference is recognized, this recognition is not the outcome of these moments; it is, rather, part of a process that acts as a means towards partaking in the event. We interpret his satisfaction as representative of a more fulsome respect which, again, is often process rather than outcome based (cf. Van Quaquebeke, Henrich, and Eckloff 2007).

It is noteworthy that Farida's, Samira's, and Hassan's experiences all involve some type of prior preparation. Their neighbours, friends, and colleagues take care around the type of meat, where to purchase it, and how to cook it, as well as how the presence of alcohol should be negotiated. In other cases, however, these moments are more spontaneous and ephemeral. This extemporaneity is visible when Ouria, the reporter, recounts an embrace with a colleague. Her male colleague, on returning to work after a chemotherapy treatment, spontaneously embraced her, which trespassed her sense of *mahram* (the men whom she can touch, based on who is marriageable and who is not). Ouria explains, "It was a colleague who had cancer and who came back after chemo. Chemo, that's it. And he came close to me and, listen, at that moment I did not think. I said, 'Well, there's no problem. The intention is not to French kiss [*frencher*]!' [laughs]." Ouria brought up this example as part of a wider discussion of how she negotiates physical contact with men who are not relatives. Note how in greeting her colleague and accepting his hug, she suspends her beliefs about noncontact between unrelated men and women to share with him this moment of empathy, joy, and relief over his relative health. She understands this unexpected moment as representing an encounter between two human beings that is devoid of sexual meaning.

Ouria's story also makes visible a dimension that is present in all such moments of respect. Ouria deliberately overlooks her own beliefs around proper interaction and entitlement to "rightness" to engage with her colleague (on this see Beaman 2014a: 98 and Rothenberg 2010: 101 on what she calls "wilful overlooking"). Farida and her husband decide to attend the block party and accept the presence of alcohol. These actions carry an agonistic dimension, as they require a brief abandonment of one's sense of truth (Connolly 1991, 2005; Beaman 2014a). Connolly (2005: 123) characterizes this "agony [as one] grow[ing] out of mutual appreciation for the ubiquity of faith to life and the inability of the contending parties, to date, to demonstrate the truth of one's faith over other life candidates." At the same time, this agonistic dimension is conducive to fostering a shared experience. It is *the* element that opens up a space for uncertainty, spontaneity, and creativity. It also speaks to the complexity and fragility of these interactions that require participants to "absorb the agony of having elements of [their] own faith called into question by others" (124). We recognize that such an absorption must be reciprocal, with an uneven give and take. In some situations the agony is absorbed, and in others it is a position that is offered. As Connolly points out, the process of becoming is complex and variable.

Alina, who moved to St. John's with her husband and child for his job, recalls her encounter with her nonreligious neighbour. Her experience further conveys the intricacies of adopting a state of being that embraces the vulnerable posture that is required by agonistic respect (see Skerrett 2004). Such a position is not easy, and vulnerability is often a key factor in these exchanges: by entering into relations, whether spontaneous and fleeting exchanges or more enduring relationships, respect, caring, and neighbourliness require that one embrace a certain vulnerability, perhaps even humility:

And I even remember my neighbour, who happened to be a retired man in his, maybe close to seventy years old. Very well-educated man.

And he was not a, he did not believe in any religion. He was not even questioning the presence of God. [...] One day he asked me, "Do you know the direction of the qibla [direction of prayer, towards Mecca]? I know you are performing daily prayers, but I am just curious as to, you know, whether you are praying in the right direction?" I said, I mean, like, "I think it's roughly this way." And then, believe it or not, like he spends a few hours on the computer to calculate scientifically where the qibla exactly is. So the next morning when I woke up, there was a picnic table right next to, in our common front yard. [laughs] I saw an arrow on that picnic table showing me the direction of the qibla. I found it so sweet, so nice. And he came to my door, and he said, "You know, if one day, you know, we are questioned about what we did in this life, you can at least refer to me, you know, showing me the right direction. I'm saving you from praying in the wrong direction." So it was so friendly, full of humor, and, you know, it was beautiful.

This exchange between Alina and her neighbour is enabled by the fact that her neighbour suspends his nonbelief to engage and support her practice. Alina also opens herself to the beauty of the gift of her neighbour's caring and does not take offence at his interference in her spiritual life (see also Beaman 2014a: 99). In this encounter, marked by vulnerability, Alina and her neighbour suspend their own convictions to recognize each other's differences.

The point is not that our participants are flattening their beliefs or practices (or that they have doubts about the truths of their faiths), but that beliefs and practices are variable, flexible, and invoke multiple registers. The lives of our participants and the people with whom they often interact are replete with mundane moments of interpretation, uncertainty, and spontaneity. Again, these exchanges speak to the fluidity and messiness that characterize multifaceted identities, an idea that is well conveyed by Salomon and Walton (2012: 408), who write about how stark categories do not reflect lived realities: "Perhaps religion is always the product of a creative symbiosis of insiders and outsiders, populated by individuals who cannot simply be placed into the rigid categories of believer and unbeliever." In this way religion (here, Islam) is a verb, marked by creativity and fluidity.

In sum, thinking through some of the arithmetic that precedes the sense of mutuality by our participants in these moments is an invitation to realize that coexistence is not solely about the [successful] management of individual differences on which academic and governmental analyses tend to focus. We suggest that this mutual respect is a process that enables the building and cultivating of shared experiences, whereby living *well* together and emotionally or sincerely engaging with others in a plural society is part and parcel of the everyday.

Thinking about Mutual Respect: Fragile and Power Laden

As we have noted, because these moments are often marked by spontaneity, are episodic, and carry an agonistic dimension, they are fragile. While our interviewees might feel comfortable with an arrangement with a specific group of people at a particular moment in time or in a specific period of their lives, under other circumstances particular arrangements might not make sense or seem appropriate. Indeed, the conditions to (re)produce moments of mutual exchange may no longer exist. The everyday is replete with power relations (see D. Smith 1987: 89) so that in some cases the balance of power and context make the conditions that encourage these moments impossible to replicate.

Thus far we have spoken about the mundaneness of everyday life, which is concurrently informed by moments of heightened debate and exception. As sociologist of religion Nancy Ammerman (2007: 5) succinctly puts it, the everyday "may have to do with mundane routines, but it may also have to do with the crises and special events that punctuate those routines." What Schielke and Debevec (2012) call grand schemes are thus not separate from daily life but serve contiguously in its construction. Societal debates and controversies clearly frame difference in its construction and presence. Thirty-one-year-old Karim sophisticatedly shows how exceptional debates contribute to the fragility of everyday interactions. Karim, born and raised in Montreal and of Pakistani and French Canadian descent, shares his family's experience of organizing a sugar-shack outing for a group of approximately two thousand people, all members of a Muslim association. Sugar-shack outings are popular in Quebec in the spring. They are fun and convivial events, where family and friends meet to have a meal complemented by maple syrup and traditional French Canadian songs and dances.[7] Karim explains how they organized the details of the event with the sugar-shack owners by phone prior to the visit. The owners rented them the sugar shack for the day, and the group brought their own halal meat to cook on site. The activity's organization was uneventful, and the group deemed the outing a success. In Karim's account, the sugar-shack rental was an ordinary transaction between a client and business owners. As he explains, "They [the owners of the sugar shack] were super cool about it, yeah. They were, they were a great *cabane à sucre* to go to." Yet, a year after this unremarkable and enjoyable experience, reports circulated in the media of Muslims "imposing" their religion in a different sugar shack, notably making "demands" that a halal menu be served to everyone and that the common dance floor be used as a prayer space.[8]

In its final report, the Bouchard-Taylor Commission concludes that the media narratives depicting demanding Muslims at sugar shacks were inaccurate. The commissioners found that, as with the example provided by Karim, the mediatized visit to the Mont-Saint-Grégoire shack in 2007 had been sensibly negotiated (Bouchard and Taylor 2008: 57; Barras, Selby, and Beaman 2018). Nevertheless, the supposedly unreasonable demands captured in this inaccurate news rigidified popular discourse that questioned ad hoc decisions to meet visitors' dietary and/or prayer needs. The sugar-shack halal and prayer space demands became an emblematic example of how Muslims make too many unreasonable demands in Quebec (for more on this discourse of demand, see Chapter 4; Barras 2016). Moreover, the imagined unreasonableness within the Mont-Saint-Grégoire sugar-shack controversy affected the ability of Karim's family to continue organizing this annual outing, even to a different sugar shack. Even though their group was not at the centre of the media frenzy, Karim explains that the sugar-shack owners subsequently refused to engage in dietary negotiations like those that had taken place beforehand. Karim is empathetic to their plight, noting, "Yeah, it's, it's, I mean, understandable, you know? It [negotiation] has been a headache for them." In this case, the public debate shifted the terms of the previously positively experienced interaction, whereas before this media frenzy, religious difference was an element among others that had to be negotiated to ensure the success of the business transaction and, ultimately, of the event; after this accommodation crisis, the group's religious needs became magnified. Their request to bring their own meat became "a headache," a deal breaker. The conditions that could have assured that this interaction begat a moment of respect no longer existed.

Along with context, in the stories outlined in this chapter respect also depends on who partakes in the encounter and on the modalities of the encounter. As Banu Gökariksel and Anna Secor (2015: 26) note in their discussion of the conditions of respect for devout Sunni Muslim women in contemporary Turkey,[9] "in some situations, even respect cannot enable the building of bridges across difference [...] what counts as respect is not given but rather constituted within the particular socio-spatial relationships of [...] communities sharing neighborhoods, workspaces, and public life." Gökariksel and Secor explain how the "devout, headscarf wearing Sunnis" in their focus groups admitted that even if they successfully mediate social boundaries (which, in urban Turkey, the authors categorize as interactions among Sunni, Alevi, and secular communities), the women often remain "closer to those who were similar to themselves." The inability to build "bridges across difference" is partly related to the fact that understandings of what respect means changes in function of positionality (26).

In effect, diverse viewpoints around the meaning of respect factor into why, in some contexts, cultivating moments of respect is difficult and can be lived by participants in these exchanges as moments of misrecognition that weaken their self-respect and self-esteem (Tully 2000: 470). These difficulties can be sensibly brokered but, again, with a *délicatesse* and allowance for awkwardness. Amira, a thirty-two-year-old professional who immigrated to Canada when she was five and now works as a manager in the education sector, considers herself to be a "spiritual" but not devout Muslim. She speaks about how it is difficult for her to find social environments that she feels are conducive to shared moments to flourish. Like we saw with Akeem in Chapter 1, she says that because she is a visible minority and of Middle Eastern origin, people tend to assume that she is a practising Muslim. She mentions that she often feels that her practices (and/or nonpractices) are judged by others. Social pressure to draw boundaries between acceptability and unacceptability makes it difficult for her to find those whom she calls "cool Muslims."

For Amira, cool Muslims accept people as they are, with their beliefs and un-beliefs (cf. Tully's third point above). Her sense of this pressure complicates how she engages with other Muslims, especially more devout ones, as religious difference becomes a clear boundary marker. She says that religious difference is often made into a "big thing," also among the Muslims she knows. The chasm can be transformed into an uncomfortable challenge, which necessarily complicates the "building of bridges" across differences (Gökariksel and Secor 2015: 26).

Perhaps precisely because of her acute awareness of the intricacies that mark her everyday relationships in a variety of contexts, moments of mutual respect are memorable for Amira. She shares one of these exchanges with us: a dinner with a young woman from Jordan. Amira claims that religiosity was not made into a "big thing" because the exchange was devoid of judgments:

> I remember meeting a young woman from Jordan. And so she's, like, "I don't really know a lot of people." And I said, "You know, let's be friends." I made that decision. And so we went out, um, we went out to a pizza place. And the first question I said, the way I said, like, "OK, we're about to order. And this is the *awkward question* now: Are you ready?" And she's, like, "I know. I don't drink, and I don't eat pork." So she already knew what I was about to ask her. And I said, "OK, I do both." And she's, like, "OK." This person and I had already developed an understanding, kind of unsaid, um, unvocalized understanding of, I'm respecting of, of the culture, and you're respecting of the culture but we're going to do our, each do our own thing. We sat in a place where I drank a glass of wine and had a pizza with prosciutto on it, and she had a vegetarian pizza and a glass of juice. And it was perfectly OK. (our emphasis)

Amira's positive interaction over dinner with a new friend is facilitated by an "awkward question." It is precisely Amira's willingness to broach the question that set the terrain for both women to potentially engage in a moment characterized by equality and openness. This brief moment requires that both women step out of their comfort zones, thanks to what Amira calls an unvocalized understanding between them.[10] Nevertheless, in placing their meal requests with their waiter, the dynamic of the dinner and the possibility of seeking to transform and judge the other looms. Other interviewees convey concerns around misunderstandings of respect and power asymmetries. Nayla, of Palestinian origin and who works in Montreal as a financial analyst, emphasizes how her sense of respect is different from those of her colleagues. She does not share her religious beliefs with them and does not wear a headscarf because, in her words, she wants to avoid "constantly fight[ing] for my rights." And yet, in her interview she describes the hurdles she still faces in negotiating work events with alcohol. Nayla illustrates an example of barriers to mutual respect when she recounts attending a workplace wine-tasting, which was a team-building event. She found the theme of the event offensive but felt obliged to participate to demonstrate that she was part of the team. For her, worse than simply attending, a number of colleagues were insistent that she should drink wine:

NAYLA: We had a team-building event, and it was at a wine tasting ... it's a winery ... I don't know what you call it. And I think I was, I was the only one who was Muslim. Everybody else drinks. And I guess because I was a minority, they didn't ask if somebody doesn't drink. Actually, maybe they didn't even know if I drank or not. And I find that was hard because ...

INTERVIEWER: Because you had to go ...

NAYLA: Yes, I had to go, and it was, like, a very important event, and it's, like, you're not allowed, even if you get, you can't take a day off because you're paid for that day, so it was very hard, very hard to say no.

INTERVIEWER: And so you went ...?

NAYLA: I went, but I didn't drink. I still participated in the event. Um, there was a team building, that I told them that I don't drink. I'm being rude but I, I had to, like, um, I didn't want to be rejected. I still wanted to be part of that group, because in a company it is important to maintain relationships.

INTERVIEWER: And so, how did they react to the fact that you weren't drinking? Did they react in any way or did they just, uh ...

NAYLA: They tried to make me drink! [laughs] Many, many times. Many, many times!

INTERVIEWER: By saying, "Oh, please try?"

NAYLA: Yes, yes! Many, many times. Yeah. And it's hard to say "No, no, no, no." But, and I tried to joke about it to make it light, not to, so that they don't take it in, um, an offensive way?

INTERVIEWER: And from that point onwards did they, uh, make any effort to ...

NAYLA: Oh, they always tried! Nonstop. It's not that they, the people I work with, they were alcohol lovers, like, they ...

INTERVIEWER: And how do you, how do you feel about that?

NAYLA: Oh my, no, because I have, I want them to respect my beliefs, my religion, so I have to respect theirs too. And I cannot, I don't like imposing, um, things on them, so. And relationships are very important for me at work. I'm very social, so I try to maintain it, and I try to be flexible.

Power relations are highly visible in this account. Nayla is a minority on a number of scores: as a woman, as a visible minority, as a Muslim, and as a nondrinker. She thinks she may be the only Muslim at her company and generously imagines this is why her colleagues do not consider the possibility that she might feel uncomfortable at a wine-tasting event. They do not engage with her difference or respect her unwillingness to drink, even when she indicates her unwillingness through jokes and more overtly. For Nayla, this outing magnified her putative difference. Quite the opposite from its team-building goal, the day trip is marked in her memory as an unpleasant event where nonrecognition was exclusionary (on the connection between nonrecognition and exclusion, see Young 1990; Tully 1995, 2000). Nayla does not feel as though she is part of the team. Thus, while her vision of respect entails empathy for her colleagues and their values – "I don't like imposing [...] things on them" to avoid putting them in an uncomfortable position – this understanding is far from mutual. The "socio-spatial relationships" (see Gökariksel and Secor 2015: 26) structuring the environment, in this case the winery and the drunkenness of some colleagues, impede mutual respect.

Yet, this outing did not necessarily need to have been a negative and exclusionary one. Let us imagine for a moment how it could have unfolded differently. Perhaps suggestions for a team-building event could have been collected from the employees. Even supposing that the winery visit was the event of choice, a baseline supposition that perhaps not everyone would want to drink alcohol should have been part of its planning. Rules of basic courtesy were ignored. No one should have had the authority to force alcohol, nor should it have been acceptable to comment on whether and what others were drinking. The question that might be asked is how to create an atmosphere of religious accessibility in which employees could enjoy themselves but make drinking alcohol a less central part of the team-building exercise. Even recognizing that things went as far as they did, taking the time to *listen* to (not simply to hear) Nayla's gentle refusal to taste wine (see Tully 2000: 94 on the importance of listening) and accept her position without wanting to transform or judge her would have been equally important in crafting a moment of respect, or at least salvaging a structurally disrespectful situation. For some of her colleagues, refraining from insisting that she drink would have required a suspension of their sense of rightness to support her abstinence, a gesture which resembled her openness to attend the event (see Beaman 2014a: 99). She would not be paid for the day if she were absent. Acknowledging her multiple signs of discomfort would have been an essential move towards mutuality and towards accepting her as she is (and not positioning her as they think she is or should be or, worse, bullying her). Better would have been not to create the discomfort in the first place.

Other participants in our study found themselves in somewhat similar situations, where alcohol was present in their work environment but where they felt they were treated with greater *délicatesse*. For instance, thirty-five-year-old Caroline points to how she appreciates that her boss gave her a bottle of sparkling apple juice instead of a bottle of Champagne (that was given to all other employees) at the annual Christmas party.[11] Caroline explains how this switch allowed her to participate in the office toast and to feel included: "It's really cool because it gives us the impression that we're celebrating like you guys [*comme vous autres*], and that we say 'cheers,' and that way we're not excluded [*pis qu'on fait chin-chin tsé pis on est pas à part*]." In this case, Caroline does not feel judged or under pressure to change. She can *chin-chin* (toast) with her colleagues. Respect seems to be a given in her interactions with her officemates and her boss. Overall, we observed in our participants a genuine sense of desire to work out such situations, and in most cases our participants' experiences reflected a shared toast like Caroline's rather than the exclusion that Nayla experienced.

***

The everyday lives of our participants are replete with moments in which difference is negotiated with relative ease. Farida describes her neighbours' care to locate halal meats for a shared barbecue. Samira describes her friend's discreet facilitation of Samira's evening prayer and food restrictions at a dinner party. Hassan is delighted he can try his colleague Géraldine's traditional Québécois dish when she modifies the recipe. Ouria describes overlooking her discomfort with embracing a nonrelative male colleague, appreciating his joy following the end of his cancer treatments. Alina tells us about a neighbour who carefully marks the qibla on a picnic table between their front doors. Caroline is pleased when her boss includes her in Christmas gifting and thoughtfully purchases a nonalcoholic beverage. Conversely, Karim shares how negotiations break down reserving a sugar shack for a Muslim association following the mediatization of unreasonable accommodation in Quebec. And Nayla describes her profound discomfort when she and her officemates attend a team-building activity at a winery. These stories describe moments in the lives of our participants and explore the conditions that render mutual respect both possible and impossible. This shift in focus from overprivileging demands to thinking about the more common sentiment of respect, we believe, is significant. Although documenting events where religious difference is constructed as a problem and the source of discrimination is essential, conflict is, nonetheless, only part of the story. Moments of respect – even if sometimes agonistic or awkward – are equally part and parcel of the everyday lives of Muslim Canadians.

Yet, as mentioned, these moments have been the focus of little scholarly and public attention. There are several reasons for this omission, including that these are harder to document as they are fleeting and often unremarkable and might, therefore, be understood as less sensational. There are also geopolitical, racialized, and (post)colonial politics undergirding the absence of these common narratives in the public imagination.

Based on our exploration in this chapter, we would add that thinking about these moments also allows us to consider the emotions and the contexts that are present in moments when individuals sincerely engage with each others' moral universes. Examining these interactions can allow us to consider how care, generosity, respect, happiness, and playfulness, but also awkwardness, frustration, and agony are woven through these quotidian moments. We think this shift in focus is significant. Documenting their delicateness, flexibility, and creative potential can allow us to imagine alternatives in situations like Nayla's, where respect falls apart.

Focusing on mundane social interactions offers new insights to principles that otherwise remain abstract and theoretical. Let us return to Farida's experience of her street's barbecue party. Delving into that example makes clear the participants' generosity, the power asymmetries laden in the event, the efforts made to redress them, and the flexibility required to facilitate the sharing of a moment. The recognition of difference (that Farida's family eat halal and do not drink alcohol) is not lived here as the outcome of the process. Rather, it is understood as an element (an important one) to achieve mutual respect, to live well, and have fun together. Scholars and policy-makers often approach this recognition as an end in itself. We see this everyday example differently, however. Navigation and negotiation here should be understood as part of a process. Reflecting on the emotions and conditions that enable moments of respect to unfold allows us to think differently about the intricacies that mark the politics of interactions in the everyday.

Conclusion

Stories make us more alive, more human, more courageous, more loving.

– Madeleine L'Engle

Every moment happens twice: inside and outside, and they are two different histories.

– Zadie Smith, *White Teeth*

Sometimes reality is too complex. Stories give it form.

– Jean-Luc Godard

On the Importance of Multi-Layered Narratives

Beyond Accommodation has sought to unravel often overlooked facets of religious diversity in Canada. Our book's primary objective has been to focus on more mundane and less exceptional stories than those frequently reported by the media and by scholarly accounts but that are, nevertheless, evocative of power dynamics, generosity, awkwardness, and respect. We have chosen to forefront these narratives precisely because they capture the complexities evoked by Godard in the epigraph above. Through the stories they have shared, the participants in our study give form to the textured lived realities of Muslims in Canada specifically, and to the contemporary Canadian social fabric more generally.

We analyze these narratives through a number of different lenses: through the vantage point of Muslim-associated figures; through narratives of settlement, immigration policy, and scholarly knowledge production; through secular discourses embedded in stories about time, space, and embodied practices; through the arithmetic of navigations and negotiations; and, finally, through experiences of mutual respect. We have structured our analysis around these narratives that layer and shape our interlocutors' experiences. Their stories – that take place inside and outside, as Zadie Smith notes in her novel *White Teeth* – are also conduits for power structures and hegemonies that frame the quotidian meaning making of our participants, sometimes in ways that they cannot control.

We identify the recurrence of figures such as the Terrorist, the Imperilled Muslim Woman, and the Enlightened Muslim Man in our participants' narratives of everyday life. The figures often emerge as Islamophobic- and, at times, as Islamophilic-related burdens that can be easily recognizable but, nonetheless, exceedingly difficult to dismantle. In contrast to scholarly work on similar figures, we map them as activating one another, as not only binary, but also as racialized and gendered. We show how a number of our participants feel obliged to invoke the figures themselves. Recall Sheila, who makes reference to the Enlightened Muslim Man and the Liberated Muslim Woman in trying to pre-emptively address widespread stereotypes about the patriarchal basis of her recently adopted religious tradition following her marriage to Akbar. Participants uniformly express frustration and discouragement at the pervasiveness of these figures that trap them in flattened, caricatured, and one-dimensional realities. Ouria articulates anger with those who engage with her and remain fixated on her headscarf. She says, "No one accepts [*on n'acceptera pas*] that you speak about the economy or the environment or arts and culture. But you can speak about being a Muslim, and you stop there." The Imperilled Muslim Woman figure overdetermines Ouria's identity in rigid ways, including her response. Ouria and other participants express concern about how their anger and other emotions and their work to call out and divest these power structures could be received. Negatively perceived reactions could be associated with character traits embodied by figures (e.g., the Terrorist). The figures thus powerfully impede interactions and discipline ways of being and feeling.

Taken as a whole, the figures tell an important story of both systematic and subtle discriminations. Put differently, although we identify recurring nonevents that evidence navigation and negotiation, the figures and their prevalence shed light on an, at times, pugnacious typecasting that significantly shapes our interlocutors' everyday lives.

An important contextualizing factor in our study is the changing narrative around settlement, immigration policy, and knowledge production about Muslims in Canada, which we chart through the stories of Shaben and Ibnouzahir. Both are active in community organizations, and both note harsh Canadian winters. Contrasting their narratives illustrates how their families' arrivals in different centuries and political eras impact their experiences of religiosity. Shaben's grandfather, Big Sam, who migrated from what is now Syria at the turn of the twentieth century, appeared to encounter facility in securing work in the fur trade and in launching trading businesses and a general store. Almost one hundred years later, Ibnouzahir's father, who migrated from Morocco, was like many of Canada's Muslim immigrants (see p. 75) in that he was both highly educated and, despite his best efforts, unemployed for years after settling. Gender had a further impact. Shaben was the first parliamentarian to take his oath of office using a Qur'an. But his Muslimness and involvement in religiously based community organizations did not appear to pejoratively impact his political career. Ibnouzahir's own post-migration life at a public high school in post-9/11 Montreal meant that her decision to wear (or not) a headscarf was often interpreted as a political act. Remembering and retelling narratives such as these family histories are important counterimpulses to contemporary emphasis on newcomers and quandaries about integration. We also believe they can help to displace the disciplining impulses of the figures we have identified by contributing to a narrative of shared history.

In addition to considering familial narratives of migration and settlement as lenses through which to identify changing immigration patterns, we also map a shift in the scholarly work on Muslims in Canada: from a focus on ethnicity and racisms to a post-2001 focus on problematized religiosity. We note only a handful of qualitative studies to date that have emphasized quotidian life. In part, we see this knowledge production as reflecting prevalent narratives about Islam in Canada, in which we too participate.

While the broader cultural and structural narratives that frame our participants' lives and experiences are important, it is their stories of everyday life that capture our attention. For this reason, our methodological approach is crucially important. Locating these narratives is not straightforward and is likely why these kinds of stories have received less scholarly attention. When nonevent moments take place – that is, when moments of religiosity are successfully navigated and/or negotiated – they are often forgotten. For instance, Sabah, whom we met in the Introduction and who sought to secure a gender-segregated swim time in her apartment building's pool, had not remembered her navigation and negotiation of this question with her building manager until prompted by a question about sports in her everyday life and, notably, until we gave her a few moments in our interview to recall the interaction.

Our methodological approach also aims to decentre religiosity as our sole focus. We wanted to interview a range of Muslim Canadians, so we recruited beyond mosques and religious centres. We endeavoured to focus our interview questionnaire on places and situations rather than on the classic five pillars approach. Our interlocutors speak, therefore, about being Muslim, but not necessarily. They also differ in relation to other characteristics, like ethnicity, able-bodiedness, educational backgrounds, gender, socioeconomic status, and sexual orientation. Still, we realize that Muslim is a category that relates to concerns with racialization, immigration, national identities, postcoloniality, expressions of sexuality, extremism, and radicalism (cf. Selby and Beaman 2016). At the same time as we consider these politics, we make space for the voices of participants who emphasize a desire to get on with it.

The core themes in this book emerged from the experiences of our participants, including the nature and shape of secularism in Canada. Early in our analysis of the transcripts as a whole, we noted how concerns and engagements with the secular were interwoven in nearly all our interview data. Granted, the three of us have long-standing interests in this topic, but we were nevertheless surprised by the number who emphasized how the secular conditioned and framed what we see as power and its attending institutions. Again, drawing on their narratives, it is clear that the category of the secular shapes and regulates acceptable religion in social life through various sites, including the holiday party, prayer spaces, and appropriate social interactions between women and men. Nour, whom we introduced at the beginning of Chapter 3, describes her unease with the label of "holiday party" for the December celebration thrown for the staff at her school. She notes, "People call it the holiday party because they want to accommodate everybody, but I'm, like, you know what, it's a Christmas party." Narratives like hers demonstrate how the secular is (re)produced in our participants' lives and also the tangible ways in which all live with, adapt to, and, for some, outwardly critique these power structures.

We define secularism as a series of "legal and political claims and projects that are deeply implicated in the definition and management of religion" (Hurd 2012: 955). We locate the contemporary Canadian framework of reasonable accommodation as one of those secular projects and have been attentive to what this framework does to religion. Our guiding questions have been: What does this project tell us about religion and, in particular, about Islam? How does the secular structure religion and manage it? How do minorities fare in these accounts? More specifically, with Hassan (who we first met in Chapter 3) in mind, we ask: What are the costs of using a reasonable accommodation framework for him and for his unidentified colleague who made the request to not work on Friday to attend Friday prayer? In which ways did Hassan's generous acceptance to be a workplace spokesperson for a religious tradition impact his identity and the way he is perceived by his colleagues? Answering these questions helps us circumscribe and substantiate our critiques of the reasonable accommodation project. Because of his visible religious identity, his willingness to dispense knowledge and to seek out normative determinations about Islam, and his personal connections in the Muslim community in which he participates, Hassan is considered – by his employer and by himself – to be authorized to make decisions about religious matters.[1] We describe Hassan's unofficial designation as theological arbiter, aiming to focus not on whether the request of him is reasonable, but on the parameters, power differentials, and language in which the role is invoked. We argue that the assumptions undergirding his willing appointment as arbitrator subtly reflect problems laden in the notion of reasonable accommodation, which we see as essentializing and rendering Muslim identities as static and hypervisible in a geopolitical moment in which Muslimness is already problematized.

We argue that Hassan finds himself in this position because the reasonable accommodation model requires institutions to evaluate and arbitrate on the reasonability of religious demands made by self-identified religious individuals who often do not benefit from the contours of culture. As arbitrator, Hassan necessarily collapses multitudinous expressions of Islam into a narrow version of its traditions and, more significantly, into a version that works within the corporation's policies. We suggest that this narrowness does disservice to the range of practices among Muslims (in Montreal and in his workplace), and that this theologically articulated myopathy is typical of how the reasonable accommodation model operates. A similar burden of education also often falls on individuals who make requests, as they must describe and explain their practices. Even if some frame this education as *da'wa*, an effort to spread the "correct" knowledge of Islam, many of our participants are regularly called upon to justify practices, holidays, and beliefs. Moreover, as we note repeatedly, this required essentialization of Islam occurs alongside asymmetrical power relations.

While we critique what we call the discourse of demand lodged in the reasonable accommodation framework, we nonetheless recognize the possibilities laden within it. First, its ad hoc nature has the potential to promote the consideration of requests on a case-by-case basis. Recent legal projects in the province of Quebec aim to move away from this case-by-case approach to rigidify and specify allowable religious symbols, as occurred in France and Belgium more than a decade ago. This focus is clearly visible in Bill 62, which was passed into law in October 2017. Second, the discourse of demand cannot be solely attributed to the mechanisms in this framework. Narrow characterizations of Muslimness reflect a recent broader trend towards a singular focus on religious identity in scholarship and public discourse, which we discuss at length in this book (see Dressler and Mandair 2011; Hurd 2012, 2015; Dessing et al. 2013). And third, we recognize that Hassan's position and status in this company's HR department accords him a certain power. He appreciates the role. However, not all our participants find themselves in such positions of privilege to make decisions that enable what we call mutual respect. Those with executive titles are able to avoid these categorizations more than those in less authoritative positions. Remember Sabrina, whose managerial position enables her to organize a laser tag Christmas party instead of the traditional holiday dinner and drinks. She recognizes that her administrative position allows her to set the parameters of the gathering.

In general, particularly in the case of hijab-wearing women, many wish they could simply proceed through daily life without being the focus of comments, queries, or requests. Recognition without a production is a typically hoped for state of affairs. Indeed, the discourse of demand that Hassan affirms at his workplace forces individuals to trespass irreligious norms and invisibility. To have access to desired food, prayer spaces, or times, individuals must make a request, whether formally or informally, which places them already outside the parameters of normalcy. In sum, this discourse of demand forces visibility and obscures power imbalances.

By locating and rendering Muslim practices as hypervisible, reasonable accommodation produces a certain story about Canadian diversity. This story affirms a secular reflex where Christianity slides into the realm of culture and heritage and is embedded in Canadian life, and Islam remains visibly, necessarily, and, in the Foucauldian sense, confessionally "religion." Non-Christian beliefs and practices (categories which themselves are Protestant conceptualizations of religiosity, as Keane 2007 argues) are thus, in this paradigm, to be accommodated or tolerated and, in some cases, legally adjudicated. Culture, in contrast, is assessed as part of our values and heritage and thus escapes that scrutiny.

In response to these critiques of reasonable accommodation, we introduce the notions of navigation and negotiation as more apt theoretical apparatus to analyze the intricate processes that take place in moments in which religiosity and/or difference come to the fore. Indeed, when probed, many of our participants engage in a great deal of navigation that takes place prior to any negotiation, whether formal or informal. Maria undertakes a good deal of theological and emotional navigation to sort through a moment when two visiting workers whom she invites to breakfast order bacon, which, for her, is *haram* (forbidden by Islamic law). Likewise, Caroline, a young mother with full-time employment outside the home, shares the navigation that precedes her choice of daycare for her infant son. She explains how her daily commute to work, her and her husband's mental and physical health, and the importance they give to their religion factor into her internalized navigation. Caroline ends up choosing a facility that is close to home and does not offer halal meals but that does not serve pork. She decides not to enter into negotiation with the daycare about the possibility of providing halal substitutes, because this request would require that she pack her son's lunches every day, which would be too complicated. Caroline does not see this solution as ideal but as the best one for her and her family at that point in their lives, to maybe reassess when her son is a bit older: "Maybe then [when he's three or four], I'll tell myself, 'OK, it's worth it, Caroline, that you drive half an hour every day,' when he'll be old enough to understand." These women's narratives capture how navigations and negotiations are characterized by flexibility and fragility. In other words, a particular arrangement, or assemblage, can easily change as a function of one's priorities, "registers of being," and life circumstances, including, as our participants remind us on several occasions, social class, and job security.

The navigation/negotiation model offers a more flexible and reflective framework to think about everyday interactions that attempts to be mindful of the power dynamics inherent to many of these moments. It is our hope that our navigation and negotiation lens allows us to better convey the inherent textures of lived religion that get lost with the dominant framework of reasonable accommodation. Indeed, this approach lends itself to thinking through more everyday narratives that are typically ignored; debates and court cases are too often structured around evaluating the reasonableness of demands that tend to capture policy, media, and public attention, even if they reflect minority practices and concerns.

Stories that include moments of mutual respect predominate in our research findings. These moments are part and parcel of the stories that give form to our participants' everyday lives and also reflect how they experience and live Canadian diversity. In order to better conceptualize the dynamics enabling and undergirding these moments, including their fragility and processual nature, we draw on James Tully's (1995, 2000) work on recognition. Recall Alina, who generously brackets critique of her next-door neighbour when he calculates (without the facility of new

GPS applications on smartphones) the qibla for her. Alina sees power asymmetries at work – among others, her religiosity is far more visible than his atheism; she is racialized, he is not – but they both appear willing to be open to the other's worldview to share that moment.

Mindful of this wilful overlooking, we nevertheless emphasize in our analysis that these moments may, in fact, be "agonistic," to cite William Connolly (2005: 124) or, at least "awkward," to cite our participant Amira, who describes how she negotiates dinner with a new friend at a pizza place in downtown St. John's. Notably, even if they may be positively experienced, these moments of respect are not always easy.

Many of these interactions involve an awkward moment. Farida describes how "one of the neighbours [in her cul-de-sac] had just asked me casually, 'Where do you buy your meat from?'" as she and neighbours planned a communal barbeque when she lived in the Greater Toronto Area. The question required the neighbour to knock on her door, ask her where she buys meat, and then go purchase it at a halal butcher shop. It is rather awkward, requiring what Samira calls a certain *délicatesse* that helps produce the conditions of mutual respect and a convivial shared neighbourhood moment, where they also successfully negotiate the presence of alcohol.

In a last narrative exercise, we take as a cautionary tale Nayla's experience of a team-building wine-tasting event with her colleagues. Because it happens during a paid workday, it is "very hard, very hard to say no." The young financial analyst describes the event as offensive and exclusionary. She does not want to make her religiosity an object of discussion and tries to deflect some of the issues of disrespect with humour. In the end, she attends the outing without drinking alcohol and suffers as colleagues pressure her and laugh at her expense. Basic courtesy is ignored and negotiation thwarted. We take Nayla's narrative to imagine how a more mutually respectful moment could have occurred. While his focus is on formal demands, Tully's work on the processes of recognition offers a compelling lens to think about moments of respect. For Nayla, this recognition could have included having her voice heard without seeking to transform or judge her and having the power differentials in the situation acknowledged. These processes may have also transformed her colleagues' beliefs and practices. Though we have tried to draw attention to the positive outcomes our research has uncovered, we heard narratives of exclusion and alienation such as Nayla's.

We have thus shown how shifting attention to various narrative lenses alters our vision and the knowledge we produce. In conceiving of these interviews and this research project, we have been cognizant of how Islam is the site of a great deal of scholarly and popular production and consumption. Our intent has been to weave these narratives together to create a different framework that, we hope, offers better alternatives to the focus on hypervisible forms of Islam and failed accommodations. Our participants' narratives about their experiences also allow us to conceptualize a deep reading of cultural and structural forces that impinge upon our interlocutors' lives and choices. They shed light on both the contours of power in public life in Canada and the varieties of lived Islam (cf. Deeb 2015) in two cities.

Like Lídia Jorge's (2015) urging to tell a more positively spun story of the Portuguese Carnation Revolution, in 1974, in her novel *Les Mémorables* (see our book's opening epigraph), we too seek to focus on more positive narratives – that sometimes include nonevents and often reveal elements of navigation, negotiation, and mutual respect – to reimagine "myth[s] currently prevalent in society" (Jorge 2015, our translation). We hope that analyzing these moments of mundane navigation and negotiation serves as a critique of the reasonable accommodation framework and facilitates more critical engagement with dominant myths in Canadian society around diversity. The figures and secular projects tell part of this dominant myth, but they are only part of a much more complex and vibrant patchworked story.

Notes

Epigraph

1 From a radio interview with Lídia Jorge on her book, *Les Mémorables* (2015), on France Inter, June 1, 2015, https://www.franceinter.fr/emissions/l-humeur -vagabonde/l-humeur-vagabonde-01-juin-2015; our translation.

Introduction

1 Translations from French are our own. We have included the original French phrases in brackets in some interviews to indicate translation and to share phrases less easily translated. *Pis*, for instance, is a Québécois expression that is slang for *et puis* ("and") or *puis* ("so"). Ellipses without brackets indicate pauses in speech; ellipses with brackets indicate speech we have omitted.

2 All participants' names have been anonymized. We removed specific identifiers where we thought the participants might be more easily identified, particularly in St. John's, which has a smaller Muslim population. The demographic information given for participants was current at the time of interview.

3 *Halal* denotes that which is permissible according to Islamic law, itself a centuries-old and varied, complex system of interpretation of the tradition's central revealed text, the Qur'an, and the Hadith, a collection of the sayings and actions attributed to the Prophet Muhammad. Generally, conceptualizations of halal refer to food and drink (such as the avoidance of alcohol and pork), as well as matters of daily life (for more on contemporary interpretations, see J. Fischer 2011).

4 Bill 60, *Charter affirming the values of State secularism and religious neutrality and of equality between women and men, and providing a framework for accommodation requests*, 1st Sess, 40th Leg, Quebec, 2013 (1st reading November 7, 2013). In 2010

the provincial Liberal Party introduced a bill (Bill 94, *An Act to establish guidelines governing accommodation requests within the Administration and certain institutions*, 1st Sess, 39th Leg, Quebec, 2010 (later dismissed) that sought to regulate the presence of face covering in Quebec society and to develop a particular framework for religious reasonable accommodation. Bill 60 should be understood in relation to this first piece of legislation (Jahangeer 2014; Dalpé and Koussens 2016).

5 Bill 62, *An Act to foster adherence to State religious neutrality and, in particular, to provide a framework for religious accommodation requests in certain bodies*, 1st Sess, 41st Leg, Quebec, 2015. In the same vein as Bill 60, Bill 62 has sought to regulate the presence of Muslim women wearing full-face veils in Quebec society by prohibiting their ability to work for public institutions or access their services. At the time of writing this introduction, Bill 62 had been passed into law (October 2017) but was temporarily stayed in December 2017 to review its accommodation guidelines or until a constitutional challenge could be heard. For more information on how the bill links with other attempts to legislate religion in the province, see Fahmy 2016; Dabby 2017; Lefebvre and St-Laurent 2018.

6 For a thorough discussion of the development of reasonable accommodation in Canada and its limits, see Day and Brodsky 1996; Choudhry 2013. See also Bribosia, Ringelheim, and Rorive (2010: 144–45), who note that "the concept of reasonable accommodation first appeared in Canada during the 1980s. This common law principle was introduced by courts specialized in the interpretation of the Canadian Human Rights Act, before being applied by ordinary courts and eventually confirmed by the Supreme Court for the first time in *Ontario Human Rights Commission (O'Malley) v Simpson-Sears Limited*, decided in 1985."

7 *Multani v Commission scolaire Marguerite-Bourgeoys*, [2006] 1 SCR 256 [*Multani*].

8 Though reasonable accommodation was central in the *Multani* decision, in *Alberta v Hutterian Bretheren of Wilson Colony*, [2009] SCR 567, the Supreme Court explicitly moved away from it as a legal standard. Nonetheless, the *Multani* decision is important because it marks the moment when the notion of reasonable accommodation broke away from law and entered public discourse, in particular as it was taken up by the Bouchard-Taylor Commission hearings in Quebec in 2007. Reasonable accommodation subsequently became endemic in media coverage and popular discourse about how to manage diversity in Canada. While it has not been used as a legal principle in recent Supreme Court decisions on religion such as *R v N.S.*, 2012 SCC 72, [2012] 3 SCR 726 [*R v N.S.*] or *Mouvement laïque québécois v Saguenay (City)*, [2015] 2 SCR 3, it is still present as common language in those decisions, in particular in the summaries of the arguments made by the applicants and the respondents.

9 The *Multani* decision is a good example of how reasonable accommodation models tend to frame religion in ways that do not necessarily correspond to lived religion. Indeed, this decision implicitly connected Multani's religiousness to an ideological orthodoxy with which he and his family felt uncomfortable (Stoker 2007).

10 We see religiosity as a signifier in that it is historically, socially, and culturally constructed. These constructions are real insofar as they produce effects on human lives and societies (see Beckford 2003: 7, 24; Taira 2013). This moderate constructionist approach calls into question a "proper" or normative Islam and acknowledges how power, privilege, and status are "legitimated by the religious traditions that are socially defined as authentic" (McGuire 2008: 190). In this vein, we understand expressions of Islam not as normative concepts, but as constructed and changing, a guideline that Talal Asad (1986: 15) counts as "apt performance." In this reading, Islam is a discursive arena occupied by conflicting perspectives over what counts as appropriate. For example, "Islamic piety" does not necessarily refer to rigid or conservative viewpoints, but to a set of multiple epistemological procedures, discourses, and practices that are considered authoritative and are thus given a prescriptive legitimacy (see Fadil 2011: 93; Schielke and Debevec 2012: 6).

11 The academic study of Islam has been influenced by an historical and textual emphasis in the discipline of religious studies. Akin to what some have called Muslim studies, we concentrate on the lived rather than solely on the written components of the tradition. We take seriously what makes some social events and individual actions "religious" for our interlocutors and how these definitions are shaped by various cultural and institutional contexts and normative theological ideas. We include micropolitics and aspects of identity that are not necessarily "Islamic" but are constitutive of people's daily lives (see similar theoretical discussion in Soares and Osella 2009; Dessing et al. 2013: 2).

12 See note 20 below on the relatively small percentage of Canadian Muslims who attend mosque regularly.

13 In her introduction to *Islam in the Hinterlands*, Jasmin Zine (2012a: 27) describes what she sees as "academic forms of colonialism in which the narratives and lived experiences of Muslims have been co-opted by those who do not share in this identity." We do not see our work in this book in this light; nor do we share A. Hughes's (2015: 46) characterization of what he calls "Islamic Religious Studies," which positions religious insiders as caretakers of the tradition. In perhaps different ways than Zine, we see implications for some of the concerns raised by our interlocutors in our own lives and contexts, even if we are not Muslim.

14 In Chapter 2, we chronicle several qualitative research projects that examine aspects of Muslim life in the Greater Toronto Area (A. Hussain 2001; Zine 2008a, 2008b), Montreal (Eid 2007; Mossière 2013; Barras 2016), Metro Vancouver (Dossa 1994, 2002, 2009), and the Edmonton metropolitan region (Waugh and Wannas 2003; Waugh 2012). Canadian cities under 1 million in population have not received significant attention.

15 This secularization process manifested itself in different ways, including the deconfessionalization of school boards in Newfoundland in 1997 and of pastoral care in hospitals in Quebec since the early 2000s (Sharify-Funk and Guzik 2017). Yet, despite these initiatives, our participants' narratives point to the fact that Catholicism

continues to be embedded in Newfoundland and Quebec societies (see Chapter 3 for more on this power dynamic).

16 In addition, 22.6 percent of Montreal's population are immigrants, considerably more than the 4 percent in St. John's (Statistics Canada 2016), which reflects ways in which there may be more services in Montreal for newcomers.

17 See Haggerty and Gazso 2005; McDonough and Hoodfar 2005; Razack 2007; Caidi and MacDonald 2008; Hanniman 2008; Gazso and Haggerty 2009; Jamil and Rousseau 2012; Patel 2012; Bramadat and Dawson 2014.

18 A 2002 study by the same organization also found that 56 percent of respondents reported anti-Muslim incidents in the year following September 11, 2001, and 61 percent reported kindness or support from friends and colleagues of other faiths in the post-9/11 period (Council on American-Islamic Relations–Canada 2004: 6).

19 This climate is reinforced through legal projects. On June 20, 2014, Bill C-24 became law in Canada (*Strengthening Canadian Citizenship Act*, SC 2014, c 22), allowing citizenship to be rescinded for those with dual citizenship for reasons other than fraud and without a live hearing or the right to appeal (see Adams, Macklin, and Omidvar 2014). In June 2015, Bill C-51 received royal assent to officially become Canada's *Anti-Terrorism Act*. It amends the Canadian *Criminal Code* and broadens the mandate of the Canadian Security Intelligence Service (CSIS) in ways that some have argued curtails civil liberties. CSIS may now physically disrupt "acts of terrorism" and has policing power (see Forcese and Roach 2015; Watters 2015).

20 Most Canadian Muslims do not attend mosque regularly. A 2016 opinion survey of six hundred Muslim Canadians suggests that 48 percent attend mosque weekly, up 7 percent from 2006 (Environics 2016: 17). Zaman (2008: 466) and Cesari (2006) suggest that as many as 80 percent of American Muslims do not attend mosque regularly.

Chapter 1

1 The Hadith encapsulate the sayings, deeds, and descriptions of the Prophet Muhammad. For many, the Sunna, or the example of the Prophet that is recorded in the Hadith, establishes normative precendents for Muslims. The Hadith have engendered their own science to determine their legitimacy. They are second in importance to the Qur'an, the revealed text of the traditions of Islam, and are regularly used in legal interpretations.

2 According to 2001 Statistics Canada data, Muslims in Canada have the highest unemployment rate by religious group. On average they experience two months of unemployment every year and make $20,000 less than non-Muslim Canadians (cited in Kazemipur 2014: 121). Pew data in 2007 examining poverty rates in six countries (the United States, France, Germany, Spain, Britain, and Canada) found the largest gap between Muslim and non-Muslim poverty rates to be in Canada (123).

3 Courses like these invariably – and, we will suggest, problematically – focus on the pillars, often without mention of context, history, or doctrinal differences.

4 We have expressly chosen throughout this book to not describe "Western" phenomena. We see this descriptor as privileging Huntingtonian language that reifies binaries and always excludes Muslims by positioning them outside the West.

5 In this chapter we are not interested in determining whether those who believe and/or practise a religious tradition – here Islam – are patriarchal or violent in ways that affect women especially. In fact, we are unaware of a nonpatriarchal space with which to compare and question the assumption that so-called secular norms better protect women. In her critique of how secularism is positioned to ward against religious patriarchies, Beaman (2014b: 239) argues that locating patriarchy (or terrorism) as only a "religious" problem fails to acknowledge its pervasiveness and violence in "secular" societies.

6 For another criticism of this binary, see Orsi 2003.

7 Arshad, Setlur, and Siddiqui (2015) found that only 8 percent of the headlines in the *New York Times* (between 1990 and 2014) containing the words Islam/Muslim were scored positively. They concluded that in this twenty-five-year period, "Islam" and "Muslim" had higher incidents of pejorative association than did other religious groups or benchmarked terms such as "cancer" and "alcohol." See also Furseth 2017 for a discussion of shifts in media coverage of Muslims in Nordic countries.

8 Racial and religious forms of identity are socially constructed and multilayered and are both chosen and ascribed. *Islamophobia* refers to what Bleich (2011: 1581) describes as "indiscriminate negative attitudes or emotions directed at Islam or Muslims" (see also Cohen 2002; Allen 2010; Kumar 2012). Bleich's inclusion of the qualifier "indiscriminate" in his definition is significant in that it allows us to distinguish between attitudes and emotions directed at Islam or Muslims that are negative and those that are phobic. We recognize how the notion of Islamophobia does not adequately account for pervasive normative and exclusionary structures of power that are foundational to these interactions.

9 See Morgan and Poynting (2012: 5) and their description of a globalized "radical Muslim folk devil."

10 Within the *enjeux* or battleground of the 2004 French debates on the ban of conspicuous religious signs in public schools, these authors enumerate other related neo-Orientalist and good/bad binaries, including modernity/tradition, progression/regression, equality/inequality, and the Republic/communautarianism (Guénif-Souilamas and Macé 2004: 12). Guénif-Souilamas (2006) subsequently shows how these gendered figures serve to legitimize discriminatory and racist policies that affect France's disadvantaged suburban regions. The two figures (which offer specificity on the "Patriarch" and the "Imperilled Woman") bolster a Republican Feminism built on subduing the so-called Arab boy and saving the Arab girl.

11 More precisely, Razack discusses how the facile figure of the Imperilled (niqabi) Woman successfully sold the US intervention in Afghanistan in 2001 to the American public. Legal projects in Canada related to the niqab also depict these dynamics. Anti-niqab discourse in Canada from 2011 to 2015 is illustrative of this triad, namely in controversies around Bill 94 and Bill 60, prohibiting women from wearing the niqab in Quebec and attempting a federal ban on face coverings during citizenship ceremonies. In these examples, niqab-wearing women were described as unable to "integrate" in Canadian society because of their overt/ fundamental religiosity imposed by controlling men. In response to the debate on their exclusion from citizenship ceremonies, former Canadian prime minister Stephen Harper (cited in Chase 2015) invoked these figures in asking, "Why would Canadians, contrary to our own values, embrace a practice at that time that is not transparent, that is not open and frankly is rooted in a culture that is anti-women?" Natasha Bakht (2006: 70) similarly maps the ubiquity of the "Imperilled Muslim Woman and Dangerous Muslim Man" in discourses present in the so-called Sharia debate in the province of Ontario, 2003–05.

12 Razack (2004: 163) analyzes how figures are enacted by Muslims and non-Muslims in public discourse in a Norwegian context in which young Muslim women are in situations of forced marriage. She signals that Norwegian Muslim male and female youth do not inhabit "an unproblematic position as victims of their families and communities, although it is certain that they are also victims."

13 The anti-niqab discourse, illustrated by controversies around prohibiting women from wearing the niqab during citizenship ceremonies, is an example. There have been a number of legislative efforts in Quebec specifically aiming to bar women in niqab from receiving or delivering public services. For example, in June 2015, the Quebec government tabled Bill 62 that sought to ban both public servants from wearing face coverings at work and members of the public from covering their faces when receiving government service (for more on Bill 62, see Introduction, note 5). Additionally, it would set out a framework for dealing with accommodation requests. The niqab became the focus of rather contentious debate in Canadian political and media discussion during the 2015 federal election campaign, becoming so salient that it was a topic raised in the party leaders' debate.

The attention was amplified by the case of Zunera Ishaq, a woman seeking to take the citizenship oath while wearing her niqab. Ms. Ishaq successfully challenged the government's 2011 policy that banned the wearing of niqabs during citizenship oath ceremonies (see *Ishaq v Canada (Citizenship and Immigration)*, [2015] 4 FCR 297, 2015 FC 156). The Federal Court of Appeal dismissed the government's appeal in a fast-tracked decision (*Canada (Citizenship and Immigration) v Ishaq*, 2015 FCA 194), so that Ms. Ishaq could take the citizenship oath (which she did) and vote before October 19, 2015. Recall the former prime minister's opposition to the niqab as "anti-women" (see note 11 above). It was pitched as a way to save niqab-wearing women from sartorial and other implied subjugations.

14 In Canada, this initiative is officially called Passenger Protect. Implemented in 2007, it is said to include between five hundred and two thousand names (Public Safety Canada 2016; Sagan 2016).

15 But even if it is presented as harmless, humour is deeply political and difficult to dislodge because it "is intricately linked to power-laden ideologies and unequal social structures" (Sue and Golash-Boza 2013: 1594).

16 Others have called this practice "résumé whitening" (see Kang et al. 2016). In his overview of the early Muslim community in Edmonton, amateur historian Richard Awid (2010: 45, 55), whose father helped build the Al Rashid Mosque in 1938, shows the "Canadianization" of individuals in the early community's "Arabic" names, like Ali Ahmed Omar Aboughoushe (who becomes Ali Omar), Mohammed Khalil Ali Nogedi (who is later known as Bud Alley), and Mahmoud Saaid El Hage Ahmed Abilama and Rikia Haidar (now known as Mahmoud and Mary Saddy).

17 The study also found that 56 percent of respondents reported anti-Muslim incidents in the year following September 11, 2001; 61 percent reported kindness or support from friends and colleagues of other faiths (Council on American-Islamic Relations–Canada 2004: 6). Azeezah Kanji (2016) cites a purported Royal Canadian Mounted Police (RCMP) 2009 document, "Radicalization: A Guide for the Perplexed" that states, "virtually all of the planned or actual terrorist attacks in Western Europe and North America since 9/11 have been carried out by young Muslims." Kanji argues that this RCMP publication is an example of a broader phenomenon of law enforcement that links terror with Muslims in ways that have left white supremacist groups unscathed.

18 Another poll (B. Anderson and Coletto 2016) found that 79 percent of Canadians believed that Muslim Canadians experience some or a great deal of discrimination. Indigenous people were next, with 67 percent of Canadians believing they experience discrimination. At the same time, however, 46 percent of Canadians have an unfavourable view of Islam, and in 2017, Statistics Canada reported that hate crimes against Muslims rose 60 percent from 2014 to 2015 (cited in Harris 2017; recall also the vociferous rhetoric about Muslim Canadians in the 2015 federal election).

19 Notably, the number of respondents with a favourable view of Muslims has grown twofold in the province of Quebec from 2009 to 2017 (B. Anderson and Coletto 2016); similarly, an Environics (2016) poll found that 84 percent of Muslims polled believe they are treated better in Canada than are Muslims in other Western countries, up from 77 percent who expressed this view in the same survey in 2006.

20 *Anti-terrorism Act, 2015,* SC 2015, c 20.

21 *Criminal Code,* RSC 1985, c C-46.

22 In 1984, when the Canadian Security Intelligence Service (CSIS) was established, it acted in an advisory capacity and as an intelligence-gathering agency to collect and share information with the RCMP. As of June 2015, CSIS is now able to physically disrupt acts of terrorism and has policing power (see Watters 2015; also Forcese and Roach 2015).

23 In Montreal, two days prior to the Ottawa shooting, a man the RCMP said was "known to counter-terrorism authorities" and was said to have "become radicalized" drove his car into two members of the Canadian Forces, killing one of them (Bell 2014).

24 For examples of this media coverage, see Associated Press 2015; CTV.ca News Staff 2015a, 2015b.

25 Amarnath Amarasingam (2015) undertook interviews with Canadian foreign fighters. Australian media focused on ISIS female recruits (see Varandani 2015); France is said to have the highest number of radicalized youths in Europe, with more than one thousand counted as joining extremist groups in Syria and Iraq in 2014 (Heyer 2014).

26 Terrorist incidents in this period included the "Sydney Siege" in Australia, in December 2014, where a hostage-taking in a café left two people and the gunman dead (see Sanchez et al. 2014).

27 Liam Harvey-Crowell's (2015) interviews with fifteen Muslim university students for his thesis research in St. John's on their web use similarly confirm a fear of being watched and detained. One of Harvey-Crowell's participants, "Oswald," captures one potential ending following the *Anti-terrorism Act, 2015*:

I mean [former Prime Minister Stephen] Harper did change laws to detain people easier and stuff. It is very frightening to think that someone could look at something I accidentally clicked on or read something, just because it is so crazy online. And they think this is the stuff this guy is reading, and then all of a sudden you are in Guantanamo Bay. (Cited in Harvey-Crowell 2015: 73)

28 This line of questioning also reflects how the secular norms that outline private and public spaces are necessarily trespassed by Muslim women (Fernando 2014a; Selby 2014).

29 Dalia generously explained to her seatmate how long she has skied so that he could learn that Muslims are active in winter sports. She said to him, "I mean, now you know that I do that [snowboard]. The next Muslim that you see, you will have an attitude change, and she'll notice it." In Chapter 4 we discuss at greater length the ways some of our participants, like Dalia, draw on education as part of their everyday negotiation strategies.

30 *Zero Tolerance for Barbaric Cultural Practices Act*, SC 2015, C 29.

31 At the time of writing, a Google search of Zunera Ishaq's name produced a series of entries, the second being "zunera ishaq-husband."

32 We think that it is important to bring this literature into second-wave feminist discussions of women's agency, as well as into the research of those who study women and religion more generally. Particularly fruitful in the former is work in feminist legal studies. Robin West (1988, 2003) argues that liberal and critical legal scholarship privilege autonomy and separation that are in turn linked to freedom (or the freedom to choose). West is critical of a lack of recognition of

connectedness or relationality. As legal scholar Rebecca Johnson (2002: 125) so succinctly puts it, "much contemporary legal thought reflects a profound commitment to a conception of the self as relatively autonomous and self-directing. Thus the rhetoric of choice is of central symbolic value in Western liberal society." The law imagines women (especially when they are religious) as either choosing badly or having no choice (see also Beaman 2008).

33 The works of Jakobsen and Pellegrini (2004, 2008) and Mahmood (2005, 2009) thus resonate with those of Neitz (1987); Davidman (1991); Kaufman (1991); Palmer (1994); Gallagher (2003).

34 See, for example, Daly 1973. Social scientific research has consistently shown that women in conservative religious groups have complex understandings of gender roles, women's oppression, and religious demands (see Davidman 1991; Olshan and Schmidt 1994; Beaman 1999, 2008; Gallagher 2003). Scholars consider how piety, agency, and the human subject are layered and situated and, most importantly, are not captured by the "binary model of subordination and resistance" (Jacobsen 2011: 74; see also Mahmood 2005, 2009; Douglas 2010; Hemmings 2011; Jouili 2011; Pham 2011; Scharff 2011).

35 We describe scholarship that has analyzed Khadr's situation in Chapter 2.

36 The government also distanced itself from Mohamed Fahmy, the Canadian Al Jazeera journalist who, in 2013, was arrested and jailed in Egypt under accusations that he and colleagues were supporting the Muslim Brotherhood. Fahmy was released in September 2015 after being granted a pardon by the Egyptian president. He was a dual citizen of Canada and Egypt (though in order to be released he had to renounce his Egyptian citizenship). His dual citizenship was used to justify non-intervention from the Canadian government, perhaps implying that the good citizen is Canadian only (CBC News 2015a; Commisso 2014). Maher Arar's case, described in the Introduction, is also an example of this interplay between the figure of the Foreigner and the Bad Citizen.

37 For example, philosopher Cressida Heyes (2007) demonstrates how Western women are disciplined and normalized to undertake a never-ending task of bodily perfection, with self-disciplining techniques like dieting and cosmetic surgery.

38 Questions around visibility and invisibility and how they relate to the politics of secularism are discussed more extensively in Chapter 3.

39 Estimates in France suggest that approximately one third of niqabis are white converts (Selby 2014).

40 We elaborate on the discourse of demand in Chapters 4 and 5. See also Barras 2016.

41 These Canadian norms are described in the country's citizenship guide (see Citizenship and Immigration Canada 2012). Under the rubric of gender equality, the guide states, "Canada's openness and generosity do not extend to barbaric cultural practices that tolerate spousal abuse, 'honour killings,' female genital mutilation, forced marriage or other gender-based violence." The invocation of barbarism and

culture explicitly names some forms of gender violence and not others. This guide for proper citizenship invokes the Patriarch, the Foreigner, and the Imperilled Woman.

42 Selby (2016a) notes the academic trend since 2005 (and the significance of Mahmood's 2005 book on a female piety movement in Cairo) to describe Muslim practice with the terms *Islamic piety, revolution,* and/or *revival.* Anthropologists Benjamin Soares and Marie-Nathalie LeBlanc (2015) insightfully critique the overuse of revival in academic contexts related to Islam and observe that its proliferation has rendered the term analytically useless. A similar critique could be made about the term piety.

43 The page "Hadith 03: Islam Is Built on 5 Pillars," on the website Honey for the Heart (https://honeyfortheheart.wordpress.com/40-hadith/hadith-03-islam-is-built-on-5-pillars/) claims the Hadith can be attributed to one of the "rightly guided" Caliphs, Abdullah ibn Umar al-Khattab.

44 In addition to the Islamophobic and Orientalist elements in the debate, others (Phillips 2007; Bhargava 2011) have shown that orthodox, rather than liberal, clerics are often positioned as experts on religious practice in policy debates, which problematically grants power to the more powerful members or gatekeepers in communities and often overemphasizes maleness.

45 Faith-based arbitration remained under the radar until the end of 2003, when the leader of the Islamic Institute of Civil Justice (IICJ) held a press conference to announce it would hold "Sharia courts" for "good Muslims" (Selby and Korteweg 2012; see also Reda 2012; Ali 1995). The Boyd Report (Boyd 2004), which followed a government-mandated commission to study the debate and make formal recommendations, solicited positions from a number of actors both for and against faith-based arbitration. Its author, Marion Boyd, concluded that faith-based family law arbitration should be allowed, with some caveats. Despite Boyd's careful balancing of interests, and despite studies that showed imams' involvement in mediation and not arbitration (Macfarlane 2012b), in their promotion of their *Darul-Qada* ("Islamic Court of Justice") the IICJ monopolized the pro-side of the debate in the media. Boyd's reasoning for maintaining faith-based arbitration (FBA) in Ontario was ignored as subsequent international protests at Canadian embassies against Sharia courts in September 2005 referenced patriarchal violence and human rights atrocities. With mounting international pressure, on September 11, 2005 (a Sunday, not typically reserved for government press releases), then Ontario provincial premier Dalton McGuinty announced, "There will be no Shariah law in Ontario. There will be no religious arbitration in Ontario. There will be one law for all Ontarians," thus barring FBA for all religious groups. The frightening image of Sharia invoked by the leader of the IICJ was thus silenced and solidified. An amendment in February 2006 (the *Family Statute Law Amendment Act*) legally ended faith-based arbitration in Ontario, even if qualitative research by religious studies scholar Christopher Cutting (2012) and legal scholar Julie Macfarlane (2012a)

demonstrates that, because arbitration was never widely used (informal mediation was far more common), very little has changed. See also Emon 2009 for an overview of Islamic law in Canada.

46 We return to how Caroline navigates this daycare conundrum in Chapter 5.

47 This collapsing of everyday practice also reveals other factors, including nervousness in early interviews and, perhaps, our non-Muslimness, which we consider in the methodological section of our Introduction.

Chapter 2

1 In June 2016, the Edmonton Public School District announced that two elementary schools in the city were named after Ms. Hamdon and Dr. Lila Fahlman, who we introduce later in this chapter (see Simons 2016).

2 Our thanks to Katherine Bullock who, owing to her friendship with Hilwie's son's family in Edmonton, determined the name of the women's organization.

3 Another version of this narrative claims that it was the Arabian Muslim Association, formed in January 1938, of which six of thirty-two members were women, who pulled together the funds (see Waugh 1980: 126; Hamdani 2007: 6). Edmonton community historian Richard Awid (2010: 34) suggests that the Ladies' Muslim Auxiliary was founded in February 1941.

4 Academic institutionalization came two decades later. McGill University, in Montreal, established its Institute of Islamic Studies in 1952. The founding director, Wilfred Cantwell Smith, recruited a number of scholars of Islam, including Fazlur Rahman Malik (see A. Hussain and J.S. Scott 2012; Salwa n.d.). One of the Institute's first graduates, Hammudah Abdalati, became the first full-time imam at the Al Rashid Mosque in Edmonton, in 1960.

5 We see the juxtaposition of the figures introduced in the last chapter and these stories of community presence as containing both continuities and disjunctures. As Asad (1986) and others have shown, one central continuity is tracing a narrative focused expressly on Islam. But we also expect the reader will experience disjointedness in her reading. In this vein, we intend the figures mentioned earlier to be held in tension with parts of the narratives told here.

6 Zuhair Kashmeri's (1991) book examines the impact of the 1990–91 Gulf War on Canadian Arabs; Jenna Hennebry and Bessma Momani's (2013) edited volume examines the stigmatized experiences of Arab Canadians. Rakib Buckridan (1994) investigates Muslims from Trinidad. Parin Dossa (1994, 1999) offers case studies of elderly Ismai'ili Canadians. Kristin McLaren (1999) turns to Indonesian Muslims in Canada. Berns McGown (1999) considers the transnational lives of Somalis in London and Toronto. Paul Eid (2003, 2007) focuses on the multiple identities of second-generation Arab Canadians in Montreal (see also Asal 2016). Faiza Hirji (2010) looks to South Asian youth in British Columbia. Based on quantitative data, Lakhdar Brahimi (2011) compares the economic integration of Algerians, Moroccans, and Tunisians in Quebec. Shaha El-Geledi and Richard

Bourhis (2012) study the impact of representations of the veil for Arab Muslims.

7 Notably, many of the studies that take an everyday, empirical field-research approach are masters' theses and doctoral dissertations that explore specific Muslim ethnic groups or communities (including Buckridan 1994; McLaren 1999; Akter 2010; Nagra 2011b; R. Smith 2011; Downie 2013; Rochelle 2013; Cassin 2014; Hameed 2015; Harvey-Crowell 2015; Williams 2015).

8 The territory was initially inhabited by First Nations people, including the Blackfoot Confederacy and the Plains, Woodland Cree, and Chipewyan peoples. The Hudson Bay Company had "acquired" the territory in 1670.

9 Kelly (1998) observes that zero Muslims were recorded in the 1881 and 1891 censuses.

10 Waugh et al. (2015) note that the town of Lac La Biche still has the largest number of Muslims per capita in Canada.

11 According to Awid (2000: 34), Alexander Hamilton learned Cree in order to trade with local Indigenous peoples in the Lac La Biche area following a failed three years of homesteading in Edam, Saskatchewan. When the fur trade collapsed with the First World War, he sold Ford vehicles and operated an Imperial Oil gas station, before opening a store (later sold to the Hudson's Bay Company in 1946), a mink ranch, and a butcher shop. In his retirement, Hamilton travelled south to Arizona and Hawaii to escape the cold Canadian winters and went on *hajj* (pilgrimage to Mecca that is to be undertaken if one is financially and physically able).

12 Like his great-uncle before him, Nadir is active in his city's mosque and is of Lebanese origin. He immigrated to Edmonton first with some of his immediate family and then to St. John's to begin doctoral studies eleven years later. Nadir explains, "I always ask for my rights."

13 The family's narrative describes how Amina left behind her youngest daughter in the care of relatives in Lebanon. Tragically, in the four-and-a-half year period in which Amina was marooned in Mexico, this younger daughter went missing.

14 Six passengers died in the air crash. Fortunately, a police officer had broken protocol before the flight and removed the handcuffs from the convict, Paul Archambault. Archambault is said to have carried Shaben from the wreckage. Larry and Alma's daughter Carol, a Middle East–based journalist, wrote a book about how she accidentally found out about the crash by reading about it in the *Jerusalem Post* (her parents did not want to worry her) and about the bond that formed between the four survivors at the crash scene (C. Shaben 2013). Two years after the plane crash, Larry Shaben survived a severe beating by two young men whom he and Alma had tried to assist on the side of a highway in northern Alberta.

15 The Canadian government counted 8,549 interned persons during this period (as described in the "Enemy Aliens, Prisoners of War: Canada's First World War Internment Operations, 1914–1920" exhibit at Banff National Park, Parks Canada,

September 6, 2013; see: https://www.pc.gc.ca/en/pn-np/ab/banff/decouvrir-discover/ histoire-history/internement-internment.

16 It is important to note that even though, as we saw in the newspaper clippings, the construction and opening of the Al Rashid Mosque was celebrated by local governmental officials, the interwar period was not reflective of a trend in growth or in government-sponsored interest in the settlement of Muslim Canadians. The mosque was renamed in 1946 as the Canadian Islamic Centre of Edmonton, also indicating the multifunctional use of the space. The first wedding celebrated in the mosque was for Hilwie and Ali Hamdon's daughter Helen and her husband Eddie Youssef, in 1948 (Hamdani 2007: 8). Daood Hamdani (2015:4) describes the mosque's symbolic importance, arguing that its "influence extended far beyond their small numbers and whose descendants have produced prominent personalities in the Canadian public life."

17 An Environics poll (2016: 8) reports that when Canadian Muslims were asked to name their least favourite thing about Canada, the weather (31 percent) emerged first, up from 24 percent ten years earlier. A 2006 study found that 94 percent of Muslim Canadians adopted "Canadian values" (Environics 2006: 90).

18 The 1967 points system selected immigrants based on factors such as education, occupational demand, age, health, and destination in Canada (see Dewing 2009; Kelly 1998: 87).

19 Prior to 1981, one could tick the "Other" checkbox and write in "Muslim." More people, however, are willing to check a box than to write out their affiliation under "Other."

20 We make this approximation based on worldwide data where Shi'ias are said to account for 15 percent of the Muslim population and by making assumptions based on country of origin.

21 The Shi'ia Imami Ismai'ili community grew in 1972 when, following a Ugandan expulsion order, the community's leader, the Aga Khan, contacted then Prime Minister Pierre Elliott Trudeau to negotiate the acceptance of approximately six thousand Ismai'ili refugees. An influx of Ismai'ili immigrants from Kenya, Zaire, Madagascar, and South Asia continued throughout the 1970s, largely to Ontario. The number of Shi'ias also grew, with some fleeing Iran in the 1970s (see Aga Khan 2008) and Iraq and Afghanistan beginning in the 1980s (A. Hussain and J.S. Scott 2012). Sheila McDonough and Homa Hoodfar (2005: 133, 137) note vibrant Canadian Ismai'ili communities in Canada in the 2000s. Approximately ninety thousand Ismai'ilis live in Canada, the majority in Quebec and Ontario, with an estimated twenty thousand in Alberta (see Shirley 2001; Sharify-Funk and Dickson 2013). Scholarship on Shi'ism has typically focused on Ismai'ilis rather than on the largest branch of Shi'ias, Twelvers, who believe in twelve divinely ordained leaders (see Dharamsi 2014; Karim 2014). Dossa (2002) and Josiane Le Gall (2003) surveyed Canadian Shi'ias, and May Al-Fartousi's (2013, 2015) work examines Shi'ia young women's experiences in public schools. N. Jiwani and G. Rail's (2010) study is a

discourse analysis based on ten informal conversations with Shi'ia women (themselves falling within three Shi'ia sects), between the ages of twenty and twenty-six, in Ottawa and Toronto about how they understand physical activity and religiosity.

22 Ahmadis trace their origins to the teachings of Mirza Ghulam Ahmad (1835–1908), in British India, at the end of the nineteenth century. Deryl Maclean (2010: 73) estimates there are twenty-five thousand Ahmadis in Canada, most of whom settled as refugees after 1974, when they were declared non-Muslims in Pakistan (owing primarily to their belief in the Messianism of their founder).

23 Karim H. Karim (2013) takes his readers inside Shi'ia *jamatkhanas* (private places of worship). Shi'ia mosques are typically spaces open to the wider non-Ismai'ili community and *jamatkhanas* remain private. The Aga Khan Museum established in Toronto, in 2014, includes a distinctly separate *jamatkhana* on a higher elevation than the public part of the complex (Karim 2013: 160).

24 In 2005, the Global Centre for Pluralism, along prestigious Sussex Drive in Ottawa, Ontario, was inaugurated by the group's spiritual leader, the Aga Khan, and Canada's then Governor General, representative of the Queen of England, Adrienne Clarkson. The Aga Khan Canadian Foundation remains active in political and humanitarian projects (see Aga Khan Foundation of Canada 2015). Ismai'ili Rahim Jaffer was the first known Muslim elected to the federal government, in 1997; Yasmin Ratansi became the first Muslim woman elected to the federal parliament, in 2004; and Naheed Nenshi was voted as mayor of Calgary in 2010.

25 *Canadian Multiculturalism Act*, RSC 1985, c 24 (4th Supp).

26 Earle Waugh, Baha Abu-Laban, and Regula Qureshi (1983: 1) claim their North American focus on Islam was "the first of its kind." In their 1994 book, Yvonne Haddad and Jane Smith include Canadian data. Waugh, Sharon McIrvin Abu-Laban, and Qureshi (1991) later edited an overview of the traditions of Islam in family and community life.

27 The original mosque was located next to the Royal Alexandra Hospital, which sought to expand in 1988. As was the case fifty years earlier, a fundraising committee was struck, this time made up largely of Canadian Council of Muslim Women members. They financed moving and restoring the first building to an outdoor historical park, Fort Edmonton, in 1991 (Lorenz 1998). A new Al Rashid Mosque was built, which is one of six mosques in present-day Edmonton that serve more than twenty thousand Muslims (Dayrit and Milo 2015).

28 *Canadian Charter of Rights and Freedoms*, Part I of the *Constitution Act, 1982*, being Schedule B to the *Canada Act 1982* (UK), 1982, c11.

29 This is not specific to Canada. European scholars also note that until the 1990s, ethnicity was the central prism through which immigrant communities were studied (see, for example, Knippenberg 2005; Yukleyen 2010; Selby 2014).

30 Along with immigrants from Syria, Lebanon, Pakistan, Bangladesh, and India, Arab Muslims immigrated in greater numbers during this period, particularly to

Ontario and Quebec, following the Iran-Iraq War (1980–88) and the Gulf War (1990–91) (Kaba 2002; A. Hussain and J.S. Scott 2012). Other groups fleeing persecution who arrived in Canada included refugees from Ethiopia, Eritrea, Somalia, Sudan, Albania, Kosovo, and Bosnia.

31 Drawing on Statistics Canada's 2011 National Household Survey data, Hamdani (2014: 6) notes that while demographic trends among Muslims in Canada showed a small decline in those who marry, marriage remained the traditional family structure. Fourteen percent were female single-parent families, and 2.6 percent of Muslim couples lived in common-law arrangements. Put otherwise, 11 percent of Muslim children in Canada lived in a single-parent household, and in 90 percent of these families that parent was the mother (Hamdani 2014: 11; 2015).

32 Similar to France, the Québécois Muslim community is largely of Maghrebian origin (McDonough and Hoodfar 2005; Fortin, LeBlanc, and Le Gall 2008; R. Brown 2016b). Between 2007 and 2011, Algerians constituted the province's highest number of migrants (Brahimi 2011; Castel 2012). Algerians in Quebec hold the highest unemployment rate (13.7 percent in 2006) and have a higher level of family regroupment immigration (Hachimi Alaoui 2006; Grenier and Nadeau 2011; Mossière and Meintel 2010; Brahimi 2011; Rousseau et al. 2013).

33 The Bouchard-Taylor report discusses these types of difficulties at greater length (see Bouchard and Taylor 2008: chap. 11).

34 Because their dossier was managed by the province of Quebec, their fluency in French bolstered their application.

35 For more information on mental health and immigration in Canada, see Robert and Gilkinson 2012; Metropolis Project 2010.

36 Sarah Wayland (1997) and David Seljak (2005) have written about Muslim private schools in Ontario. Razack (1995, 1998) examines the racialization of South and East Asian students who are mostly Muslim. Much of the work of sociologist Zine (2000, 2001, 2002, 2006, 2007, 2008a, 2008b), who has published the most on Muslims in Canada, focuses on her participants' abilities to express their religiosity in public and Islamic schools, with attention to young hijabi women's experiences in the Greater Toronto Area (especially 2012b). Marie McAndrew, Béchir Oueslati, and Denise Helly (2007) have also examined how Islam is treated and experienced by young people in French Québécois high schools (see also Oueslati, McAndres, and Helly 2011). Amina Triki-Yamani and Marie McAndrew (2009) focus on young Muslims in CEGEPs in Montreal. Nadeem Memon (2012) turns to the pedagogies within Islamic schools in Ontario, while Al-Fartousi (2015) considers the experiences of younger Shi'ia women.

37 Muslims make up 7.7 percent of Toronto's population (see Statistics Canada 2013). More generally, the Greater Toronto Area is home to approximately half of Canada's new immigrant population (52.4 percent; see City of Toronto n.d.). Most Muslim Canadians live in Brampton, Scarborough, and Mississauga, suburbs to the east

and west of the Toronto city core that became part of the amalgamated mega-city of Toronto in 1997.

38 Unmosqued Muslims refers to those who see themselves as practising but do not attend mosques. Scott Flower and Deborah Birkett (2014: 4) note how starting in the 2010s, in an era of increased concern and securitization regarding domestic terrorist activity and radicalization, converts have been increasingly scrutinized in the media.

39 By law, Canadian federal and provincial governments leave the administration and governance of mosques to local governing committees, which must have boards of directors and an electing membership. Numerous Muslim organizations operate within Canada, including the Muslim Association of Canada (established in 1997), the Muslim Students' Association (established in 1963), the Canadian Islamic Congress (founded in 1994), the Muslim Canadian Congress (established in 2001), the Canadian Council of Muslim Women (established in 1982), the Islamic Society of North America (established in 1982), and the Canadian Council on American-Islamic Relations (established in 2000). Most Muslim community organizations in Canada are located in the Greater Toronto Area, which is home to more than sixty ethnocultural groups (Toronto Muslims n.d.).

40 Religious studies scholar Laurie Lamoureux Scholes (2002: 414) depicts the establishment of and the CCMW's participation in public debates primarily through workshops, theological information brochures, and policy papers (see also Alvi and McDonough 2002). The group has also spearheaded *imamah*, or female-led prayer initiatives, in Canada (as detailed in Sharify-Funk and Haddad 2012).

41 Scholars have collaborated on numerous publications with the CCMW and a number are available online, including V.A. Behiery and A.M. Guenther (2000) on Islam; Pascale Fournier (2004) on Islamic jurisprudence at the time of divorce; Daood Hamdani (2005, 2007, 2014) on Muslim women and life in Canada; Nuzhat Jafri (2006) and Jasmin Zine and Zabedia Nazim (2010) on anti-Islamophobia and anti-racisms; and Lynda Clarke (2013) on niqab wearers.

42 Anthropologists Camilla Gibb and Celia Rothenberg (2000) compare the diasporic experiences of Harari and Palestinian women in Toronto, while through in-depth interviews Dossa (2002) analyzes the mental health experiences of immigrant Iranian women. Dossa (2008) also studies the migration narratives of Afghan women and later (2014) analyzes the transnational post-war lives of Afghan women at home and in the Vancouver area, largely by considering their domestic lives and cooking practices. Nasrin Akter (2011) interviews Bangladeshi Muslim women on the East Coast, and Qamer Hameed (2015) interviews 1.5- and second-generation Muslims of a variety of backgrounds living in Winnipeg.

43 For more general reflections on the impact of 9/11 for Muslim Canadians, see Khalema and Wannas-Jones 2003; Helly 2004a, 2004b; Yousif 2005; Sheridan 2006; Bakht 2008; LeBlanc, Le Gall, and Fortin 2008; Nagra 2011a, 2011b; and Jamil and Rousseau 2012. Razack (2008) captures this moment from a feminist critical race

perspective. In general, Razack takes a postcolonial perspective on Muslim cultural politics in contemporary Canada. Zine takes a similar approach, but from a sociological perspective. Her early qualitative work on Islam in schools was followed by an edited volume (Zine 2012a). Other scholars have adopted postcolonial perspectives in their work related to Islam in Canada, namely Evelyn Hamdon (2010), who turns to Muslim identity and Islamophobia. Denise Helly (2010, 2011) examines what she calls *Orientalisme populaire* and locations of Islamophobia in Quebec. Golnaz Golnaraghi and Albert Mills (2013) take up public discourse at the moment of the proposed Bill 94 in the province of Quebec in 2010 that proposed banning face coverings when seeking public services.

44   On this point, significant literature was published in a specific period and includes Dossa 1999, 2002; Kurd 1999; Gibb and Rothenberg 2000; S. Hussain 2002; Shahnaz Khan 2002; Lamoureux Scholes 2002; Zine 2002; and Reitmanova and Gustafson 2008.

45   On the meanings of the hijab, see Hadj-Moussa 2004; Ruby 2004; Haddad 2005; Jafri 2005; Atasoy 2006; and Al-Fartousi 2015. On "de-veiling," see Kullab 2012. On marriage and the *mahr*, see, for example, Fournier 2004, 2006, 2010; and Selby 2016b. On forced marriage, see Razack 2004; and Korteweg 2013. On polygamy, see Milot 2008; and Saris and Daoust 2014. On divorce in southern Ontario, see Macfarlane 2012a, 2012b. On divorce in Montreal, see Saris and Amor 2011. On divorce in Canada, see Fournier 2007 and Cross 2013.

46   See, especially, Korteweg 2012 and Beaman 2012b.

47   See note 57 below.

48   See Haggerty and Gazso 2005; Razack 2007; Hanniman 2008; Gazso and Haggerty 2009; Leuprecht and Winn 2011; Jamil and Rousseau 2012; Patel 2012; and Bramadat and Dawson 2014. Drawing on 120 anonymous surveys and 16 interviews with Muslim university students, Nadia Caidi and Susan MacDonald (2008) show stigmas that the students navigate post-9/11. They note the homogenization of all Muslims into one perspective. Jamil and Rousseau (2012: 373) emphasize the class dimensions of this discrimination. Working-class immigrant communities more often ride a bus, for instance, making encounters in the public sphere more likely than for those who own vehicles.

49   His young age, the interrogation methods, his confession, his guilty plea related to war crimes, his Canadian citizenship, a civil suit against the Canadian government for conspiring with the United States and abusing his rights, and the 2017 financial settlement have been the subject of a great deal of academic study and debate (see Jamison 2005; R.J. Wilson 2006; Dore 2008; Shephard 2008; Grover 2009; Mendes 2009; R.J. Wilson 2009; Macklin 2010; McGregor 2010; Roach 2010; Ryan 2010; Rangaviz 2011; R. Smith 2011; Y. Jiwani 2011; Williamson 2012; R.J. Wilson 2012).

50   The "Toronto 18" refers to eleven men and four youths arrested on June 2, 2006 (two others were arrested who were already serving prison terms, another was

arrested two months later), accused of participating in plots to attack Parliament Hill, among other locations. That these were the first arrests after the 9/11-related anti-terrorist legislation and that these threats to Canada were "homegrown" raised the spectre of radicalization (Sharify-Funk and Dickson 2013: 193).

51 Sociologist James Beckford and legal scholar Ilona Cairns (2015: 40) contrast the institutional understanding of Muslim chaplains in prisons in Canada and England and Wales. In their sample of seven Canadian male Muslim chaplains, one held the position as a full-time job. The remainder were volunteers or paid by their faith communities. The Muslim chaplains they interviewed primarily noted issues with access to communal prayer time due to prison staffing issues, lack of space, and concern with congregation without proper supervision (46).

52 Much of the scholarly writing on the 2003–05 Sharia debate in Ontario (Almas Khan 2005; Thornback 2005; Bakht 2006, 2007a, 2007b; Clarke and Cross 2006; Korteweg 2006; Bunting and Mokhtari 2007; Razack 2007; Korteweg 2008; Sharify-Funk 2009; A. Brown 2010, 2012; Reda 2012; Korteweg and Selby 2012; Zine 2012b; Razavy 2013; Selby 2013) critiques the ways Muslims were represented. Legal scholars Jean-Mathieu Potvin and Anne Saris (2009) and Helly et al. (2011) examine private arbitration practices among Muslims in Montreal, and Saris and Potvin (2013) do so in Canada, more generally. Others have considered the impact of Member of the National Assembly Fatima Houda-Pepin's motion (quickly passed) before the Quebec provincial government to ban Sharia courts in the province. Most compellingly, interviews conducted with Muslims and imams in Ontario by Julie Macfarlane (2012a, 2012b) and Christopher Cutting (2012) show that the debate's premise was erroneous: religiously based family law arbitration is not something that Canadian Muslims engage in or that Muslim Arbitration Boards conduct. Mediation services, however, are widely used and available.

53 The 2007 Bouchard-Taylor Commission in Quebec has also been the subject of a good deal of work (see Brodeur 2008; Mahrouse 2010; Sharify-Funk 2010; Lefebvre and Beaman 2012; Barras 2016).

54 For work on the Quebec-France comparison related to Islam, see Karine Côté-Boucher and Ratiba Hadj-Moussa 2008; Géraldine Mossière 2010, 2013; Lépinard 2015; and Selby 2014.

55 For more specific comparisons related to hijab and niqab politics in the two contexts, see Caylee Hong 2011; Meena Sharify-Funk 2011; Bakht 2012; Nafay Choudhury 2012; Kyle Conway 2012; Pascale Fournier and Erica See 2012; David Koussens, Stéphane Bernatchez, and Marie-Pierre Robert 2012, 2014; Clarke 2013; Fournier 2013; Naama Ofrath 2013; and Saris 2014.

56 In a 4–2–1 split decision in 2012, the Supreme Court of Canada ruled that the courts should make determinations on the niqab on a case-by-case basis, considering the sincerity of the religious belief, trial fairness, and alternative accommodations available (in *R v N.S.* 2012). See Bakht 2009, 2010, 2015a; Beaman 2011; Robert Leckey 2013; Safiyeh Rochelle 2013; Chambers and Roth 2014; *R v N.S.* 2012.

57 Occasional *Globe and Mail* columnist Sheema Khan's *Of Hockey and Hijab: Reflections of a Canadian Muslim Woman* (2009) is a compilation of previously published opinion pieces on her life in Canada. The tone of her opinion pieces ranges from laughter at the game of hockey to this response, in 2015, following the announcement of former prime minister Harper's election promise of a phone line to report "barbaric cultural practices": "Never in 50 years have I felt so vulnerable. For the first time, I wonder if my children will have the opportunity to thrive as I did" (Sheema Khan 2015). Irshad Manji's (2005) best-selling autobiography has been translated into thirty languages. Manji was nominated for an Emmy award for her documentary, *Faith without Fear* (Manji and McLeod 2007). Manji has been critiqued by a number of scholars, in particular by Razack (2008), who reads her work as a neo-Orientalist portrayal of gender politics in Islam. Djemila Benhabib's (2009) *Ma vie à contre-Coran* is a comparable example from Quebec. In 2012 and 2014, Benhabib ran unsuccessfully as a member of the National Assembly for the Parti Québécois (see a critique in Barras 2018).

58 Young Muslim Canadians have mobilized on social media, including Twitter feeds with hashtags such as #jesuishijabi (see Agence QMI 2015; Funk n.d., 2017) and #muslimsactually; and through videos such as one created by Winnipeg's Snow Angel Films (Saira Rahman and Nilufer Rahman 2015). Drawing on interviews conducted in Montreal, Toronto, and Ottawa with second-generation Muslims ages eighteen to twenty-seven, Ramji (2014) shows how the majority of her respondents used the internet to find answers to religious questions rather than directing their religious questions towards their local mosque/community or imam.

59 See Council on American-Islamic Relations–Canada 2004: chap. 1.

60 See Sunier (2014: 1142) on how securitization has impacted policy priorities and research agendas in Europe.

61 Fourteen nationwide focus groups revealed a sense of horror at the terrorist attacks as well as significant distress about unfair negative stereotyping of Muslims and their difficulties in travel (McDonough and Hoodfar 2005: 148; see also Hamdani 2005).

62 This trend is also visible in the rise of scholarly treatment of forms of "radicalization" and "deradicalization."

63 A handful of studies have examined the portrayal of Muslim Canadians in Canadian government reports (see A. Brown 2010, 2012; Selby 2013, 2016a; Barras 2016).

64 In *Chroniques d'une musulmane indignée* (2015b), Ibnouzahir writes about her family's journey to Canada and dedicates a large portion of the book to observations from her humanitarian work. Still, media interviews focused almost exclusively on her relationship to the hijab, namely that she wore one for a few years and later removed it (some interview examples: Bennis, Ibnouzahir, and Awada 2015; ADR-Tele 2016).

65 By conducting phone interviews with 455 Muslims in Ottawa and by holding focus groups across Canada, specifically with the Canadian Uyghur community, to

account for regional and minority differences, Leuprecht and Winn (2011) sought to understand what the Canadian Muslim community thought about Canada and the world around them. In their focus groups, they found that Muslim Canadians were concerned about Canadian security agencies. The most significant issue raised by their respondents was prejudicial hiring practices by Canadian employers, especially in Quebec.

66 Based on their findings from questionnaires, focus groups, and surveys mostly focused on Toronto and Montreal, Moghissi, Rahnema, and Goodman (2009: 17) argue that "the experience of immigrants has many dimensions, and that it cannot be reduced to a single element such as religion."

67 Waugh has also written *Al Rashid Mosque: Building Canadian Muslim Communities*, to be published in 2018 by the University of Alberta Press.

68 A small study by Selby (2016b) of young Sunni women in the Greater Toronto Area at the time of their *mahr* negotiation similarly found that while engaging with *fiqh* was important to them, they made little distinction between schools of Islamic law.

69 The thirty members of the Canadian Council of Imams, established in 1990, meet every month to discuss issues that affect Muslims in Canada and are working towards formalizing some fatwās, or legally unbinding edicts, for this context (see Agence France-Presse 2010; Canadian Council of Imams 2012).

70 The study (September 2004–April 2006) included ninety-seven youths, aged eighteen to twenty-seven, who had at least one immigrant parent, were either born in Canada or arrived in Canada before the age of ten, and who lived or studied in the urban areas of Toronto, Ottawa, or Montreal (Beyer and Ramji 2013).

71 Katherine Bullock (2015: 91) analyzes the responses of three Canadian female converts to the 1960s sitcom *I Dream of Jeannie*. The women reported significant tension between their memories of watching the program as children and their feelings towards the program's Orientalist tropes post-conversion.

72 In 2011, 44 percent of Muslims between the ages of twenty-five and sixty-four held a university degree, compared with the national average of 26 percent (cited in Hamdani 2015: vii). Also in 2011, 13.9 percent (sixty-six thousand) of Muslims were unemployed, compared with the national average of 7.8 percent (Hamdani 2005: 24). Hamdani notes a problem of underemployment, which is more difficult to quantify. See also Paul Eid's (2012) study that shows this phenomenon at work in Quebec.

73 The highest rates of poverty are for Muslims from Western Asia and the Middle East, India, Pakistan, and Eastern Africa – for whom the poverty rates are in the range of 40 to 50 percent. In his book on Muslims in Canada, drawing on 2001 data, Kazemipur (2014) suggests that this economic disparity is the most significant discriminatory issue affecting Muslims in Canada (see also Hamdani 1986).

Chapter 3

1 Legal scholar Stephen Feldman (1998) writes a powerful critique of the celebration of religious holidays in public institutions such as schools and traces the

development of the modern conceptualization of the state and its links to Christianity (see also Forbes 2007).

2 This scenario also reflects Nour's separation of her teaching and religious lives, where she frames her religious intention (in wearing her hijab) within a logic of regulation. In so doing, she resituates her religious practice so that it is always invested with certain public politics.

3 This, too, though, may not be as simple as Nour assesses it: the move to the holiday discourse may fold in the Christian celebration of Christmas, but there may also be a move towards something broader and inclusive (mirroring, perhaps, the Nordic celebration of Yule) that has yet to fully emerge.

4 See Fournier and See (2012), who map the expanding boundaries of the public in relation to the proposed legislation of Bill 94 that would have limited the wearing of religious symbols.

5 The language of neutrality is often used to qualify space, time, and policies that favour a Christian imaginary (on this point see, for instance, Asad 2003; Jakobsen and Pellegrini 2004, 2008; Gilliat-Ray 2005; Sullivan 2005; Bender and Klassen 2010; Beaman 2013a).

6 That it was not part of our interview schedule (or questionnaire) may reflect our positions as non-Muslim Caucasian and Christian-identified women researchers. In other words, this omission is surely due to our own privileged experiences of the holidays.

7 Akin to Knott's (2013) notion of decoupling the secular and the profane, Erin Wilson's (2012: 96–97) distinction between "either/or" and "both/and" approaches to religion has helped us think about the complexities and subtleties of how people themselves see their own lives and practices, like Dalia. Indeed, Wilson invites us to move beyond the dualist framework whereby religion and secularism can only be understood according to an either/or framework (either something is religious or secular but cannot be both) and instead suggests we adopt a more relational both/and framework that recognizes the relations between multiple concepts.

8 Notably, Sabrina does not seem to be perturbed by the perception of the potential violent undertones of the laser tag activity.

9 For more on how participants' abilities to negotiate vary as a function of their social position, see Barras, Selby, and Beaman (2016: 108).

10 In the Bouchard-Taylor Commission report, the sugar-shack story was one example that was examined. This 2007 controversy in Quebec involved the negotiation of Muslim prayer and dietary needs at a maple syrup shack and restaurant. The commissioners found that the organization of the prayer space had been carefully and amicably negotiated with the business owners prior to the visit of a Muslim community group (Bouchard and Taylor 2008: 72). The controversy and subsequent rigid guidelines following the media portrayal, however, created a conflictive situation that previously had been no big deal. In this way, the commission and the media brouhaha around the sugar-shack story focused on problematic visible

prayer and dietary substitutions, creating the problem (see Barras, Selby, Beaman 2018).

11　Interestingly, in controversies regarding prayer space at McGill University and École de Technologie Supérieure, in Montreal, both institutions argued that they were not obliged to provide prayer rooms because of their secular mandate (see Cauchy 2006; Eidabat 2014). It is equally noteworthy that at McGill, Catholics are able to pray in two different sites (Newman Center and the Birks Chapel) and Jews in the Hillel House (see Zehiri 2009; Libin, Kay, and Gurney 2011; Kay 2013; Eidabat 2014). The image of Muslim prayer as a practice infringing on public space is not limited to Canada. France, for instance, prohibited Muslims from praying in the streets in 2011, after repeated reports of Muslims prostrating collectively in the street (Agence France-Presse 2011a, 2011b). While on a campaign trail in December 2010, French National Front leader Marine Le Pen compared the Parisian street prayers to German Nazi occupation, a position with which 39 percent of French citizens allegedly agreed (Bretton 2010) and a statement for which she was accused (and acquitted in 2015) of hate speech. Deeming outdoor prayer "unacceptable," the French interior minister announced that a former barracks in the Porte des Poissonniers district in Paris's periphery would better accommodate the large prayer-attending community, especially in the month of Ramadan. Out of sight, out of mind.

12　This might be because scholars tend to focus on public controversies and legal cases (see Jeldtoft 2014 on this point). This perspective is somewhat replicated in Jouili's (2015) association of the secular with constraint in her book-length treatment of second-generation Maghrebian female youths in Germany and France.

13　To claim a space for prayer can engender situations that are difficult and conflict-ridden, something that many of Jouili's interlocutors preferred to avoid. This is why most opt to conform themselves more or less to normative conduct in secular public spheres, hiding their prayer from this scene (Jouili 2009: 461). Yet, as we explore through our participants' stories, analyzing prayer arrangements through a public/private prism, in which making one's religion visible in the public realm is read/lived as transgression, is limiting. It overlooks numerous narratives in which this ordering of space is not identified as central and as the variable explaining prayer arrangements, or in which this ordering is experienced differently. Jouili does underline that her focus is precisely on analyzing practices in relation to "public spheres experienced as restrictive" (465). This emphasis might explain the dominance of the conflict variable in her discussion and analysis of how hostile prayer environments become sites of contestation (460).

14　To be clear, we are not taking a position on whether prayer space should be available anytime/anywhere. Rather, we are interested in examining the implications of this rigid discourse for our participants, as it implies that they want and are formally asking for dedicated prayer spaces.

15 We focus on prayer space in this section, but we heard similar stories about flexible negotiations around other religious practices, such as eating halal and the Eid holiday (see Chapters 4 and 5).

16 We saw another facet of the spatial location of prayer and its intersection with the secular when our interviewees talked about multifaith spaces. These are usually designated as inclusive and universal, yet often include Christian symbols or a Christian-privileged organization of space (with no place for footwear or ablutions and with pews and an altar). In one telling narrative, Aydin, aged twenty-nine, notes that the general hospital where he works as a resident has a prayer room with "benches and stuff" and where Christian images and iconography remain. He uses it on occasion to pray, but the configuration is not well-suited for his needs. He did not know it had been renamed a multifaith chapel until he showed it to Barras, who noticed an official sign designating it as such. Before that point, Aydin had assumed that it was officially a Christian chapel because of how it was spatially organized. Its Christian specificity is overlooked by the multifaith chapel moniker.

17 Foucault's (2003: 252) work on governmentality is especially attentive to the regulation of sexuality, which he notes is the precise point where "the disciplinary and the regulatory, the body and the population, are articulated." Following this point and other theorists who have since taken up Foucault's work (Fassin 2006; Göle 2015: 178), we are interested in how the secular maps on to configurations of sexuality expressed through social interaction.

18 Plainly stated, as already seen in our discussion of Muslim prayer, our Muslim participants' religiosity is often the foregrounded part of their identities in their interactions with others, whether desired or not.

19 See Riis and Woodhead (2010) for a book-length discussion of the role of emotion in religion from a sociological standpoint. Though Riis and Woodhead focus on symbols, practices are equally subject to an analysis of the social context in which they occur and the emotion that attaches to them.

20 Fadil (2009) discusses this concern in her study of how Muslim Belgian Maghrebi women manage emotionally laden and potentially socially transgressive practices, like not shaking hands.

21 The Québécois government created the Conseil du Statut de la Femme in 1973 to defend women's rights in the province. In their 2011 document *Affirmer la laïcité, un pas de plus vers l'égalité réelle entre les femmes et les hommes* [Affirming secularism, a step towards real equality between men and women], the Conseil du Statut de la Femme endorses Bill 94's importance with examples from Quebec's historical relationship with the Catholic Church. Still, despite this careful couching, the timing of the report makes its target clear (see Selby 2014).

22 Our participants' emphasis on the hypervisibility of their headscarves resonates with the findings in other studies (e.g., J.R. Bowen 2007; J.W. Scott 2007; Selby 2012b; Jeldtoft 2013; Barras 2014).

23 Recall the story of Dalia in Chapter 1, when she was interrogated on a ski lift.

24 Vincent Geisser (2010: 43) has aptly described the post-9/11 period in the West as being characterized by "hijabophobia," or the irrational rejection of the hijab. This sentiment has been well-charted in social scientific literature, which shows how non-Christian religious signs are perceived as superseding all other personal philosophical positions (see, for instance, Mahmood 2005; Fadil 2009; Silvestri 2011).

25 In a number of Western European nation states, Muslim bodies have increasingly acted as negative points of reference for secular projects. In her linkage of the secular and religious to bodies in contemporary European debates, Schirin Amir-Moazami (2016: 149) convincingly argues that the secular body in the German context "gains currency *through* the discursification of the Muslim body."

Chapter 4

1 The kirpan is a central article of faith for male Sikhs. Categorizing the kirpan is complex. Is it a ceremonial or religious sword, knife, or dagger?

2 The court decided on a compromise to accommodate the student: the kirpan could be worn as long as it was sealed and secured so that the sheath would not be accessible (Stoker 2007; Lavoie 2015).

3 The degree to which receiving societies should accommodate has been a core focus of the literature on interculturalism, which has been extensively developed in Quebec (see Bouchard 2012). It has also been taken up in Europe, namely in a report by Foblets and Schreiber (2013) that, while focused on Belgium, has many similarities with the Bouchard-Taylor Commission report (Bouchard and Taylor 2008).

4 Jamil and Rousseau (2012) show that after 9/11, Muslims in Montreal who used public transportation were more likely to encounter prejudice and discrimination than those who drove.

5 Dorothy Smith (1987: 110) offers a useful warning about taking our participants' narratives at face value: "We cannot rely upon them [our participants] for an understanding of the relations that shape and determine the everyday. Here then is our business as social scientists for the investigation of these relations and the exploration of the ways they are present in the everyday."

6 Jeldtoft's (2013) chapter discusses in broad terms how Islam and Muslims are depicted in "Western imaginaries," and includes public and academic discourses.

7 In Canada, these reports, commissions, and bills focus on high-profile cases, like the Bouchard-Taylor Commission in 2007 and its report (Bouchard and Taylor 2008), the Boyd Commission on family law arbitration (Boyd 2004), as well as Bill 94 and Bill 60 in Quebec. There are a myriad of similar examples outside Canada, particularly laws and legal proposals (and the reports that typically precede these laws) to ban the visible Muslimness of niqabs and burqas (e.g., France, in 2010; Belgium, in 2011), headscarves (e.g., France, in 2004), and minarets (e.g., Switzerland, in 2009).

8   See note 23 in Chapter 1.

9   It is relevant to highlight that Deeb and Harb (2013: 18–19) explicitly speak of "rubric" (and not "register," a term used by Schielke 2009a). Because they are interested in capturing how a moral subject (re)defines him/herself, they consider that rubric allows them to better capture the primary sets of values within a register.

10 The fragility conveyed by the notion of working consensus is explored at greater length in Chapter 5.

11 Geographical location affects the navigation and negotiation of our participants in school settings. In cities such as Montreal or Toronto, parents can send their children to full-time private Muslim schools, which is not an option in St. John's. It is estimated that in 2010 there were thirty-seven full-time Muslim schools in Ontario, twenty-four of which were in the Greater Toronto Area (Memon 2010: 111). McAndrew (2010: 44) notes that in 2008 the total enrollment of students in private Muslim schools recognized by the Government of Quebec was 1,621 students. Memon (2010: 111) counts eight Islamic schools in Montreal.

12 Given the high cost of childcare, some of our participants elect for the mothers to stay home with preschool children. We do not have any same-sex couples or stay-at-home fathers in our sample, and only our female participants discuss childcare. Childcare arrangements differ in the Montreal and St. John's contexts because Quebec is the only Canadian province to subsidize public daycares. The participants we describe in this section are mostly in Montreal. There is little religious diversity or negotiation available around religion-inspired requests related to daycares in St. John's. The authors know of one Montessori-based provider in St. John's that has vegan and vegetarian options, but with eight spots and a higher price point, it is less accessible. Most Muslims in St. John's in our sample who need childcare use Memorial University of Newfoundland's on-campus daycare (which offers some dietary flexibility but has not omitted non-halal foods; it also has limited spots starting at age two) or the children remain at home (with a parent, relative, or nanny).

13 See note 11 above.

14 In France, for instance, there have been heated controversies since the 1980s around the menus (and lack of choice on menus) offered in cafeterias [*cantines*] in public schools (Lecomte 2015). While there have been explicit efforts to not serve a halal menu, in practice some canteens offer a vegetarian option and others a menu option without pork (on these negotiations, see Bouzar 2014).

15 Educating non-Muslims (or *da'wa*, a call to proselytize) often motivates study, which can render participants more knowledgeable about the traditions of Islam (see Jouili and Amir-Moazami 2006). A number of scholars who examine Muslim minorities locate this proselytization in what has been called the Islamic revival movement (see Roy 2002; Fernando 2010, 2014b; Jouili 2011, 2015).

16 This point resonates with Caitlin Downie's (2013) discussion of this strategy in St. John's. In her thesis, Downie argues that her participants mobilize an education strategy as a way to ward off judgments, negative experiences, and Islamophobia. She found this tactic most prevalent in two situations: "in instances of ignorance where people do not know about Islam and thus explanation is necessary, and secondly in instances of criticism of Islam thus one feels compelled to defend one's beliefs and practices" (73).

17 Anna's encounter with this teacher happened during the mid-1990s debates in Quebec, where there were attempts to ban headscarves in schools (see Ciceri 1998). Her teacher openly supported a possible ban. This scenario captures an example where Anna's everyday is influenced by a "grand scheme" (on grand schemes, see Schielke and Debevec 2012).

18 Khaled Beydoun (forthcoming) outlines four ways in which Muslim Americans have responded to President Trump's mandate against Muslims and finds four forms of "Acting Muslim": confirming affiliation, conforming to a "Moderate" Muslim approach, covering up their beliefs, or outrightly concealing it.

19 For a detailed discussion of the importance of acknowledging power asymmetries, see Chapter 5.

20 One of our participants, Faizah, worked as a teacher's assistant in a similar high school to the one Aadil's children attended. In our interview, she shared a parallel situation in which parents wanted their daughters to wear hijab in gym class. She tried to mediate between the vice-principal and the parents before the latter took their request to the school board. Faizah says, "I just explained [to the parents] that the whole thing [not allowing hijabs in gym classes] is related to safety. Sometimes the immigrants are a little bit, sometimes they even expect some level of resistance to their practices. So I was just trying to explain that there are rules of safety and, you know, liabilities and things like that." Faizah is also a first-generation immigrant. She tries to negotiate a working consensus. Notably, in a similar case, Faizah presents the headscarf as less of a religious sign and more as a way to "induce their children to behave in a certain way [...] to induce things like manners or stuff like that." Faizah sees a number of registers (religiosity, modesty, sexuality, good manners) revolving around these parents' desire that their girls not remove their scarves in gym class.

21 Visible religious garments – notably hijabs – for players and referees have come under question in a number of controversies in Quebec. Following the case of an eleven-year-old soccer player in Laval, Quebec, in February 2007, the Quebec Federation of Soccer banned hijabs in soccer tournaments and games for "security" reasons (see CBC News 2007b). This ban was lifted in 2012 after FIFA officially ruled against it (see Curtis 2012; CBC News 2012), with certain conditions (FIFA 2013).

22 For more information on the closure of this swimming pool, see CBC News 2013.

23 Women-only access to a public swimming pool is fragile. Even if a pool has a dedicated women's-only time slot, this policy can be challenged by the

reactions of other swimmers, or by the broader political context (on the example of the YMCA in Côte-des-Neiges, a neighbourhood in Montreal, see CBC News 2013).

24 Bouthillier (2013) describes a group of Muslim women in Laval who rent a public pool for three hours on Saturday and Sunday evenings (after the pool is closed for regular swimming) for women's-only swimming (boys under the age of five are admitted). The pool director explains that the centre refused to turn off security cameras but does cover the windows on request.

25 Montreal's weekly newspaper *La Presse* covered an August 2008 story of a lifeguard at a YMCA pool in Montreal who sought to wear her burkini to work and captured mixed responses among swimmers in the women's changeroom (Ouimet-Lamothe 2008).

26 There is a clear gendered component both latent and explicit within these negotiations. Most of the examples in this chapter detail women's experiences, particularly women who wear hijabs. Chapter 1 includes narratives of many young men who regularly experience Islamophobia. It is clear, however, that our visibly Muslim female participants experience a greater number of instances that require navigating and negotiating and therefore carry the additional emotional burden that goes with crafting these arrangements. As we discussed in Chapter 1, data documenting a rise in hate crimes confirm this suspicion.

Chapter 5

1 For instance, a mother of one, aged forty-three and a civil servant, recounts a dinner at her neighbours' home. In trying to capture the "nice atmosphere" of their shared meal, she describes a give and take that takes place as "a certain kindness that we can exchange between ourselves. To me, sitting around this table, as long as they don't impose on me their eating practices, it's not offending. It's acceptable. So it was [a moment of] mutual respect."

2 Schielke (2009b) asks this question as part of a greater reflection on the work of Saba Mahmood who, by focusing only on the discourses of pious women in Egypt, does not focus on how everyday competing claims might influence their coherence, Schielke argues.

3 Turam (2015) suggests looking at urban spaces and interactions in those spaces as fertile sites to study democratization and pluralism.

4 Hilal Elver (2012: 200–01) proposes that living well together requires more than tolerance. It includes not only a recognition of difference, but also protection of others from danger. Farida's narrative nicely exemplifies Elver's point and expands this protection to other feelings of exclusion.

5 In line with our conceptualization of the quotidian (see the Introduction), we do not locate these moments solely in the so-called private sphere. Rather, moments of coexistence and interactions related to religiosity captured in this chapter cut across these public/private spatial distinctions.

6   Social scientists have long theorized about how beliefs and practices related to food – namely what we eat and do not eat and with whom – form identities and communities through their functions of solidarity and separation. See, for example, E.N. Anderson 2005; L.C. Anderson 2010; Freidenreich 2011; R. Brown 2016a.

7   Karim's experience of successfully organizing an event at a sugar shack resonates with other Muslims' experiences in Quebec with sugar-shack owners. In an hour-long Radio-Canada program (Paquette 2014) on the subject, a sugar-shack owner and Muslim attendees stressed the fun, familial, and convivial dimensions of participating in such an outing. He highlighted these dimensions and not the menu and accommodations around dietary requirements. Not unlike Karim, the interviewed sugar-shack owner took particular pride in explaining that, for him, · his sugar shack and his guests were representative of the *mosaïque* that make up contemporary Quebec. It is a relaxed and simple place that brings people together. The owner said, "The sugar shack is a meeting place. Everyone goes. It's not expensive" (*"La Cabane à sucre c'est un lieu rassembleur. Tout le monde vient là. C'est pas cher"*). To illustrate its openness he listed an LGBTQ group, a Jehovah's Witness group, and a biker group as recent clients (Paquette 2014).

8   Following news coverage of the negotiated event at the Mont-Saint-Grégoire sugar shack, southwest of Montreal, in March 2007, the owners received hundreds of angry phone calls. They subsequently publicly stated they had made a mistake in accepting accommodation requests, particularly for the Muslim group of twenty to fifty (out of the larger group of approximately two hundred) to stop the music and temporarily use a dance floor for the ten-minute midday prayer (CTV.ca News Staff 2007; TVA Nouvelles 2007). In his critique of the media coverage of the backlash, Rachad Antonius (2013: 116) shows how provincial newspapers' images, language (with repeated use of terms like "irrational" and "hatred"), and more subtle elements like font size shaped public discourse and entrenched "respectable" racism so that emotional elements and problematized difference trumped the facts of the case.

9   Gökariksel and Secor (2015:28) discuss what they call the "gendered moral order of public space" in Turkey, which means that women who wear headscarves are particularly positioned by the demands and geopolitics of what they characterize as the "post-secular" plural public sphere. The usage of the concepts of post-secularism/post-secular has been the subject of discussion and debates (see, for instance, Beckford 2012; E. Wilson 2012).

10 In contrast, we are reminded of the narrative of a young male respondent who describes his annoyance when this looming awkward question was not asked and his pizza order was misunderstood:

> So whenever I go to restaurants they always assume that ... they always ask me, 'Are you vegetarian for religious reasons?' I think they just confuse Buddhism with Islam. And then I say, 'No. I'm not. I'm just vegetarian.' [...] I went to a pizza

place, and the guy [taking my order] was from the Middle East. And I said, 'Can I have, can I have a vegetarian pizza?' And he gave me a pizza with chicken. And I said, 'No, I want a vegetarian pizza.' And he said, 'Don't worry, it's not pork.' He just assumed that I'm Muslim so I'm ordering vegetarian because I don't want to eat pork. And I said, 'No, I'm *actually* vegetarian.' So, yeah, it gets a bit annoying.

This error could have been avoided if the order taker asked the awkward question of whether by vegetarian, he meant halal.

11   We first met Caroline in Chapter 3, when she described an altercation with her former boss over a prayer arrangement. In this Christmas party example, she is referring to a new manager.

Conclusion

1   Government employees, such as Hassan, regularly translate policies on religion in their dispensation of services (see Berger and Moon 2016 for more Canadian examples).

References

Abu-Laban, Baha. 1980. *An Olive Branch on the Family Tree: The Arabs in Canada.* Toronto: McClelland and Stewart.

Abu-Laban, Baha. 1983. "The Muslim Canadian Community: The Need for the New Survival Strategy." In *The Muslim Community in North America*, edited by Earle H. Waugh, Baha Abu-Laban, and Regula B. Qureshi, 75–93. Edmonton: University of Alberta Press.

Abu-Laban, Sharon McIrvin. 1989. "The Coexistence of Cohorts: Identity and Adaptation among Arab-American Muslims." *Arab Studies Quarterly* 11, 2/3: 45–63.

Adams, Michael. 2009. "Muslims in Canada: Findings from the 2007 Environics Survey." *Policy Research Initiatives Horizons* 10, 2: 19–26.

Adams, Michael, Audrey Macklin, and Ratna Omidvar. 2014. "Citizen Act Will Create Two Classes of Canadians." *Globe and Mail*, May 21, 2014. https://www.theglobeandmail.com/globe-debate/citizenship-act-will-create-two-classes-of-canadians/article18778296/.

ADR-Tele. 2016. "Chronique d'une Musulmane Indignée." YouTube, January 19, 2016. https://www.youtube.com/watch?v=06CV3U-XgKE.

Aga Khan Foundation of Canada. 2015. "What We Do." https://www.akfc.ca/work/what-we-do/.

Agence France-Presse. 2010. "Canadian Imams Condemn Radical Islam." *National Post*, August 13, 2010. http://nationalpost.com/holy-post/canadian-imams-condemn-radical-islam.

Agence France-Presse. 2011a. "La France interdit les prières dans la rue." *La Presse*, September 16, 2011. http://www.lapresse.ca/international/europe/201109/16/01-4448408-la-france-interdit-les-prieres-dans-la-rue.php.

Agence France-Presse. 2011b. "Plus de 100 mosquées 'en construction.'" *Le Figa-ro*, July 2, 2011. http://www.lefigaro.fr/flash-actu/2011/08/02/97001-20110802 FILWWW00332-plus-de100-mosquees-en-construction.php.

Agence QMI. 2015. "Les musulmanes du Canada lancent #JeSuisHijabi." *TVA Nou-velles*, December 4, 2015. http://www.tvanouvelles.ca/2015/12/04/les-musulmanes -du-canada-lancent-jesuishijabi.

Agrama, Hussein Ali. 2012. *Questioning Secularism: Islam, Sovereignty, and the Rule of Law in Modern Egypt*. Chicago: University of Chicago Press. https://doi. org/10.7208/chicago/9780226010700.001.0001.

Akter, Nasrin. 2010. "The Religious Lives of Immigrant Muslim Women in Can-ada: The Case of Bangladeshi Women in St. John's, Newfoundland." Master's thesis, Memorial University of Newfoundland. http://collections.mun.ca/PDFs/ theses/Akhter_Nasrin.pdf.

Akter, Nasrin. 2011. *The Religious Lives of Immigrant Muslim Women in Canada: The Case of Bangladeshi Women in St. John's*. St. John's, NL: Lambert Academic Publishing.

Al Rashid Mosque. n.d. "The History of Al Rashid Mosque." Al Rashid: A Century of Achievement (website). Accessed December 15, 2015. http://alrashidmosque. ca/history/.

Al-Fartousi, May. 2013. "Unveiling Shi'i Religious Identities: Case Studies of Hi-jab in Culturally Homogenous Canadian Schools." PhD diss., Brock University. http://dr.library.brocku.ca/handle/10464/4192.

Al-Fartousi, May. 2015. "Enhancing Contextualized Curriculum: Integrated Iden-tity in Young Shi'i Muslim Arabic-Canadian Students' Social Worlds." *Journal of Curriculum Studies* 48, 2: 1–33.

Ali, Syed Mumtaz. 1995. "Interview: A Review of the Muslim Personal/Family Law Campaign." The Canadian Society of Muslims, August 1995. http://muslimcanada. org/pfl.htm.

Allen, Chris. 2010. "Fear and Loathing: The Political Discourse in Relation to Mus-lims and Islam in the British Contemporary Setting." *Contemporary British Reli-gion and Politics* 4, 2: 221–35.

Alvi, Sajida Sultana, Homa Hoodfar, and Sheila McDonough, eds. 2003. *The Muslim Veil in North America: Issues and Debates*. Toronto: Canadian Women's Press.

Amarasingam, Amarnath. 2015. "A Clear Banner: Canadian Foreign Fight-ers in Syria; An Overview." Jihadology.net, March 4, 2015. http://jihadology. net/2015/03/04/the-clear-banner-canadian-foreign-fighters-in-syria-an-overview/.

Amiraux, Valérie. 2014a. "'Islam' et 'islamophobie.'" In *Dictionnaire des inégalités*, edited by Alain Bihr and Roland Pfefferkorn, 208–10. Paris: Armand Colin.

Amiraux, Valérie. 2014b. "Visibilité, transparence et commérage: de quelques con-ditions de possibilité de l'islamophobie ... et de la citoyenneté." *Sociologie* 5, 1: 81–95. https://doi.org/10.3917/socio.051.0081.

Amiraux, Valérie. 2016. "Visibility, Transparency and Gossip: How Did the Religion of Some (Muslims) Become the Public Concern of Others." *Critical Research on Religion* 4, 1: 37–56. https://doi.org/10.1177/2050303216640399.

Amiraux, Valérie. 2017. "Citoyens, piété et démocratie: réflexions sur le droit au secret comme condition de la vie politique." Keynote to the 34th International Society for the Sociology of Religion Conference, University of Lausanne, Switzerland, July 6.

Amiraux, Valérie, and Javiera Araya-Moreno. 2014. "Pluralism and Radicalization: Mind the Gap!" In *Religious Radicalization and Securitization in Canada and Beyond*, edited by Paul Bramadat and Lorne Dawson, 92–120. Toronto: Toronto University Press.

Amir-Moazami, Schirin. 2016. "Investigating the Secular Body: The Politics of the Male Circumcision Debate in Germany." *ReOrient* 1, 2: 147–70. https://doi.org/10.13169/reorient.1.2.0147.

Ammerman, Nancy T. 2007. "Introduction." In *Everyday Religion: Observing Modern Religious Lives*, edited by Nancy T. Ammerman, 3–18. Oxford: Oxford University Press. https://doi.org/10.1093/acprof:oso/9780195305418.003.intro.

Anderson, A. Brenda, and Franz Volker Greifenhagen. 2013. "Covering Up on the Prairies: Gender, Muslim Identity and Security Perception in Canada." In *Islamic Fashion and Anti-Fashion in Europe and North America*, edited by Emma Tarlo and Annelies Moors, 55–72. London: Bloomsbury Publishing.

Anderson, Bruce, and David Coletto. 2016. "Muslims and Indigenous People Face Most Discrimination in Canada, According to Canadians." *Abaacus Data*, December 29, 2016. http://abacusdata.ca/muslims-and-indigenous-people-face-the-most-discrimination-in-canada-according-to-canadians/.

Anderson, Eugene N. 2005. *Everyone Eats: Understanding Food and Culture*. New York: New York University Press.

Anderson, Lynne Christy. 2010. *Breaking Bread: Recipes and Stories from Immigrant Kitchens*. Berkeley: University of California Press.

Antonius, Rachad. 2008. "L'islam au Québec: les complexités d'un processus de racisation." *Cahiers de Recherche Sociologique* 46: 11–28. https://doi.org/10.7202/1002505ar.

Antonius, Rachad. 2013. "L'islam intégriste, l'hostilité à l'immigration, et la droite nationaliste: quels rapports?" In *Les nationalismes québécois face à la diversité ethnoculturelle*, edited by Rachad Antonius and Pierre Toussaint Michelle Labelle, 107–23. Montréal: Éditions de l'IEIM.

Arat-Koc, Sedef. 2006. "Whose Transnationalism? Canada, 'Clash of Civilizations' Discourse, and Arab and Muslim Canadians." In *Transnational Identities and Practices in Canada*, edited by Vic Satzewich and Lloyd L. Wong, 216–40. Vancouver: UBC Press.

Arshad, Owais, Varun Setlur, and Usaid Siddiqui. 2015. *Are Muslims Collectively Responsible? A Sentiment Analysis of the New York Times*. 416Labs. http://static1.

squarespace.com/static/558067a3e4b0cb2f81614c38/t/564d7b91e4b082df3a4e29
1e/1447918481058/nytandislam_study.pdf.

Asad, Talal. 1986. *The Idea of an Anthropology of Islam*. Occasional Papers Series. Washington: Georgetown University, Center for Contemporary Arab Studies.

Asad, Talal. 2003. *Formations of the Secular*. Stanford, CA: Stanford University Press.

Asad, Talal. 2007. *On Suicide Bombing*. New York: Columbia University Press.

Asad, Talal. 2011. "Thinking about the Secular Body, Pain, and Liberal Politics." *Cultural Anthropology* 26, 4: 657–75. https://doi.org/10.1111/j.1548 -1360.2011.01118.x.

Asal, Houda. 2016. *Se dire arabe au Canada: un siècle d'histoire migratoire*. Montreal: Les Presses de l'Université de Montréal. https://doi.org/10.4000/books.pum.3199.

Associated Press. 2015. "Canadian Police Arrest 10 at Airport on Suspicion of Leaving to Join Isis," " *The Guardian*, May 20, 2015. https://www.theguardian.com/world/2015/may/20/canadian-police-arrest-10-at-airport-on-suspicion-of-leaving -to-join-isis.

Atasoy, Yildiz. 2006. "Governing Women's Morality: A Study of Islamic Veiling in Canada." *European Journal of Cultural Studies* 9, 2: 203–21. https://doi. org/10.1177/1367549406063164.

Awid, Richard Asmet. 2000. *Through the Eyes of the Son: A Factual History of Canadian Arabs*. Edmonton, AB: Accent Printing.

Awid, Richard Asmet. 2010. *Canada's First Mosque: The Al Rashid*. Edmonton, AB: High Speed Printing.

Bader, V. 2007. "The Governance of Islam in Europe: The Perils of Modelling." *Journal of Ethnic and Migration Studies* 33, 6: 871–86. https://doi.org/ 10.1080/13691830701432723.

Bakht, Natasha. 2006. "Were Muslim Barbarians Really Knocking on the Gates of Ontario? The Religious Arbitration Controversy – Another Perspective." *Ottawa Law Review* 40th anniversary edition: 67–82. https://commonlaw.uottawa. ca/ottawa-law-review/were-muslim-barbarians-really-knocking-gates-ontario -religious-arbitration-controversy-another.

Bakht, Natasha. 2007a. "Family Arbitration Using Sharia Law: Examining Ontario's Arbitration Act and Its Impact on Women." *Muslim World Journal of Human Rights* 1, 1: 1–24.

Bakht, Natasha. 2007b. "Religious Arbitration in Canada: Protecting Women by Protecting Them from Religion." *Canadian Journal of Women and the Law* 19, 1: 119–44.

Bakht, Natasha, ed. 2008. *Belonging and Banishment: Being Muslim in Canada*. Toronto: TSAR.

Bakht, Natasha. 2009. "Objection, Your Honour! Accommodating Niqab-Wearing Women in Courtrooms." In *Legal Practice and Cultural Diversity*, edited by Ralph Grillo, Roger Ballard, Alessandro Ferrari, André J. Hoekema, Marcel Maussen, and Prakash Shah, 115–33. Surrey, UK: Ashgate. https://doi.org/10.2139/ssrn. 1336791.

Bakht, Natasha. 2010. "What's in a Face? Demeanour Evidence in the Sexual Assault Context." In *Sexual Assault in Canada: Law, Legal Practice, and Activism in a Post-Jane Doe Era*, edited by Elizabeth Sheehy, 591–12. Ottawa: University of Ottawa Press.

Bakht, Natasha. 2012. "Veiled Objections: Facing Public Opposition to the Niqab." In *Reasonable Accommodation: Managing Religious Diversity*, edited by Lori G. Beaman, 70–108. Vancouver: UBC Press.

Bakht, Natasha. 2015a. "In Your Face: Piercing the Veil of Ignorance about Niqab-Wearing Women." *Social & Legal Studies* 24, 3: 419–41. https://doi.org/10.1177/0964663914552214.

Bakht, Natasha. 2015b. "The Incorporation of Shari'a in North America: Enforcing the Mahr to Combat Women's Poverty Post-relationship Dissolution." In *The Oxford Handbook of Islamic Law*, edited by Anver M. Emon and Rumee Ahmed. New York: Oxford University Press. https://doi.org/10.1093/oxfordhb/9780199679010.013.48.

Bannerji, Himani. 2000. *The Dark Side of the Nation: Essays on Multiculturalism, Nationalism, and Gender*. Toronto: Canadian Scholars Press.

Barras, Amélie. 2014. *Refashioning Secularisms in France and Turkey: The Case of the Headscarf Ban*. New York: Routledge.

Barras, Amélie. 2016. "Exploring the Intricacies and Dissonances of Religious Governance: The Case of Quebec and the Discourse of Request." *Critical Research on Religion* 4, 1: 57–71. https://doi.org/10.1177/2050303216630066.

Barras, Amélie. 2018. "Travelogue of Secularism: Longing to Find a Place to Call Home." *European Journal of Women's Studies*. Published ahead of print, February 11, 2018. https://doi.org/10.1177/1350506818755415.

Barras, Amélie, Jennifer A. Selby, and Lori G. Beaman. 2016. "Visible Religion in Public Institutions: Canadian Muslim Public Servants." In *Religion and the Exercise of Public Authority*, edited by Benjamin Berger and Richard Moon, 95–110. Oxford: Hart Publishing.

Barras, Amélie, Jennifer A. Selby, and Lori G. Beaman. 2018. "Rethinking Canadian Discourses of 'Reasonable Accommodation.'" *Social Inclusion* 6, 2.

Beaman, Lori G. 1999. *Shared Beliefs, Different Lives: Women's Identities in Evangelical Context*. St. Louis, MO: Chalice Press.

Beaman, Lori G. 2008. *Defining Harm: Religious Freedom and the Limits of the Law*. Vancouver: UBC Press.

Beaman, Lori G. 2011. "'It Was All Slightly Unreal': What's Wrong with Tolerance and Accommodation in the Adjudication of Religious Freedom?" *Canadian Journal of Women and the Law* 23, 2: 442–63. https://doi.org/10.3138/cjwl.23.2.442.

Beaman, Lori G. 2012a. "Introduction: Exploring Reasonable Accommodation." In *Reasonable Accommodation: Managing Religious Diversity*, edited by Lori G. Beaman, 1–12. Vancouver: UBC Press.

Beaman, Lori G. 2012b. "The Status of Women: The Report from a Civilized Society." *Canadian Criminal Law Review* 16: 223–46.

Beaman, Lori G. 2013a. "Battle over Symbols: The 'Religion' of the Minority versus the 'Culture' of the Majority." *Journal of Law and Religion* 28, 1: 67–104. https://doi.org/10.1017/S0748081400000242.

Beaman, Lori G. 2013b. "Overdressed and Underexposed or Underdressed and Overexposed?" *Social Identities* 19, 6: 723–42. https://doi.org/10.1080/13504630. 2013.842671.

Beaman, Lori G. 2014a. "Deep Equality as an Alternative to Accommodation and Tolerance." *Nordic Journal of Religion and Society* 27, 2: 89–111.

Beaman, Lori G. 2014b. "'Everything is Water': On Being Baptized in Secularism." In *Secularism on the Edge: Rethinking Church-State Relations in the United States, France, and Israel*, edited by Jacques Berlinerblau, Sarah Fainberg and Aurora Nou, 237–46. New York: Palgrave Macmillan. https://doi.org/10.1057/9781137380371_18.

Beaman, Lori G. 2016. "Living Together v. Living Well Together: A Normative Examination of the SAS Case." *Social Inclusion* 4, 2: 3–13. https://doi.org/10.17645/si.v4i2.504.

Beaman, Lori G. 2017. *Deep Equality in an Era of Religious Diversity*. Oxford: Oxford University Press. https://doi.org/10.1093/oso/9780198803485.001.0001.

Beaman, Lori G., Jennifer A. Selby, and Amélie Barras. 2016. "No Mosque, No Refugees: Some Reflections on Syrian Refugees and the Construction of Religion in Canada." In *The Refugee Crisis and Religion: Secularism, Security and Hospitality in Question*, edited by Luca Mavelli and Erin Wilson, 77–96. Lanham, MD: Rowman & Littlefield.

Beaman, Lori G., and Winnifred Fallers Sullivan. 2013. "Neighbo(u)rly Misreadings and Misconstruals: A Cross-Border Conversation." In *Varieties of Religious Establishment*, edited by Lori G. Beaman and Winnifred Fallers Sullivan. New York: Ashgate Publishing.

Beckford, James A. 2003. *Social Theory and Religion*. Cambridge: Cambridge University Press. https://doi.org/10.1017/CBO9780511520754.

Beckford, James A. 2012. "SSSR Presidential Address Public Religions and the Postsecular: Critical Reflections." *Journal for the Scientific Study of Religion* 51, 1: 1–19. https://doi.org/10.1111/j.1468-5906.2011.01625.x.

Beckford, James A., and Ilona C.M. Cairns. 2015. "Muslim Prison Chaplains in Canada and Britain." *Sociological Review* 63, 1: 36–56. https://doi.org/10.1111/1467-954X.12224.

Behiery, Valérie, and A.M. Guenther. 2000. *Islam: Its Roots and Wings; A Primer*. Canadian Council of Muslim Women. http://archive.ccmw.com/resources/res_pub_islam_rootswings.html.

Bell, Stewart. 2014. "Soldier Dies after Being Run Down in Suspected Terror Attack near Montreal." *National Post*, October 20, 2014. http://nationalpost.com/news/canada/driver-who-ran-into-canadian-soldiers-near-montreal-was-known-to-counter-terrorism-officials-rcmp.

Bender, Courtney, and Pamela Klassen, eds. 2010. *After Pluralism: Reimagining Religious Engagement*. New York: Columbia University Press.

Benhabib, Djemila. 2009. *Ma vie à contre-Coran: une femme témoigne sur les islamistes*. Montreal: VLB éditeur.

Bennis, Kenza, Asmaa Ibnouzahir, and Dalila Awada. 2015. "Musulmanes, féministes et fières de l'être." Interview by Pénélope McQuade, Parce qu'on est en 2015-2016,

December 26, 2015. Radio-Canada Émissions. http://ici.radio-canada.ca/emissions/parce_qu_on_est_en_2015_2016/2015-2016/archives.asp?date=2015-12-26.

Berger, Benjamin L. 2010. "The Cultural Limits of Legal Tolerance." In *After Pluralism: Reimagining Religious Engagement*, edited by Pamela E. Klassen and Courtney Bender, 98–127. New York: Columbia University Press.

Berger, Benjamin L., and Richard Moon, eds. 2016. *Religion and the Exercise of Public Authority*. Oxford: Hart Publishing.

Berlinerblau, Jacques, Sarah Fainberg, and Aurora Nou, eds. 2014. *Secularism on the Edge: Rethinking Church-State Relations in the United States, France, and Israel*. New York: Palgrave Macmillan. https://doi.org/10.1057/9781137380371.

Berns McGown, Rima. 1999. *Muslims in the Diaspora: The Somali Communities of London and Toronto*. Toronto: University of Toronto Press. https://doi.org/10.3138/9781442677470.

Beydoun, Khaled A. Forthcoming. "Acting Muslim." *Harvard Civil Rights–Civil Liberties Law Review*.

Beyer, Peter. 2014. "Securitization and Young Muslim Males: Is None to Many?" In *Religious Radicalization and Securitization in Canada and Beyond*, edited by Paul Bramadat and Lorne Dawson, 121–44. Toronto: University of Toronto Press.

Beyer, Peter, and Rubina Ramji, eds. 2013. *Growing Up Canadian: Muslims, Hindus, Buddhists*. Montreal/Kingston: McGill-Queen's University Press.

Bhargava, Rajeev. 2011. "States, Religious Diversity, and the Crisis of Secularism." Open Democracy (website), March 22, 2011. https://www.opendemocracy.net/rajeev-bhargava/states-religious-diversity-and-crisis-of-secularism-0.

Bielefeldt, Heiner. 2013. "Misperceptions of Freedom of Religion or Belief." *Human Rights Quarterly* 35, 1: 33–68. https://doi.org/10.1353/hrq.2013.0009.

Bissoondath, Neil. 1994. *Selling Illusions: The Cult of Multiculturalism in Canada*. London: Penguin.

Blanchot, Maurice. 1962. "La Parole quotidienne." In *L'Entretien infini*, edited by Maurice Blanchot, 355–66. Paris: Gallimard.

Bleich, Erik. 2011. "What Is Islamophobia and How Much Is There? Theorizing and Measuring an Emerging Comparative Concept." *American Behavioral Scientist* 55, 12: 1581–600. https://doi.org/10.1177/0002764211409387.

Bouchard, Gérard. 2012. *L'interculturalisme: un point de vue québécois*. Montreal: Les Éditions du Boréal.

Bouchard, Gérard, and Charles Taylor. 2008. *Building the Future: A Time for Reconciliation*. Report of the Quebec Commission de Consultation sur les Pratiques d'Accommodement Reliées aux Différences Culturelles. http://collections.banq.qc.ca/ark:/52327/bs1565996.

Bourdieu, Pierre. 1977. *Outline of a Theory of Practice*. Cambridge: Cambridge University Press. https://doi.org/10.1017/CBO9780511812507.

Bouthillier, Christine. 2013. "Elles se baignent entre elles." *Le Journal de Montréal*, February 4, 2013. http://www.journaldemontreal.com/2013/02/04/elles-se-baignent-entre-elles.

Bouzar, Dounia. 2014. "Des cimetières et des cantines à Lyon: une gestion laïque de la diversité par 'l' élargissement de la norme générale." In *Quand le religieux fait conflit*, edited by Anne-Sophie Lamine, 77–94. Rennes, France: Presses Universitaires de Rennes.

Bowen, John R. 2007. *Why the French Don't Like Headscarves: Islam, the State and Public Space*. Princeton, NJ: Princeton University Press. https://doi.org/10.1515/9781400837564.

Boyd, Marion. 2004. *Dispute Resolution in Family Law: Protecting Choice, Promoting Inclusion*. Report for the Office of the Attorney General of Ontario. https://www.attorneygeneral.jus.gov.on.ca/english/about/pubs/boyd/executivesummary.html.

Brahimi, Lakhdar. 2011. "L'intégration Économique des Immigrants Maghrébins du Québec: Le cas des Algériens, Marocains et Tunisiens." Master's thesis, Université de Québec à Montréal.

Bramadat, Paul. 2014. "The Public, the Political, and the Possible: Religion and Radicalization in Canada and Beyond." In *Religious Radicalization and Securitization in Canada and Beyond*, edited by Paul Bramadat and Lorne Dawson, 3–33. Toronto: University of Toronto Press.

Bramadat, Paul, and Lorne Dawson, eds. 2014. *Religious Radicalization and Securitization in Canada and Beyond*. Toronto: Toronto University Press.

Bretton, Laure. 2010. "39% des Français approuveraient les propos de Marine Le Pen." *L'express*, December 15, 2010. https://www.lexpress.fr/actualites/2/39-des-francais-approuveraient-les-propos-de-marine-le-pen_945402.html.

Bribosia, Emmanuelle, Julie Ringelheim, and Isabelle Rorive. 2010. "Reasonable Accommodation for Religious Minorities: A Promising Concept for European Antidiscrimination Law?" *Maastricht Journal of European and Comparative Law* 17, 2: 137–61. https://doi.org/10.1177/1023263X1001700203.

Brodeur, Patrice. 2008. "La commission Bouchard-Taylor et la perception des rapports entre 'Québécois' et 'musulmans' au Québec." *Cahiers de Recherche Sociologique* 46: 95–107. https://doi.org/10.7202/1002510ar.

Brown, Alexandra. 2010. "Constructions of Islam in the Context of Religious Arbitration: A Consideration of the 'Shari'ah Debate' in Ontario, Canada." *Journal of Muslim Minority Affairs* 30, 3: 343–56. https://doi.org/10.1080/13602004.2010.515814.

Brown, Alexandra. 2012. "Managing the Mosaic: The Work of Form in 'Dispute Resolution' in Family Law: Protecting Choice, Promoting Inclusion." In *Debating Sharia: Islam, Gender Politics, and Family Law Arbitration*, edited by Anna C. Korteweg and Jennifer A. Selby, 329–50. Toronto: University of Toronto Press.

Brown, Rachel. 2016a. "How Gelatin Becomes an Essential Symbol of Muslim Identity: Food Practice as a Lens into the Study of Religion and Migration." *Religious Studies and Theology* 35, 2: 185–205. https://doi.org/10.1558/rsth.32558.

Brown, Rachel. 2016b. "Immigration, Integration and Ingestion: The Role of Food and Drink in Transnational Experience for North African Muslim Immigrants in Paris and Montréal." PhD diss., Wilfrid Laurier University.

Brown, Wendy. 2008. *Regulating Aversion: Tolerance in the Age of Identity and Empire*. Princeton, NJ: Princeton University Press.

Bryant, Darrol M. 2001. *Religion in a New Key*. Kitchener, ON: Pandora Press.

Buckridan, Rakib. 1994. "Trinidad Muslims in Canada: A Community in Transition." Master's thesis, University of Ottawa.

Bullock, Katherine. 2002. *Rethinking Muslim Women and the Veil: Challenging Historical and Modern Stereotypes*. Herndon, VA: International Institute of Islamic Thought.

Bullock, Katherine, ed. 2005. *Muslim Women Activists in North America: Speaking for Ourselves*. Austin: University of Texas Press.

Bullock, Katherine. 2010. "Hijab and Belonging: Canadian Muslim Women." In *Islam and the Veil: Theoretical and Regional Contexts*, edited by Theodore Gabriel and Rabiha Hannan, 161–80. London: The Continuum International Publishing Group.

Bullock, Katherine. 2012. "Toward a Framework for Investigating Muslim Women and Political Engagement in Canada." In *Islam in the Hinterlands: Muslim Cultural Politics in Canada*, edited by Jasmin Zine, 92–111. Vancouver: UBC Press

Bullock, Katherine. 2015. "Visible and Invisible: An Audience Study of Muslim and Non-Muslim Reactions to Orientalist Representations in *I Dream of Jeannie*." *Journal of Arab & Muslim Media Research* 8, 2: 83–97. https://doi.org/10.1386/jammr.8.2.83_1.

Bullock, Katherine. 2017. "To Make a Difference: Oral Histories of Two Canadian Muslim Women and Their Organisational Lives." In *Muslim Community Organizations in the West: History, Developments and Future Perspectives*, edited by Mario Peucker and Rauf Ceylan, 183–204. Wiesbaden, Germany: Springer VS. https://doi.org/10.1007/978-3-658-13889-9_9.

Bullock, Katherine, and Paul Nesbitt-Larking. 2013. "Becoming 'Holistically Indigenous': Young Muslims and Political Participation in Canada." *Journal of Muslim Minority Affairs* 33, 2: 185–207. https://doi.org/10.1080/13602004.2013.810116.

Bunting, Annie, and Shadi Mokhtari. 2007. "Migrant Muslim Women's Interests and the Case of 'Sharia Tribunals' in Ontario." In *Racialized Migrant Women in Canada: Essays on Health, Violence and Equity*, edited by Vijay Agnew, 233–64. Toronto: University of Toronto Press.

Cady, Linell E., and Tracy Fessenden, eds. 2013. *Religion, the Secular, and the Politics of Sexual Difference*. New York: Columbia University Press.

Caidi, Nadia, and Susan MacDonald. 2008. "Information Practices of Canadian Muslims Post-9/11." *CERIS* 34 (June): 1–17.

Canadian Council of Imams. 2012. Canadian Council of Imams (website). http://canadiancouncilofimams.com.

Canadian Islamic Congress. 2004. *CIC Media Research Reports 2001–2004*. Canadian Islamic Congress.

Carter, Sarah. 2015. "Old Stock Canadians: Arab Settlers in Western Canada." ActiveHistory.ca, October 1, 2015. http://activehistory.ca/2015/10/old-stock-canadians-arab-settlers-in-western-canada/#comments.

Cassin, Katelyn L.H. 2014. "A Multifaith Military: Religiosity and Belonging among Muslim Canadian Armed Forces Members." Master's thesis, McMaster University.

Castel, Fréderic. 2012. "Un mariage qui aurait tout pour marcher. Implantation et conditions de vie des Québécois d'origine algérienne." In *Le Québec après Bouchard-Taylor: Les identités religieuses de l'immigration*, edited by Louis Rousseau, 197–239. Quebec: Presses de l'Université du Québec.

Cauchy, Clairandrée. 2006. "L'ETS doit offrir un lieu de prière aux étudiants musulmans." *Le Devoir*, March 23, 2006. http://www.ledevoir.com/societe/ethique-et -religion/104978/l-ets-doit-offrir-un-lieu-de-priere-aux-etudiants-musulmans.

CBC News. 2007a. "Canada's Muslims, an International Comparison." CBC News, February 13, 2007, http://www.muslimpopulation.com/pdf/Canada_muslim_ International%20Comparison.pdf.

CBC News. 2007b. "Rule against Hijab Stands: World Soccer Body." CBC News.ca, March 3, 2007. http://www.cbc.ca/news/canada/ottawa/rule-against-hijab-stands -world-soccer-body-1.660585.

CBC News. 2012. "Hijabs Approved for Soccer Players by FIFA." CBC News.ca, July 5, 2012. http://www.cbc.ca/news/canada/montreal/hijabs-approved-for-soccer -players-by-fifa-1.1156215.

CBC News. 2013. "Côte-des-Neiges Under Fire for Offering Gender-Segregated Swimming." CBC News.ca, January 14, 2013. http://www.cbc.ca/news/canada/montreal/ côte-des-neiges-under-fire-for-offering-gender-segregated-swimming-1.1376097.

CBC News. 2015a. "Mohamed Fahmy, Canadian Journalist, Pardoned by Egyptian President, Released from Prison." CBC News.ca, September 23, 2015. http://www. cbc.ca/news/world/mohamed-fahmy-pardoned-egypt-1.3239822.

CBC News. 2015b. "Omar Khadr's Release on Bail 'Disappointing,' Says Public Safety Minister." CBC News.ca, May 7, 2015. http://www.cbc.ca/news/canada/ edmonton/omar-khadr-s-release-on-bail-disappointing-says-public-safety-minister -1.3064945.

CBC News. 2015c. "Zunera Ishaq, Who Challenged Ban on Niqab, Takes Citizenship Oath Wearing It." CBC News.ca, October 9, 2015. http://www.cbc.ca/news/ politics/zunera-ishaq-niqab-ban-citizenship-oath-1.3257762.

Cesari, Jocelyne. 2006. *When Islam and Democracy Meet: Muslims in Europe and in the United States.* New York: Palgrave.

Cesari, Jocelyne. 2013. "Self, Islam and Secular Public Spaces." In *Islam and Public Controversy in Europe*, edited by Nülifer Göle, 47–56. Farnham, UK: Ashgate.

Chambers, Lori, and Jen Roth. 2014. "Prejudice Unveiled: The Niqab in Court." *Canadian Journal of Law and Society* 29, 3: 381–95. https://doi.org/10.1017/ cls.2013.62.

Chase, Steven. 2015. "Niqabs 'Rooted in a Culture That Is Anti-Women,' Harper Says." *Globe and Mail*, March 10, 2015. https://www.theglobeandmail.com/ news/politics/niqabs-rooted-in-a-culture-that-is-anti-women-harper-says/ article23395242/.

Choudhry, Sujit. 2013. "Rights Adjudication in a Plurinational State: The Supreme Court of Canada, Freedom of Religion, and the Politics of Reasonable Accommodation." *Osgoode Hall Law Journal* 50, 3: 575–608.

Choudhury, Nafay. 2012. "Niqab vs. Quebec: Negotiating Minority Rights within Quebec Identity." *Western Journal of Legal Studies* 1, 1: 1–29.

Ciceri, Coryse.1998. "Le port du foulard islamique à l'école publique: analyse comparée du débat dans la presse française et québécoise francophone (1994–1995)." Master's thesis, Université de Montréal.

Citizenship and Immigration Canada. 2012. *Discover Canada: The Rights and Responsibilities of Citizenship*. http://www.cic.gc.ca/english/pdf/pub/discover.pdf.

Citizenship and Immigration Canada. 2015. "News Release: Zero Tolerance for Barbaric Cultural Practices Act Receives Royal Assent." Last modified June 18, 2015. https://www.canada.ca/en/news/archive/2015/06/zero-tolerance-barbaric -cultural-practices-act-receives-royal-assent.html?=undefined&wbdisable=true.

City of Toronto. n.d. "Toronto Facts: Diversity." Toronto.ca, accessed December 15, 2015. https://www1.toronto.ca/wps/portal/contentonly?vgnextoid=dbe867b42d 853410VgnVCM10000071d60f89RCRD&vgnextchannel=57a12cc817453410Vgn VCM10000071d60f89RCRD.

Clarke, Lynda. 2013. "Women in Niqab Speak: A Study of the Niqab in Canada." *Canadian Council of Muslim Women*. Gananoque, ON: Canadian Council of Muslim Women. http://ccmw.com/wp-content/uploads/2013/10/WEB_EN_ WiNiqab_FINAL.pdf.

Clarke, Lynda, and Pamela Cross. 2006. "Muslim and Canadian Family Laws: A Comparative Primer." Toronto: Canadian Council of Muslim Women. http:// ccmw.com/wp-content/uploads/2014/04/PRIMER.pdf.

Cohen, Stanley. 2002. *Folk Devils and Moral Panics: The Creation of the Mods and Rockers*. 3rd ed. New York: Routledge.

Commisso, Christina. 2014. "Mohamed Fahmy's Dual Citizenship Complicates Situation, John Baird Says." CTV News.ca, June 24, 2014. https://www.ctvnews. ca/world/mohamed-fahmy-s-dual-citizenship-complicates-situation-john-baird -says-1.1883108.

Connolly, William E. 1991. *Identity/Difference: Democratic Negotiations of Political Paradox*. Ithaca, NY: Cornell University Press.

Connolly, William E. 2000. *Why I Am Not a Secularist*. Minneapolis: University of Minnesota Press.

Connolly, William E. 2005. *Pluralism*. Durham, NC: Duke University Press. https:// doi.org/10.1215/9780822387084.

Connolly, William E. 2011. *A World of Becoming*. Durham, NC: Duke University Press.

Connolly, William E. 2013. *The Fragility of Things: Self-Organizing Processes, Neoliberal Fantasies, and Democratic Activism*. Durham, NC: Duke University Press. https://doi.org/10.1215/9780822377160.

Conway, Kyle. 2012. "Quebec's Bill 94: What's 'Reasonable'? What's 'Accommodation'? And What's the Meaning of the Muslim Veil?" *American Review of Canadian Studies* 42, 2: 195–209. https://doi.org/10.1080/02722011.2012.679150.

Côté-Boucher, Karine, and Ratiba Hadj-Moussa. 2008. "Malaise identitaire: islam, laïcité et logique préventive en France et au Québec." *Cahiers de Recherche Sociologique* 46: 61–77. https://doi.org/10.7202/1002508ar.

Council on American-Islamic Relations – Canada. 2004. *Presumption of Guilt: A National Survey on Security Visitations of Canadian Muslims.* Accessed June 2008. https://mmu.rl.talis.com/items/116532AE-A88B-4156-49C5-FE1BBDBD7574.html.

Cross, Pamela. 2013. "Violence against Women: Health and Justice for Canadian Muslim Women." Gananoque, ON: Canadian Council of Muslim Women. http://ccmw.com/wp-content/uploads/2013/07/EN-VAW_web.pdf.

CTV.ca News Staff. 2007. "Debate over Religious Rights Continues in Quebec." CTV News.ca, March 19, 2007. https://www.ctvnews.ca/debate-over-religious-rights-continues-in-quebec-1.233824.

CTV.ca News Staff. 2015a. "Canadian Youth with 'Identity Issues' Drawn to Radicalization: Expert." CTV News.ca, May 20, 2015. https://www.ctvnews.ca/canada/canadian-youth-with-identity-issues-drawn-to-radicalization-expert-1.2381771.

CTV.ca News Staff. 2015b. "6 Young People from Montreal Leave to Join ISIS." CTV News.ca, February 26, 2015. https://www.ctvnews.ca/canada/6-young-people-from-montreal-leave-to-join-isis-1.2255229.

Curtis, Christopher. 2012. "Quebec Soccer Federation Lifts Hijab Ban." Postmedia News, July 10, 2012. http://o.canada.com/news/quebec-soccer-federation-lifts-hijab-ban.

Cutting, Christopher. 2012. "Faith-Based Arbitration or Religious Divorce: What Was the Issue?" In *Debating Sharia: Islam, Gender Politics, and Family Law Arbitration,* edited by Anna C. Korteweg and Jennifer A. Selby, 66–87. Toronto: University of Toronto Press.

Dabby, Dia. 2017. "Opinion: Quebec Should Stop Trying to Legislate on Religion." *Montreal Gazette,* February 1, 2017. http://montrealgazette.com/opinion/columnists/opinion-quebec-should-stop-trying-to-legislate-on-religion.

Dakroury, Aliaa. 2012. "Toward Media Reconstruction of the Muslim Imaginary in Canada: The Case of the Canadian Broadcasting Corporation's Sitcom *Little Mosque on the Prairie.*" In *Islam in the Hinterlands: Muslim Cutural Politics in Canada,* edited by Jasmin Zine, 161–82. Vancouver: UBC Press.

Dalpé, Samuel, and David Koussens. 2016. "Les discours sur la laïcité pendant le débat sur la 'Charte des valeurs de la laïcité.' Une analyze lexicométrique de la presse francophone québécoise." *Recherches Sociographiques* 57, 2–3: 455–74. https://doi.org/10.7202/1038435ar.

Dalton, Melinda. 2012. "Shafia Jury Finds All Guilty of 1st-degree murder." CBC News.ca, January 29, 2012. http://www.cbc.ca/news/canada/montreal/shafia-jury-finds-all-guilty-of-1st-degree-murder-1.1150023.

Daly, Mary. 1973. *Beyond God the Father: Toward a Philosophy of Women's Liberation*. Boston: Beacon Press.

Davidman, Lynn. 1991. *Tradition in a Rootless World: Women Turn to Orthodox Judaism*. Berkeley: University of California Press.

Dawson, Lorne L. 2014. "Trying to Make Sense of Homegrown Terrorist Radicalization: The Case of the Toronto 18." In *Religious Radicalization and Securitization in Canada*, edited by Paul Bramadat and Lorne Dawson, 64–91. Toronto: University of Toronto Press.

Day, Shelagh, and Gwen Brodsky. 1996. "The Duty to Accommodate: Who Will Benefit?" *Canadian Bar Review* 75, 3: 433–73.

Dayrit, Flordeliza, and Michael Milo, prods./dirs. 2015. *A New Life in a New Land: The Muslim Experience in Canada*. Milo Productions documentary series and media project. http://www.anewlife.ca/documentary.

de Certeau, Michel. 1984. *The Practice of Everyday Life*. Translated by Steven F. Rendall. Berkeley: University of California Press.

Deeb, Lara. 2015. "Thinking Piety and the Everyday Together: A Response to Fadil and Fernando." *HAU: Journal of Ethnographic Theory* 5, 2: 93–96. https://doi.org/10.14318/hau5.2.007.

Deeb, Lara, and Mona Harb. 2013. *Leisurely Islam: Negotiating Geography and Morality in Shi'ite South Beirut*. Princeton, NJ: Princeton University Press. https://doi.org/10.1515/9781400848560.

Dessing, Nathal M., Nadia Jeldoft, Jorgen S. Nielson, and Linda Woodhead, eds. 2013. *Everyday Lived Islam in Europe*. Farnham, UK: Ashgate.

Dewing, Michael. 2009. *Background Paper: Canadian Multiculturalism*. Publication No. 2009-20-E. Rev. May 14, 2013. Ottawa: Library of Parliament. https://lop.parl.ca/content/lop/researchpublications/2009-20-e.pdf.

Dhamoon, Rita. 2009. *Identity: Difference Politics – How Difference Is Produced, and Why It Matters*. Vancouver: UBC Press.

Dharamsi, Tasnim. 2014. "Living within the Hermeneutic Circle: Interpreting the Curricular Inquiry of Canadian Secondary Ismaili Religious Education Teachers." PhD diss., Simon Fraser University.

Dore, Christopher L. 2008. "What to Do with Omar Khadr? Putting a Child Soldier on Trial: Questions of International Law, Juvenile Justice, and Moral Culpability." *J. Marshall Law Review* 41, 4: 1281–1320.

Dossa, Parin A. 1994. "Critical Anthropology and Life Stories: Case Study of Elderly Ismaili Canadians." *Journal of Cross-Cultural Gerontology* 9, 3: 335–54. https://doi.org/10.1007/BF00978218.

Dossa, Parin A. 1999. "(Re)imagining Aging Lives: Ethnographic Narratives of Muslim Women in Diaspora." *Journal of Cross-Cultural Gerontology* 14, 3: 245–72. https://doi.org/10.1023/A:1006659904679.

Dossa, Parin A. 2002. "Narrative Mediation of Conventional and New 'Mental Health' Paradigms: Reading the Stories of Immigrant Iranian Women."

Medical Anthropology Quarterly 16, 3: 341–59. https://doi.org/10.1525/maq.2002.16.3.341.

Dossa, Parin A. 2004. *Politics and Poetics of Migration: Narratives of Iranian Women in the Diaspora*. Toronto: Canadian Scholar's Press.

Dossa, Parin A. 2008. "Creating Politicized Spaces: Afghan Immigrant Women's Stories of Migration and Displacement." *Affilia* 23, 1: 10–21. https://doi.org/10.1177/0886109907310462.

Dossa, Parin A. 2009. *Racialized Bodies, Disabling Worlds: Storied Lives of Immigrant Muslim Women*. Toronto: University of Toronto Press. https://doi.org/10.3138/9781442688919.

Dossa, Parin A. 2014. *Afghanistan Remembers: Gendered Narrations of Violence and Culinary Practices*. Toronto: University of Toronto Press.

Douglas, Susan J. 2010. *Enlightened Sexism: The Seductive Message That Feminism's Work Is Done*. New York: Henry Holt.

Downie, Caitlin. 2013. "Negotiating Perceptions and Constructing Identities: Muslim Strategies in St. John's Newfoundland." Master's thesis, University of Ottawa.

Dressler, Markus, and Arvind Mandair. 2011. *Secularism and Religion-Making*. New York: Oxford University Press.

Duderija, A. 2008. "Factors Determining Religious Identity Construction among Western-Born Muslims: Towards a Theoretical Framework." *Journal of Muslim Minority Affairs* 28, 3: 371–400. https://doi.org/10.1080/13602000802548003.

Dustin, Moira, and Anne Phillips. 2008. "Whose Agenda Is It? Abuses of Women and Abuses of 'Culture' in Britain." *Ethnicities* 8, 3: 405–24. https://doi.org/10.1177/1468796808092451.

Eid, Paul. 2003. "The Interplay between Ethnicity, Religion, and Gender among Second-Generation Christian and Muslim Arabs in Montreal." *Canadian Ethnic Studies* 35, 2: 30–61.

Eid, Paul. 2007. *Being Arab: Ethnic and Religious Identity Building among Second Generation Youth in Montreal*. Montreal/Kingston: McGill-Queen's University Press.

Eid, Paul. 2012. *Mesurer la discrimination à l'embauche subie par les minorités racisés: résultats d'un "testing" mené dans le grand Montréal*. Commission des droits de la personne et des droits de la jeunesse. http://www.cdpdj.qc.ca/publications/etude_testing_discrimination_emploi.pdf.

Eidabat, Omar. 2014. "Dignity in Prayer: Muslims at McGill Still Need a Proper Prayer Space." *McGill Daily*, October 27, 2014.

El-Geledi, Shaha, and Richard Y. Bourhis. 2012. "Testing the Impact of the Islamic Beil on Intergroup Attitudes and Host Community Acculturation Orientations toward Arab Muslims." *International Journal of Intercultural Relations* 36, 5: 694–706. https://doi.org/10.1016/j.ijintrel.2012.03.006.

Eliade, Mircea. 1987. *The Encyclopedia of Religion*. New York: Macmillan.

Elver, Hilal. 2012. *The Headscarf Controversy: Secularism and Freedom of Religion*. Oxford: Oxford University Press. https://doi.org/10.1093/acprof:oso/9780199769292.001.0001.

el-Zein, Abdul Hamid. 1977. "Beyond Ideology and Theology: The Search for the Anthropology of Islam." *Annual Review of Anthropology* 6, 1: 227–54. https://doi.org/10.1146/annurev.an.06.100177.001303.

Emon, Anver M. 2009. "Islamic Law and the Canadian Mosaic: Politics, Jurisprudence, and Multicultural Accommodation." *Canadian Bar Review* 87, 2: 391–425.

Ensing, Chris. 2017. "Only Canadian Muslim Soldier to Die in WWI Honoured at Ceremony in London, Ont." *CBC News*, August 20. http://www.cbc.ca/news/canada/london/ceremony-marks-world-war-one-muslim-soldier-battle-of-hill-70-1.4253273.

Environics Institute for Survey Research [Environics]. 2006. "Muslims and Multiculturalism in Canada." *Focus Canada: The Pulse of Canadian Public Opinion*. Report of Environics Institute, 61–122. https://www.environicsinstitute.org/docs/default-source/project-documents/survey-of-canadian-muslims/final-report.pdf?sfvrsn=af5d4536_2.

Environics Institute for Survey Research [Environics]. 2016. *Survey of Muslims in Canada 2016*. Project of Environics Institute, April 30, 2016. https://www.environicsinstitute.org/projects/project-details/survey-of-muslims-in-canada-2016.

Ewing, Katherine Pratt. 2008. *Stolen Honor: Stigmatizing Muslim Men in Berlin*. Stanford, CA: Stanford University Press.

Fadil, Nadia. 2009. "Managing Affects and Sensibilities: The Case of Not-Handshaking and Not-Fasting." *Social Anthropology* 17, 4: 439–54. https://doi.org/10.1111/j.1469-8676.2009.00080.x.

Fadil, Nadia. 2011. "Not-/Unveiling as an Ethical Practice." *Feminist Review* 98, 1: 83–109. https://doi.org/10.1057/fr.2011.12.

Fadil, Nadia, and Mayanthi L. Fernando. 2015. "Rediscovering the 'Everyday' Muslim: Notes on an Anthropological Divide." *HAU: Journal of Ethnographic Theory* 5, 2: 59–88. https://doi.org/10.14318/hau5.2.005.

Fahmy, Mihad. 2016. "Opinion: Quebec's Bill on Religious Neutrality Is Anything But." *Montreal Gazette*, November 13, 2016. http://montrealgazette.com/opinion/columnists/opinion-quebecs-bill-on-religious-neutrality-is-anything-but.

Fassin, Eric. 2006. "The Rise and Fall of Sexual Politics in the Public Sphere: A Transatlantic Context." *Public Culture* 18, 1: 79–92. https://doi.org/10.1215/08992363-18-1-79.

Feldman, Stephen M. 1998. *Please Don't Wish Me a Merry Christmas: A Critical History of the Separation of Church and State*. New York: New York University Press.

Ferahain, Salwa. n.d. "History." McGill.ca, Institute of Islamic Studies. Accessed April 10, 2016. https://www.mcgill.ca/islamicstudies/about/history.

Fernando, Mayanthi L. 2010. "Reconfiguring Freedom: Muslim Piety and the Limits of Secular Law and Public Discourse in France." *American Ethnologist* 37, 1: 19–35. https://doi.org/10.1111/j.1548-1425.2010.01239.x.

Fernando, Mayanthi L. 2014a. "Intimacy Surveilled: Religion, Sex, and Secular Cunning." *Signs: Journal of Women in Culture and Society* 39, 3: 685–708. https://doi.org/10.1086/674207.

Fernando, Mayanthi L. 2014b. *The Republic Unsettled: Muslim French and the Contradictions of Secularism*. Durham, NC: Duke University Press. https://doi.org/10.1215/9780822376286.

FIFA. 2013. "FIFA Statement on Head Covers." FIFA.com, June 14, 2013. http://www.fifa.com/about-fifa/news/y=2013/m=6/news=fifa-statement-head-covers-2109325.html.

Fine, Cordelia. 2010. *Delusions of Gender: How Our Minds, Society and Neurosexism Create Difference*. New York: W.W. Norton.

Fischer, Johan. 2011. *The Halal Frontier: Muslim Consumers in a Globalized Market*. New York: Palgrave Macmillan.

Fischer, Michael M.J., and Mehdi Abedi. 1990. *Debating Muslims: Cultural Dialogues in Postmodernity and Tradition*. Madison: University of Wisconsin Press.

Fleischmann, Fenella, and Karen Phalet. 2010. *Identity Multiplicity among the Muslim Second-Generation in European Cities: Where Are Religious and Ethnic Identities Compatible or Conflicting with Civic Identities?* Berlin: Wissenschaftszentrum Berlin für Sozialforschung.

Flower, Scott, and Deborah Birkett. 2014. "(Mis)Understanding Muslim Converts in Canada: A Critical Discussion of Muslim Converts in the Contexts of Security and Society." Working Paper Series, No. 14–06. Canadian Network for Research on Terrorism, Security, and Society.

Foblets, Marie-Claire, and Jean-Philippe Schreiber, eds. 2013. *The Round Tables on Interculturalism*. Brussels, Belgium: Larcier.

Forbes, David Bruce. 2007. *Christmas: A Candid History*. Berkeley: University of California Press.

Forcese, Craig, and Kent Roach. 2015. "Legislating in Fearful and Politicized Times: The Limits of Bill C-51's Disruption Powers in Making Us Safer." In *After the Paris Attacks: Responses in Canada, Europe, and around the Globe*, edited by Edward M. Iaccobucci and Stephen J. Toope, 141–58. Toronto: University of Toronto Press.

Fortin, Sylvie, Marie Nathalie LeBlanc, and Josiane Le Gall. 2008. "Entre la *oumma*, l'ethnicité et la culture: le rapport à l'islam chez les musulmans francophones de Montréal." *Diversité urbaine* 8, 2: 99–134. https://doi.org/10.7202/000368ar.

Foucault, Michel. 2003. *The Essential Foucault*. Edited by Paul Rabinow and Nikolas S. Rose. New York: New Press.

Foucault, Michel. 2007. *Security, Territory, Population: Lectures at the Collège de France, 1977–1978*. Edited by Michel Senellart. New York: Palgrave Macmillan.

Fournier, Pascale. 2004. *The Reception of Muslim Family Law in Western Liberal States*. Gananoque, ON: Canadian Council of Muslim Women. http://beta.ccmw.com/wp-content/uploads/2013/04/pascale_paper.pdf.

Fournier, Pascale. 2006. "In the (Canadian) Shadow of Islamic Law: Translating Mahr as a Bargaining Endowment." *Osgoode Hall Law Journal* 44, 4: 649–77.

Fournier, Pascale. 2007. "La femme musulmane au Canada: profane ou sacrée?" *Canadian Journal of Women and the Law* 19, 2: 227–42.

Fournier, Pascale. 2010. *Muslim Marriage in Western Courts: Lost in Transplantation*. Farnham, UK: Ashgate.

Fournier, Pascale. 2013. "Headscarf and Burqa Controversies at the Crossroad of Politics, Society and Law." *Social Identities* 19, 6: 689–703. https://doi.org/10.1080/13504630.2013.842669.

Fournier, Pascale, and Erica See. 2012. "The 'Naked Face' of Secular Exclusion: Bill 94 and the Privatization of Belief." *Windsor Yearbook of Access to Justice* 30, 1: 63–76. https://doi.org/10.22329/wyaj.v30i1.4360.

Freidenreich, David. 2011. *Foreigners and Their Food: Constructing Otherness in Jewish, Christian and Islamic Law*. Berkeley: University of California Press. https://doi.org/10.1525/california/9780520253216.001.0001.

Funk, Cory. n.d. "The 50 Most Tweeted Words under #M103 Tell a Story about Contemporary Islamophobia in Canada." *Tessellate Institute*. http://tessellateinstitute.com/wp-content/uploads/2017/03/Article-M103-Cory-Funk-5.pdf.

Funk, Cory. 2017. "Hashtagging Islam: #JeSuisHijabi, Social Media, and Religious/Secular Identities in Winnipeg and St. John's, Canada." Master's thesis, Memorial University of Newfoundland, http://research.library.mun.ca/12900/.

Furseth, Inger, ed. 2017. *Religious Complexity in the Public Sphere. Comparing Nordic Countries*. New York: Springer.

Gagnon, Lysiane. 2006. "Noël, un mot tabou?" *La Presse*, December 12, 2006.

Gallagher, Sally K. 2003. *Evangelical Identity and Gendered Family Life*. Newark, NJ: Rutgers University Press.

Gans, Herbert J. 1994. "Symbolic Ethnicity and Symbolic Religiosity: Towards a Comparison of Ethnic and Religious Acculturation." *Ethnic and Racial Studies* 17, 4: 577–92. https://doi.org/10.1080/01419870.1994.9993841.

Gazso, Amber, and Kevin Haggerty. 2009. "Public Opinion about Surveillance in Post 9/11 Alberta: Trading Privacy for Security?" In *Anti-Terrorism, Security, and Insecurity after 9/11*, edited by Sandra Rollings-Magnusson, 141–59. Halifax, NS: Fernwood Publishing.

Geisser, Vincent. 2010. *Nous sommes Français et Musulmans*. Paris: Éditions Autrement.

Gerein, Keith. 2008. "Cancer Claims Larry Shaben." *Edmonton Journal*, September 7, 2008. https://www.pressreader.com/canada/edmonton-journal/20080907/281560876594012.

Gianni, Matteo. 2005. "L'intégration comme en jeu culturel a Genève: le cas de la minorité musulmane." In *Histoire de la politique de migration, d'asile et d'intégration en Suisse depuis 1948*, edited by Hans Mahnig and Sandro Cattacin, 344–74. Zürich: Seismo.

Gibb, Camilla, and Celia Rothenberg. 2000. "Believing Women: Harari and Palestinian Women at Home and in the Canadian Diaspora." *Journal of Muslim Minority Affairs* 20, 2: 243–59. https://doi.org/10.1080/713680360.

Gilliat-Ray, Sophie. 2005. "From 'Chapel' to 'Prayer Room': The Production, Use and Politics of Sacred Space in Public Institutions." *Culture and Religion* 6, 2: 287–308. https://doi.org/10.1080/01438300500226448.

Goffman, Erving. 1956. *The Presentation of the Self in Everyday Life*. New York: Random House.

Gökariksel, Banu, and Anna Secor. 2015. "Post-Secular Geographies and the Problem of Pluralism: Religion and Everyday Life in Istanbul, Turkey." *Political Geography* 46 (May): 21–30. https://doi.org/10.1016/j.polgeo.2014.10.006.

Göle, Nilüfer. 2005. *Interpénétrations: L'islam et l'Europe*. Paris: Galaade Editions.

Göle, Nilüfer. 2010. *Islam in Europe: The Lure of Fundamentalism and the Allure of Cosmopolitanism*. Translated by Steven Rendall. Princeton, NJ: Princeton University Press.

Göle, Nilüfer. 2015. *Musulmans au quotidien: une enquête européenne sur les controverses autour de l'islam*. Paris: La Découverte.

Golnaraghi, Golnaz, and Albert J. Mills. 2013. "Unveiling the Myth of the Muslim Woman: A Postcolonial Critique." *Equality, Diversity and Inclusion* 32, 2: 157–72. https://doi.org/10.1108/02610151311324398.

Gova, Alnoor. 2015. "Responses to and interpretation of anti-Muslim Racism in Canada: A Community Perspective." PhD diss., University of British Columbia.

Grenier, Gilles, and Serge Nadeau. 2011. "Immigrant Access to Work in Montreal and Toronto." *Canadian Journal of Regional Science/Revue canadienne des sciences régionales* 34, 1: 19–33.

Grover, Sonja. 2009. "Canada's Refusal to Repatriate a Canadian Citizen from Guantanamo Bay as a Violation of the Humanitarian Values Underlying the Principle of Non-Refoulement: A Reanalysis of Omar Ahmed Khadr v the Prime Minister of Canada." *High Court Quarterly Review* 5, 2: 42–48.

Guénif-Souilamas, Nacira. 2006. "The Other French Exception: Virtuous Racism and the War of the Sexes in Postcolonial France." *French Politics, Culture & Society* 24, 3: 23–41.

Guénif-Souilamas, Nacira, and Éric Macé. 2004. *Les Féministes et le Garçon Arabe*. Paris: Édition de L'Aube.

Hachimi Alaoui, Myriam. 1997. "L'exil des Algériens au Québec." *Revue Européenne des Migrations Internationales* 13, 2: 197–215. https://doi.org/10.3406/remi.1997.1558.

Hachimi Alaoui, Myriam. 2001. "'Exilés' ou 'immigrés'? Regards croisés sur les Algériens en France et au Québec." *Confluences Méditerranée* 39, 4: 107–17. https://doi.org/10.3917/come.039.0107.

Hachimi Alaoui, Myriam. 2006. "Carrière brisée, carrière de l'immigrant. L'expérience montréalaise" *Diversité urbaine* 1, 5: 111–23.

Haddad, Yvonne Yazbeck. 1977. "Muslims in Canada: A Preliminary Study." In *Religion and Ethnicity*, edited by Harold Coward and Leslie Kawamura, 71–100. Waterloo: Wilfrid Laurier Press.

Haddad, Yvonne. 2005. "The Study of Women in Islam and the West: A Select Bibliography." *Hawwa* 3, 1: 111–57. https://doi.org/10.1163/1569208053628546.

Haddad, Yvonne Yazbeck, and Jane Smith. 1994. "Muslim Communities in North America: Introduction." In *Muslim Communities in North America*, edited by Yvonne Yazbeck Haddad and Jane Smith, xvii–xxx. Albany: State University of New York Press.

Hadj-Moussa, Ratiba. 2004. "Femmes musulmanes au Canada: altérité, paroles et politique de l'action." *Canadian Review of Sociology/Revue canadienne de sociologie* 41, 4: 397–418. https://doi.org/10.1111/j.1755-618X.2004.tb00784.x.

Haggerty, Kevin, and Amber Gazso. 2005. "Seeing beyond the Ruins: Surveillance as a Response to Terrorist Threats." *Canadian Journal of Sociology* 30, 2: 169–87. https://doi.org/10.2307/4146129.

Hajjat, Abdellali. 2012. *Les frontières de l'identité nationale. L'injonction à l'assimilation en France métropolitaine et coloniale*. Paris: La Découverte.

Hajjat, Abdellali, and Marwan Mohammed. 2013. *Islamophobie: comment les élites françaises fabriquent le 'problème musulman.'* Paris: La Découverte.

Hall, Stuart. 1996. "The Question of Cultural Identity." In *Modernity: An Introduction to Modern Societies*, edited by Stuart Hall, David Held, Don Hubert, and Kenneth Thompson, 595–635. Malden, MA: Blackwell.

Hamdani, Daood Hassan. 1986. "Income Disparity between Muslims and Non-Muslims in Canada." *Journal Institute of Minority Affairs* 7, 1: 214–24. https://doi.org/10.1080/13602008608715975.

Hamdani, Daood. 1997. "Canada's Muslims: An Unnoticed Part of Our History." *Hamdard Islamicus* 20, 3: 97–100.

Hamdani, Daood. 1999. "Canadian Muslims on the Eve of the Twenty-First Century." *Journal of Muslim Minority Affairs* 19, 2: 197–209.

Hamdani, Daood. 2005. *Triple Jeopardy: Muslim Women's Experience of Discrimination*. Toronto: Canadian Council of Muslim Women. http://archive.ccmw.com/publications/triple_jeopardy.pdf.

Hamdani, Daood. 2007. "In the Footsteps of Canadian Muslim Women: 1837–2007." Canadian Council of Muslim Women. http://ccmw.com/wp-content/uploads/2014/04/footsteps_brochure.pdf.

Hamdani, Daood. 2014. "Canadian Muslim Women: A Decade of Change – 2001 to 2011." Toronto: Canadian Council of Muslim Women. http://ccmw.com/wp-content/uploads/2014/09/Canadian-Muslim-Women.pdf.

Hamdani, Daood. 2015. "Canadian Muslims: A Statistical Review." Canadian Dawn Foundation, March 29, 2015. Accessed December 15, 2015. https://muslimlink.ca/directory/ottawa/religious/local-orgs/745-cdn-dawn.

Hamdon, Evelyn Leslie. 2010. *Islamophobia and the Question of Muslim Identity: The Politics of Difference and Solidarity*. Halifax, NS: Fernwood.

Hameed, Qamer. 2015. "Grassroots Canadian Muslim Identity in the Prairie City of Winnipeg: A Case Study of 2nd and 1.5 Generation Canadian Muslims." Master's thesis, University of Ottawa.

Hanniman, Wayne. 2008. "Canadian Muslims, Islamophobia and National Security." *International Journal of Law, Crime and Justice* 36, 4: 271–85. https://doi.org/10.1016/j.ijlcj.2008.08.003.

Haque, Eve. 2012. *Multiculturalism within a Bilingual Framework: Language, Race, and Belonging in Canada*. Toronto: University of Toronto Press.

Harris, K. 2017. "Hate Crimes against Muslims Up 60%, StatsCan Reports." CBC News.ca, June 13, 2017. http://www.cbc.ca/news/politics/hate-crimes-muslims-statscan-1.4158042.

Harvey-Crowell, Liam. 2015. "The Impact and Perception of Islam and Authority Online among Muslim University Students in St. John's, NL." Master's thesis, Memorial University of Newfoundland.

Heelas, Paul, and Linda Woodhead. 2005. *The Spiritual Revolution: Why Religion Is Giving Way to Spirituality*. Malden, MA: Wiley-Blackwell.

Hefner, Robert W. 1998. "Multiple Modernities: Christianity, Islam, and Hinduism in a Globalizing Age." *Annual Review of Anthropology* 27, 1: 83–104. https://doi.org/10.1146/annurev.anthro.27.1.83.

Helly, Denise. 2004a. "Flux migratoires des pays musulmans et discrimination de la communauté islamique au Canada." In *L'islam entre discrimination et reconnaissance. La présence des musulmans en Europe occidentale et en Amérique du Nord*, edited by Ural Manço, 257–88. Paris: Éditions l'Harmattan.

Helly, Denise. 2004b. "Le traitement de l'islam au Canada. Tendances actuelles." *Revue Européenne des Migrations Internationales* 20, 1: 47–73. https://doi.org/10.4000/remi.274.

Helly, Denise. 2010. "Orientalisme populaire et modernisme: Une nouvelle rectitude politique au Canada." *The Tocqueville Review/La revue Tocqueville* 31, 2: 157–93. https://doi.org/10.1353/toc.2010.0011.

Helly, Denise. 2011. "Les multiples visages de l'islamophobie au Canada." *Nouveau cahiers du socialisme* 2, 1: 99–106.

Helly, Denise, Valérie Scott, Marianne Hardy-Dussault, and Julie Ranger. 2011. "Droit familial et parties 'musulmanes': des cas de *kafálah* au Québec, 1997–2009." *McGill Law Journal* 56, 4: 1057–112. https://doi.org/10.7202/1005852ar.

Hemmings, Clare. 2011. *Why Stories Matter: The Political Grammar of Feminist Theory*. Durham: Duke University Press.

Hennebry, Jenna, and Bessma Momani, eds. 2013. *Targeted Transnationals: The State, the Media, and Arab Canadians*. Vancouver: UBC Press.

Heyer, Julia Amalia. 2014. "The Lost Children: France Takes Stock of Growing Jihadist Problem." Spiegel Online, November 6, 2014. http://www.spiegel.de/

international/europe/france-struggles-to-deal-with-young-jihadist-exodus-to
-syria-a-1001254.html.

Heyes, Cressida. 2007. *Self-Transformations: Foucault, Ethics, and Normalization.* Oxford: Oxford University Press. https://doi.org/10.1093/acprof:oso/9780195310535. 001.0001.

Hirji, Faiza. 2010. *Dreaming in Canadian: South Asian Youth, Bollywood, and Belonging.* Vancouver: UBC Press.

Hirschkind, Charles. 2011. "Is There a Secular Body?" *Cultural Anthropology* 26, 4: 633–47. https://doi.org/10.1111/j.1548-1360.2011.01116.x.

Hirschkind, Charles, and Saba Mahmood. 2002. "Feminism, the Taliban, and the Politics of Counter-Insurgency." *Anthropological Quarterly* 75, 2: 339–54. https://doi.org/10.1353/anq.2002.0031.

Hong, Caylee. 2011. "Feminists on the Freedom of Religion: Responses to Quebec's Proposed Bill 94." *Journal of Law and Equality* 8: 27–62.

Hughes, Aaron. 2004. "Mapping Constructions of Islamic Space in North America: A Frame-Work for Further Inquiry." *Studies in Religion/Sciences religieuses* 33, 3–4: 339–57. https://doi.org/10.1177/000842980403300304.

Hughes, Aaron W. 2015. *Islam and the Tyranny of Authenticity: An Inquiry into Disciplinary Apologetics and Self-Deception.* Sheffield: Equinox.

Hughes, Melissa K. 2003. "Through the Looking Glass: Racial Jokes, Social Context and the Reasonable Person in Hostile Work Environment Analysis." *Southern California Law Review* 76, 6: 1437–82.

Huntington, Samuel P. 1996. *The Clash of Civilizations and the Remaking of World Order.* New York: Touchstone.

Hurd, Elizabeth Shakman. 2012. "International Politics after Secularism." *Review of International Studies* 38, 5: 943–61. https://doi.org/10.1017/S0260210512000411.

Hurd, Elizabeth Shakman. 2013. "Rescued by Law? Gender and the Global Politics of Secularism." In *Religion, the Secular, and the Politics of Sexual Difference*, edited by Linell E. Cady and Tracy Fessenden, 211–28. New York: Columbia University Press.

Hurd, Elizabeth Shakman. 2015. *Beyond Religious Freedom: The New Global Politics of Religion.* Princeton, NJ: Princeton University Press. https://doi.org/10.1515/9781400873814.

Hussain, Amir. 2001. *The Canadian Face of Islam, Muslim Communities in Toronto.* PhD diss., University of Toronto. http://www.collectionscanada.gc.ca/obj/s4/f2/dsk3/ftp05/NQ63783.pdf.

Hussain, Amir. 2004. "Muslims in Canada: Opportunities and Challenges." *Studies in Religion/Sciences Religieuses* 33, 3/4: 359–79.

Hussain, Amir. 2015. "(Re)presenting: Muslims on North American Television." *Contemporary Islam: Dynamics of Muslim Life* 4, 1: 55–75.

Hussain, Amir, and Jamie S. Scott. 2012. "Muslims." In *The Religions of Canadians*, edited by Jamie S. Scott, 167–218. Toronto: Toronto University Press.

Hussain, Samira. 2002. "Voices of Muslim Women: A Community Research Project." Canadian Council of Muslim Women. http://ccmw.com/wp-content/uploads/2014/04/Voices-of-Muslim-Women.pdf.

Ibnouzahir, Asmaa. 2015a. "Asmaa Ibnouzahir et la peur du niqab." Interview on Radio-Canada.ca, September 28, 2015. http://ici.radio-canada.ca/emissions/plus_on_est_de_fous_plus_on_lit/2013-2014/chronique.asp?idChronique=384645.

Ibnouzahir, Asmaa. 2015b. Chroniques d'une musulmane indignée. Anjou, QC: Éditions Fides.

Jacobsen, Christine M. 2011. "Troublesome Threesome: Feminism, Anthropology and Muslim Women's Piety." Feminist Review 98, 1: 65–82. https://doi.org/10.1057/fr.2011.10.

Jafri, Ismat. 2005. Muslim Women's Equality Rights in the Justice System: Gender, Religion and Pluralism. The Canadian Council of Muslim Women. http://ccmw.com/wp-content/uploads/2014/04/Public-Policy-Workshop-Report.pdf.

Jafri, Nuzhat. 2006. "The Canadian Council of Muslim Women: Engaging Muslim Women in Civic and Social Change." Canadian Woman Studies/Les cahiers de la femme 25, 3/4: 97–100.

Jahangeer, Roshan. 2014. "Towards an Inclusive Secularism and a Transformative Model of Community Engagement in Québec." Tessellate Institute. http://tessellate institute.com/publications/towards-an-inclusive-secularism-and-a-transformative -model-of-community-engagement-in-quebec/.

Jakobsen, Janet R., and Ann Pellegrini. 2004. Love the Sin: Sexual Regulation and the Limits of Religious Tolerance. Boston: Beacon Press.

Jakobsen, Janet R., and Ann Pellegrini, eds. 2008. Secularisms. Durham, NC: Duke University Press.

Jakobsh, Doris. 2011. "Studying the Sikhs: Thirty Years Later ... Where Have We Come, Where Are We Going?" In Sikhism in Its Global Context, edited by Pashaura Singh, 62–84. Delhi: Oxford University Press.

James, William Closson. 1998. Locations of the Sacred: Essays on Religion, Literature, and Canadian Culture. Waterloo, ON: Wilfrid Laurier University Press.

James, William Closson. 1999. "Dimorphs and Cobblers: Ways of Being Religious in Canada." Studies in Religion/Sciences religieuses 28, 3: 273–89.

Jamil, Uzma, and Cécile Rousseau. 2012. "Subject Positioning, Fear, and Insecurity in South Asian Muslim Communities in the War on Terror Context." Canadian Review of Sociology/Revue canadienne de sociologie 49, 4: 370–88. https://doi.org/10.1111/j.1755-618X.2012.01299.x.

Jamison, Melissa A. 2005. "Detention of Juvenile Enemy Combatants at Guantanamo Bay: The Special Concerns of the Children." UC Davis Journal of Juvenile Law & Policy 9, 1: 127–70.

Jeldtoft, Nadia. 2011. "Lived Islam: Religious Identity with 'Nonorganized' Muslim Minorities." Ethnic and Racial Studies 34, 7: 1134–51. https://doi.org/10.1080/01419870.2010.528441.

Jeldtoft, Nadia. 2013. "The Hypervisibility of Islam." In *Everyday Lived Islam in Europe*, edited by Nadia Jeldtoft, Nathal M. Dessing, Jorgen S. Nielsen, and Linda Woodhead, 23–38. Farnham, UK: Ashgate.

Jeldtoft, Nadia. 2014. "Lived Islam: Religious Identity with 'Non-Organized' Muslim Minorities." In *Methods and Contexts in the Study of Muslim Minorities: Visible and Invisible Muslims*, edited by Nadia Jeldtoft and Jorgen S. Nielsen, 25–43. New York: Routledge.

Jiwani, Nisara, and Geneviève Rail. 2010. "Islam, Hijab and Young Shia Muslim Canadian Women's Discursive Constructions of Physical Activity." *Sociology of Sport Journal* 27, 3: 251–67. https://doi.org/10.1123/ssj.27.3.251.

Jiwani, Yasmin. 2011. "Race, Gender, and the 'War on Terror.'" *Global Media Journal–Canadian Edition* 4, 2: 13–31.

Jiwani, Yasmin, and Homa Hoodfar. 2012. "Should We Call It Honour Killing? No. It's a False Distancing of Ourselves from a Too-Common Crime: The Murder of Females." *The Gazette*, January 31, 2012.

Johansen, Birgitte, and Riem Spielhaus. 2012. "Counting Deviance: Revisiting a Decade's Production of Surveys among Muslims in Western Europe." *Journal of Muslims in Europe* 1, 1: 81–112. https://doi.org/10.1163/221179512X644060.

Johnson, Rebecca. 2002. *Taxing Choices: The Intersection of Class, Gender, Parenthood, and the Law*. Vancouver: UBC Press.

Jorge, Lídia. 2015. *Les mémorables*. Paris: Métailié.

Jouili, Jeanette S. 2009. "Negotiating Secular Boundaries: Pious Micro-Practices of Muslim Women in French and German Public Spheres." *Social Anthropology* 17, 4: 455–70. https://doi.org/10.1111/j.1469-8676.2009.00082.x.

Jouili, Jeanette S. 2011. "Beyond Emancipation: Subjectivities and Ethics among Women in Europe's Islamic Revival Communities." *Feminist Review* 98, 1: 47–64. https://doi.org/10.1057/fr.2011.4.

Jouili, Jeanette S. 2015. *Pious Practices and Secular Constraints: Women in the Islamic Revival in Europe*. Stanford, CA: Stanford University Press.

Jouili, Jeanette S., and Schirin Amir-Moazami. 2006. "Knowledge, Empowerment and Religious Authority among Pious Muslim Women in France and Germany." *The Muslim World* 96, 4: 617–42. https://doi.org/10.1111/j.1478-1913.2006.00150.x.

Kaba, Lansiné. 2002. "Americans Discover Islam through the Black Muslim Experience." In *Islam in North America: A Sourcebook*, edited by Michael A. Köszegi and J. Gordon Melton, 25–33. New York: Garland Publishing.

Kang, Sonia K., Katherine A. DeCelles, András Tilcsik, and Sora Jun. 2016. "Whitened Résumés: Race and Self-Presentation in the Labor Market." *Administrative Science Quarterly* 61, 3: 469–502. https://doi.org/10.1177/0001839216639577.

Kanji, Azeezah. 2016. "How Has 'Allah' Become Code for 'Terrorism'?" *Toronto Star*, March 18, 2016. https://www.thestar.com/opinion/commentary/2016/03/18/how-has-allah-become-code-for-terrorism.html.

Karim, Karim H. 2003. *Islamic Peril: Media and Global Violence*. Montreal: Black Rose Books.

Karim, Karim H. 2004. "Muslim Participation in the Canadian Public Sphere." In *Muslims in the West: From Sojourners to Citizens*, edited by Yvonne Haddad, 262–77. New York: Oxford University Press.

Karim, Karim H. 2009. "Changing Perceptions of Islamic Authority among Muslims in Canada, the United States and the United Kingdom." *IRPP Choices* 15, 2. http://irpp.org/research-studies/choices-vol15-no2/.

Karim, Karim H. 2011. "At the Interstices of Tradition, Modernity and Post-modernity: Ismaili Engagements with Contemporary Canadian Society." In *A Modern History of the Ismailis*, edited by Farhad Daftary, 265–94. London: IB Tauris.

Karim, Karim H. 2013. "Pluralism, Migration, Space and Song: Ismaili Arrangements of Public and Private Spheres." In *Diverse Spaces: Identity, Heritage, and Community in Canadian Public Culture*, edited by Susan Ashley, 148–70. Cambridge: Cambridge Scholars Publishing.

Karim, Karim H. 2014. "The Aga Khan Development Network: Shia Ismaili Islam." In *Global Religious Movements across Borders*, edited by Stephen M. Cherry and Helen Rose Ebaugh 143–60. London: Ashgate.

Karim, Karim H., and Mahmoud Eid. 2012. "Clash of Ignorance." *Global Media Journal–Canadian Edition* 5, 1: 7–27.

Kashmeri, Zuhair. 1991. *The Gulf Within: Canadian Arabs, Racism and the Gulf War*. Toronto: James Lorimer and Company.

Kaufman, Debra Renee. 1991. *Rachel's Daughters: Newly Orthodox Jewish Women*. Newark, NJ: Rutgers University Press.

Kay, Barbara. 2013. "Accommodation of a Different Order." *National Post*, September 17, 2013. http://nationalpost.com/opinion/barbara-kay-accommodation-of-a-different-order.

Kazemipur, Abdolmohammad. 2014. *The Muslim Question in Canada: A Story of Segmented Integration*. Vancouver: UBC Press.

Kazemipur, Abdolmohammad. 2017. "Muslim Immigration to North America: The Rise of New Challenges and the Need for New Perspectives." In *Twenty-First-Century Immigration to North America: Newcomers in Turbulent Times*, edited by Victoria Esses and Donald E. Abelson, 206–32. Montreal/Kingston: McGill-Queen's University Press. https://doi.org/10.2307/j.ctt1w6tdzn.11.

Keane, Webb. 2007. *Christian Moderns: Freedom and Fetish in the Mission Encounter*. Berkeley: University of California Press.

Kelly, Patricia. 1998. "Muslim Canadians: Immigration Policy and Community Development in the 1991 Census." *Islam and Christian-Muslim Relations* 9, 1: 83–102. https://doi.org/10.1080/09596419808721140.

Kernerman, Gerald. 2005. *Multicultural Nationalism*. Vancouver: UBC Press.

Khalema, Nene Ernest, and Jenny Wannas-Jones. 2003. "Under the Prism of Suspicion: Minority Voices in Canada Post-September 11." *Journal of Muslim Minority Affairs* 23, 1: 25–39. https://doi.org/10.1080/13602000305928.

Khan, Almas. 2005. "Interaction between Shariah and International Law in Arbitration." *Chicago Journal of International Law* 6, 2: 791–802.

Khan, Aga. 2008. *Where Hope Takes Root: Democracy and Pluralism in an Interdependent World.* Toronto: Douglas and McIntyre.

Khan, Shahnaz. 2002. *Aversion and Desire: Negotiating Muslim Female Identity in the Diaspora.* Toronto: Women's Press.

Khan, Sheema. 2009. *Of Hockey and Hijab: Reflections of a Canadian Muslim Woman.* Toronto: Mawenzi.

Khan, Sheema. 2015. "Fifty Years in Canada and Now I Feel Like a Second Class Citizen." *Globe and Mail*, October 7, 2015, updated March 25, 2017. http://www.theglobeandmail.com/opinion/fifty-years-in-canada-and-now-i-feel-like-a-second-class-citizen/article26691065/.

Klassen, Pamela. 2015. "Fantasies of Sovereignty: Civic Secularism in Canada." *Critical Research on Religion* 3, 1: 41–56. https://doi.org/10.1177/2050303215584230.

Knippenberg, Hans, ed. 2005. *The Changing Religious Landscape of Europe.* Amsterdam: Spinhuis.

Knott, Kim. 2005. "Researching Local and National Pluralism: Britain's New Religious Landscape." In *Religiöser Pluralismus: Empirische Studien und Analytische Perspektiven*, edited by Martin Baumann and Samuel M. Behloul, 45–68. Bielefeld, Germany: Transcript Verlag. https://doi.org/10.14361/9783839403501-003.

Knott, Kim. 2009. "From Locality to Location and Back Again: A Spatial Journey of the Study of Religion." *Religion* 39, 2: 154–60. https://doi.org/10.1016/j.religion.2009.01.003.

Knott, Kim. 2010a. "Cutting through the Postsecular City: A Spatial Interrogation." In *Exploring the Postsecular: The Religious, the Political and the Urban*, ed. Kim Knott, 19–38. Leiden, The Netherlands: Brill. https://doi.org/10.1163/ej.9789004185449.i-406.11.

Knott, Kim. 2010b. "Theoretical and Methodological Resources for Breaking Open the Secular and Exploring the Boundary between Religion and Non-Religion." *Historia Religiounum* 2: 115–33.

Knott, Kim. 2013. "The Secular Sacred: In Between or Both/And?" In *Social Identities between the Sacred and the Secular*, edited by Abby Day, Giselle Vincett, and Christopher R. Cotter, 145–60. New York: Routledge.

Korteweg, Anna C. 2006. "The Sharia Debate in Ontario." *ISIM Review* 18 (Autumn): 50–51.

Korteweg, Anna C. 2008. "The Sharia Debate in Ontario: Gender, Islam, and Representations of Muslim Women's Agency." *Gender and Society* 22, 4: 434–54. https://doi.org/10.1177/0891243208319768.

Korteweg, Anna C. 2012. "Understanding Honour Killing and Honour-Related Violence in the Immigration Context: Implications for the Legal Profession and Beyond." *Canadian Criminal Law Review* 16, 2: 33–58.

Korteweg, Anna C. 2013. "The 'Headrag Tax': Impossible Laws and Their Symbolic and Material Consequences." *Social Identities* 19, 6: 759–74. https://doi.org/10.1080/13504630.2013.842674.

Korteweg, Anna C., and Jennifer A. Selby, eds. 2012. *Debating Sharia: Islam, Gender Politics, and Family Law Arbitration*. Toronto: University of Toronto Press.

Koussens, David, Stéphane Bernatchez, and Marie-Pierre Robert. 2012. *Quelles balises au port du voile intégral dans les institutions publiques québécoises*. Quebec: Fondation du barreau du Québec.

Koussens, David, Stéphane Bernatchez, and Maire-Pierre Robert. 2014. "Le voile intégral: Analyse juridique d'un objet religieux." *Canadian Journal of Law and Society/ La Revue Canadienne Droit et Société* 29, 1: 77–92. https://doi.org/10.1017/cls.2013.49.

Kullab, Samya. 2012. "The Politics of Deveiling: Manal Hamzeh and *The Hijab Cycle*." *Women in Theatre* 1, 3. http://jps.library.utoronto.ca/index.php/wit/article/view/19175/15920.

Kumar, D. 2012. *Islamophobia and the Politics of Empire*. Chicago: Haymarket Books.

Kurd, Rahat. 1999. "Reading Rights: A Woman's Guide to the Law in Canada." Canadian Council of Muslim Women. Accessed May 11, 2015. http://ccmw.com/reading-rights-a-womans-guide-to-the-law-in-canada/.

Labelle, Michelin, and François Rocher. 2009. "Immigration, Integration and Citizenship Policies in Canada and Quebec: Tug of War between Competing Societal Projects." In *Immigration and Self-Government of Minority Nations*, edited by Richard Zapata-Barrero, 57–85. Brussels: Peter Lang.

Lamine, Anne-Sophie. 2014. "Introduction: La diversité religieuse, source de tensions sociales? Visibilités publiques, concurrences et disputes internes: jeux d'échelles au coeur de nouveaux antagonismes." In *Quand le religieux fait conflit*, edited by Anne-Sophie Lamine, 7–12. Rennes, France: Presses Universitaires de Rennes.

Lamoureux Scholes, Laurie. 2002. "The Canadian Council of Muslim Women." *Journal of Muslim Minority Affairs* 22, 2: 413–25.

Lavoie, Bertrand. 2015. "Dynamiques discordantes dans la régulation de la liberté de religion au Canada." *Regulating Religion*, Winter 2015. http://religionanddiversity.ca/media/uploads/bertrand_lavoie_web_final2.pdf.

Le Gall, Josiane. 2003. "Le rapport à l'islam des musulmanes shi'ites libanaises à Montréal." *Anthropologie et Sociétés* 27, 1: 131–48. https://doi.org/10.7202/007005ar.

LeBlanc, Marie Nathalie, Josiane Le Gall, and Sylvie Fortin. 2008. "Être musulman en Occident après le 11 septembre: présentation." *Diversité urbaine* 8, 2: 5–11. https://doi.org/10.7202/000307ar.

Leckey, Robert. 2013. "Family Law and the Charter's First 30 Years: An Impact Delayed, Deep, and Declining but Lasting." *Canadian Family Law Quarterly* 32, 1: 21–52.

Lecomte, Christian. 2015. "A Chalon, le menu sans porc est une atteinte à la laïcité." *Le Temps*, August 21, 2015. https://www.letemps.ch/monde/2015/08/21/chalon-menu-porc-une-atteinte-laicite.

Lefebvre, Solange. 2010. "Le Canada, entre unité et diversité." In *Les religions sur la scène mondiale*, edited by Solange Lefebvre and Robert R. Crépeau, 81–99. Quebec: Presses de l'Université Laval.

Lefebvre, Solange, and Lori G. Beaman. 2012. "Protecting Gender Relations: The Bouchard-Taylor Commission and the Equality of Women." *Canadian Journal for Social Research* 2, 1: 85–104.

Lefebvre, Solange, and Guillaume St-Laurent, eds. 2018. *Dix ans plus tard: la Commission Bouchard-Taylor, succès ou échec?* Montreal: Québec Amérique.

Lépinard, Eléonore. 2015. "Migrating Concepts: Immigration Integration and the Regulation of Religious Dress in France and Canada." *Ethnicities* 15, 5: 611–32. https://doi.org/10.1177/1468796814529939.

Leuprecht, Christian, and Conrad Winn. 2011. "What Do Muslim Canadians Want? The Clash of Interpretations and Opinions". In *True North in Public Policy*. Ottawa: The MacDonald-Laurier Institute. https://www.macdonaldlaurier.ca/files/pdf/What-Do-Muslim-Canadians-Want-November-1-2011.pdf.

Lewis, Bernard. 1990. "The Roots of Muslim Rage." *The Atlantic Monthly*, September.

Libin, Kevin, Barbara Kay, and Matt Gurney. 2011. "Dedicated Prayer Rooms at Odds with Secular Schools." *National Post*, February 11, 2011. http://nationalpost.com/full-comment/dedicated-prayer-rooms-at-odds-with-secular-schools/.

Litchmore, Rashelle V.H., and Saba Safdar. 2016. "Young, Female, Canadian and Muslim: Identity Negotiation and Transcultural Experiences." In *Purple Jacaranda: Narrations on Transcultural Identity Development*, edited by Claude-Hélène Mayer and Stephen Wolting, 59–67. Munster, Germany: Waxmann.

Lorenz, Andrea W. 1998. "Canada's Pioneer Mosque." *Aramco World* 49, 4: 28–31.

"M-103: If Canadians, Not MPs, Voted in the House, the Motion Condemning Islamophobia Would Be Defeated." Angus Reid Institute, March 23, 2017. http://angusreid.org/islamophobia-motion-103/.

Macfarlane, Julie. 2012a. *Islamic Divorce in North America*. Oxford: Oxford University Press. https://doi.org/10.1093/acprof:oso/9780199753918.001.0001.

Macfarlane, Julie. 2012b. *Understanding Trends in American Muslim Divorce and Marriage: A Discussion Guide for Families and Communities*. Washington, DC: Institute for Social Policy and Understanding. https://www.ispu.org/wp-content/uploads/2016/08/ISPU-Report_Marriage-II_Macfarlane_WEB.pdf.

Macfarlane, Julie. 2015. "'Difference' or 'Sameness': Law, Social Ordering and Islamic Marriage and Divorce in North America." *Australian Journal of Family Law* 29, 3: 172–87.

Macklin, Audrey. 2010. "Comment on Canada (Prime Minister) v. Khadr (2010)." *Supreme Court Review* 51: 295–331.

Maclean, Derryl. 2010. "Religion, Ethnicity, and the Double Diaspora of Asian Muslims." In *Asian Religions in British Columbia*, edited by Larry DeVries and Dan Overmyer Don Baker, 64–84. Vancouver: UBC Press.

Mahmood, Saba. 2005. *The Politics of Piety: The Islamic Revival and the Feminist Subject*. Princeton, NJ: Princeton University Press.

Mahmood, Saba. 2009. "Feminism, Democracy, and Empire: Islam and the War on Terror." In *Gendering Religion and Politics: Untangling Modernities*, edited by Hanna Herzog and Ann Braude, 193–215. New York: Palgrave Macmillan. https://doi.org/10.1057/9780230623378_9.

Mahmood, Saba. 2015. *Religious Difference in a Secular Age: A Minority Report.* Princeton, NJ: Princeton University Press.

Mahrouse, Gada. 2010. "'Reasonable Accommodation' in Québec: The Limits of Participation and Dialogue." *Race & Class* 52, 1: 85–96. https://doi.org/10.1177/0306396810371768.

Mamdani, Mahmood. 2002. "Good Muslim, Bad Muslim: A Political Perspective on Culture and Terrorism." *American Anthropologist* 104, 3: 766–75. https://doi.org/10.1525/aa.2002.104.3.766.

Mamdani, Mahmood. 2004. *Good Muslim, Bad Muslim: America, the Cold War, and the Roots of Terror.* New York: Three Leaves Press.

Mamodaly, Adil, and Alim Fakirani. 2012. "Voices from Shia Imami Ismaili Nizari Muslim Women: Reflections from Canada on Past and Present Gendered Roles in Islam." In *Women in Islam: Reflections on Historical and Contemporary Research*, edited by Terrence Lovat, 213–36. New York: Springer. https://doi.org/10.1007/978-94-007-4219-2_15.

Manji, Irshad. 2005. *The Trouble with Islam Today: A Muslim's Call for Reform in Her Faith.* New York: St. Martin's Griffin.

Manji, Irshad, and Ian McLeod, writers. 2007. *Faith without Fear: Irshad Manji's Quest.* VHS/DVD. Directed by Ian McLeod. Montreal: National Film Board of Canada.

Marcotte, Roxanne D. 2010. "Muslim Women in Canada: Autonomy and Empowerment." *Journal of Muslim Minority Affairs* 30, 3: 357–73. https://doi.org/10.1080/13602004.2010.515816.

Massey, Doreen. 1993. "Politics and Space/Time." In *Place and the Politics of Identity*, edited by Michael Keith and Steve Pile, 139–59. New York: Routledge.

McAndrew, Marie. 2010. "The Muslim Community and Education in Quebec: Controversies and Mutual Adaptation." In "The Education of Muslim Minority Students: Comparative Perspective." Special issue, *Journal of International Migration and Integration* 11, 1: 41–58. http://www.chereum.umontreal.ca/activites_pdf/session3/McAndrew_%20Muslim%20Community(2).pdf.

McAndrew, Marie, Micheline Milot, Jean-Sébastien Imbeault, and Paul Eid, eds. 2008. *L'accommodement raisonnable et la diversité religieuse à l'école publique. Normes et pratiques.* Montreal: Fides.

McAndrew, Marie, Béchir Oueslati, and Denise Helly. 2007. "L'évolution du traitement de l'islam et des cultures musulmanes dans les manuels scolaires québécois de langue française du secondaire." *Canadian Ethnic Studies* 39, 3: 173–88. https://doi.org/10.1353/ces.0.0036.

McDonough, Sheila. 2000. "The Muslims of Canada." In *The South Asian Religious Diaspora in Britain, Canada, and the United States*, edited by Harold Coward, John R. Hinnells, and Raymond Brady Williams, 174–90. Albany, NY: SUNY Press.

McDonough, Sheila, and Sajida Alvi. 2002. "The Canadian Council of Muslim Women: A Chapter in the History of Muslim Women in Canada." *The Muslim World* 92, 1–2: 79–97.

McDonough, Sheila, and Homa Hoodfar. 2005. "Muslim Groups in Canada: From Ethnic Groups to Religious Community." In *Religion and Ethnicity in Canada*, edited by Paul Bramadat and David Seljak, 133–53. Toronto: Pearson Education Canada.

McGregor, Lorna. 2010. "Are Declaratory Orders Appropriate for Continuing Human Rights Violations? The Case of Khadr v Canada." *Human Rights Law Review* 10, 3: 487–503. https://doi.org/10.1093/hrlr/ngq026.

McGuire, Meredith. 2008. *Lived Religion: Faith and Practice in Everyday Life*. New York: Oxford University Press. https://doi.org/10.1093/acprof:oso/9780195172621.001.0001.

McLaren, Kristin. 1999. "Indonesian Muslims in Canada: Religion, Ethnicity and Identity." Master's thesis, University of Ottawa.

McRobbie, Angela. 2009. *The Aftermath of Feminism: Gender, Culture, and Social Change*. London: Sage.

Memon, Nadeem. 2010. "Social Consciousness in Canadian Islamic Schools?" *International Migration and Integration* 11, 1: 109–17. https://doi.org/10.1007/s12134-009-0118-8.

Memon, Nadeem. 2012. "From Mosques to Madrassas: Civic Engagement and the Pedagogy of Islamic Schools." In *Islam in the Hinterlands: Muslim Cultural Politics in Canada*, edited by Jasmin Zine, 185–207. Vancouver: UBC Press.

Mendes, Errol P. 2009. "Dismantling the Clash between the Prerogative Power to Conduct Foreign Affairs and the Charter in Prime Minister of Canada et al v. Omar Khadr." *National Journal of Constitutional Law/Revue nationale de droit constitutionnel* 26, 1: 67–83.

Metcalf, Barbara, ed. 1996. *Making Muslim Space in North America and Europe*. Berkeley: University of California Press.

Metropolis Project. 2010. "Immigrant Mental Health." Summer issue, *Canadian Issues/Thèmes canadiens*. http://www.multiculturalmentalhealth.ca/wp-content/uploads/2013/10/Immigrant_mental_health_10aug10.pdf.

Milot, Jean-René. 2008. "La polygamie au nom de la religion au Canada: L'islam est-il en cause?" *Cahiers de recherche sociologique* 46: 123–33. https://doi.org/10.7202/1002512ar.

Modood, Tariq. 2005. *Multicultural Politics: Racism, Ethnicity and Muslims in Britain*. Edinburgh: University of Edinburgh Press.

Moghissi, Haideh, Saeed Rahnema, and Mark J. Goodman. 2009. *Diaspora by Design: Muslims in Canada and Beyond*. Toronto: University of Toronto Press.

Morgan, George, and Scott Poynting, eds. 2012. *Global Islamophobia: Muslims and Moral Panic in the West*. New York: Routledge.

Mossière, Géraldine. 2008. "Reconnue par l'autre, respectée chez soi: la construction d'un discours politique critique et alternatif par des femmes converties à l'Islam en France et au Québec." *Diversité urbaine* 8, 2: 37–59.

Mossière, Géraldine. 2010. "Des femmes converties à l'islam en France et au Québec: religiosités d'un nouveau genre." PhD diss., Université de Montréal.

Mossière, Géraldine. 2011a. "Devenir musulmane pour discipliner le corps et transformer l'esprit: l'herméneutique du sujet pieux comme voie de restauration du soi." *Ethnologies* 33, 1: 117–42. http://dx.doi.org/10.7202/1007799ar.

Mossière, Géraldine. 2011b. "Religion in Québec and Otherness at Home: New Wine in Old Bottles?" *Québec Studies* 52 (October): 95–110. https://doi.org/10.3828/qs.52.1.95.

Mossière, Géraldine. 2013. *Converties à l'islam: Parcours de femmes au Québec et en France*. Montreal: Presses de l'Université de Montréal.

Mossière, Géraldine, and Deirdre Meintel. 2010. "Tradition and Transition: Immigrant Religious Communities in Urban Contexts (Québec)." In *Religion in the Practice of Daily Life*, edited by Vincent F. Biondo and Richard D. Hecht, 481–508. Westport: Greenwood and Praeger.

Nagra, Baljit. 2011a. "'Our Faith Was Also Hijacked by Those People': Reclaiming Muslim Identity in Canada in a Post-9/11 Era." *Journal of Ethnic and Migration Studies* 37, 3: 425–41. https://doi.org/10.1080/1369183X.2011.526781.

Nagra, Baljit. 2011b. "Unequal Citizenship: Being Muslim and Canadian in the Post 9/11 Era." PhD diss., University of Toronto.

Neitz, Mary Jo. 1987. *Charisma and Community: A Study of Religious Commitment within the Charismatic Renewal*. New Brunswick, NJ: Transaction Books.

Ofrath, Naama. 2013. "R v NS 2012 SCC 72 – Assessing the Contours of the Freedom to Wear the Niqab in Canada." Master's thesis, Queen's University.

Olshan, Mark A., and Kimberly D. Schmidt. 1994. "Amish Women and the Feminist Conundrum." In *The Amish Struggle with Modernity*, edited by Donald B. Karybill and Marc A. Olshan, 215–30. Hanover: University Press of New England.

Orsi, Robert. 2003. "Is the Study of Lived Religion Irrelevant to the World We Live In? Special Presidential Plenary Address, Society for the Scientific Study of Religion, Salt Lake City, November 2, 2002." *Journal for the Scientific Study of Religion* 42, 2: 169–74. https://doi.org/10.1111/1468-5906.t01-1-00170.

Orsi, Robert. 2005. *Between Heaven and Earth: The Religious Worlds People Make and the Scholars Who Study Them*. Princeton, NJ: Princeton University Press.

Oueslati, Béchir, Marie McAndrew, and Denise Helly. 2011. "Islam and Muslim Cultures in Quebec French-language Textbooks over Three Periods: 1980s, 1990s, and the Present Day." In "Teaching about Islam and the Muslim World: Textbooks and Real Curriculum," edited by Marie McAndrew, Amina Triki-Yamani, and Falk Pingel. Special issue, *Journal of Educational Media, Memory, and Society* 3, 1: 5–24.

Ouimet-Lamothe, Sophie. 2008. "Une sauveteuse en 'burkini.'" *La Presse*, August 7, 2008. http://www.lapresse.ca/actualites/200809/08/01-659695-une-sauveteuse-en-burkini.php.

Palmer, Susan. 1994. *Moon Sisters, Krishna Mothers, Rajneesh Lovers: Women's Roles in New Religions*. Syracuse, NY: Syracuse University Press.

Paquette, Mario. 2014."Halal à la cabane à sucre." Interview on *Bien dans son assiette*, Radio-Canada Émissions. Hosted by Francis Reddy. http://ici.radio-canada.ca/emissions/bien_dans_son_assiette/2013-2014/chronique.asp?idChronique=332053.

Park, Ji Hoon, Nadine G. Gabbadon, and Ariel R. Chernin. 2006. "Naturalizing Racial Differences through Comedy: Asian, Black, and White Views on Racial Stereotypes in *Rush Hour 2*." *Journal of Communication* 56, 1: 157–77. https://doi.org/10.1111/j.1460-2466.2006.00008.x.

Patel, Shaista. 2012. "The Anti-Terrorism Act and National Security: Safeguarding the Nation against Uncivilized Muslims." In *Islam in the Hinterlands: Muslim Cultural Politics in Canada*, edited by Jasmin Zine, 272–98. Vancouver: UBC Press.

Pew Research Center. 2011. *The Future of the Global Muslim Population*. Washington: Pew Research Center. http://www.pewforum.org/2011/01/27/the-future-of-the-global-muslim-population/.

Pham, Minh-Ha T. 2011. "The Right to Fashion in the Age of Terrorism." *Signs: Journal of Women in Culture and Society* 36, 2: 385–410. https://doi.org/10.1086/655979.

Phillips, Anne. 2007. *Multiculturalism without Culture*. Princeton, NJ: Princeton University Press.

Potvin, Jean-Mathieu, and Anne Saris. 2009. "La résolution de conflits familiaux chez les Canadiennes musulmanes à Montréal: un système de justice parallèle?" *Diversité urbaine* 9, 1: 119–37. https://doi.org/10.7202/037762ar.

Povinelli, Elizabeth A. 2002. *The Cunning of Recognition: Indigenous Alterities and the Making of Australian Multiculturalism*. Durham, NC: Duke University Press. https://doi.org/10.1215/9780822383673.

Powers, Lucas. 2015. "Conservatives Pledge Funds, Tip Line to Combat 'Barbaric Cultural Practices.'" CBC News.ca, October 2, 2015. http://www.cbc.ca/news/politics/canada-election-2015-barbaric-cultural-practices-law-1.3254118.

Public Safety Canada. 2016. "Safeguarding Canadians with Passenger Protect." Last modified June 20, 2016. https://www.publicsafety.gc.ca/cnt/ntnl-scrt/cntr-trrrsm/pssngr-prtct/index-en.aspx.

Rahman, Saira. 2015. "Al Rashid Mosque – The First Mosque in Canada." *A New Life a New Land: The Muslim Experience in Canada Educator's Guide*. Milo Productions. http://www.anewlife.ca/alrashid/.

Rahman, Saira, and Nilufer Rahman. 2015. *Letter to a Terrorist*. Snow Angel Films. YouTube, December 6, 2015. https://www.youtube.com/watch?v=vIYrlZhdjRc.

Ramji, Rubina. 2008a. "Being Muslim and Being Canadian: How Second Generation Muslim Women Create Religious Identities in Two Worlds." In *Women and Religion in the West: Challenging Secularization*, edited by Kristin Aune, Sonya Sharma, and Giselle Vincett, 195–205. Aldershot, UK: Ashgate.

Ramji, Rubina. 2008b. "Creating a Genuine Islam: Second Generation Muslims Growing Up in Canada." *Canadian Diversity* 6, 2: 104–9.

Ramji, Rubina. 2013. "A Variable but Convergent Islam: Muslim Women." In *Growing Up Canadian: Muslims, Hindus Buddhists*, edited by Peter Beyer and Rubina Ramji, 112–44. Montreal/Kingston: McGill-Queen's University Press.

Ramji, Rubina. 2014. "Maintaining and Nurturing an Islamic Identity in Canada – Online and Offline." In *Religion in the Public Sphere: Canadian Case Studies*, edited by Solange Lefebvre and Lori G. Beaman, 97–120. Toronto: University of Toronto Press.

Rangaviz, David. 2011. "Dangerous Deference: The Supreme Court of Canada in Canada v. Khadr." *Harvard Civil Rights–Civil Liberties Law Review* 46: 253–69.

Razack, Sherene. 1995. "The Perils of Talking about Culture: Schooling Research on South and East Asian Students." *Race, Gender, and Class* 2, 3: 67–82.

Razack, Sherene. 1998. *Looking White People in the Eye: Gender, Race, and Culture in Courtrooms and Classrooms*. Toronto: University of Toronto Press.

Razack, Sherene. 2004. "Imperilled Muslim Women, Dangerous Muslim Men and Civilised Europeans: Legal and Social Responses to Forced Marriages." *Feminist Legal Studies* 12, 2: 129–74. https://doi.org/10.1023/B:FEST.0000043305. 66172.92.

Razack, Sherene. 2007. "'Your Client Has a Profile': Race and National Security in Canada after 9/11." In *Studies in Law, Politics, and Society*, edited by Austin Sarat, 40: 3–40. Bingley, UK: Emerald Group. https://doi.org/10.1016/S1059 -4337(06)40001-6.

Razack, Sherene. 2008. *Casting Out: The Eviction of Muslims from Western Law and Politics*. Toronto: University of Toronto Press.

Razavy, Maryam. 2013. "Canadian Responses to Islamic Law: The Faith-Based Arbitration Debates." *Religious Studies and Theology* 32, 1: 101–17. https://doi. org/10.1558/rsth.v32i1.101.

Reda, Nevin. 2012. "The 'Good' Muslim, 'Bad' Muslim Puzzle? The Assertion of Muslim's Islamic Identity in the Sharia Debates in Canada." In *Debating Sharia: Islam, Gender Politics, and Religious Law Arbitration*, edited by Anna C. Korteweg and Jennifer A. Selby, 231–56. Toronto: University of Toronto Press.

Reitmanova, Sylvia, and Diana L. Gustafson. 2008. "'They Can't Understand It': Maternity Health and Care Needs of Immigrant Muslim Women in St. John's, Newfoundland." *Journal of Maternal and Child Health* 12, 1: 101–11. https://doi. org/10.1007/s10995-007-0213-4.

Reitz, Jeffrey G., Patrick Simon, and Emily Laxer. 2017. "Muslims' Social Inclusion and Exclusion in France, Québec, and Canada: Does National Context Matter?"

Journal of Ethnic and Migration Studies 43, 15: 2473–98. https://doi.org/10.1080/1369183X.2017.1313105.

Riis, Ole, and Linda Woodhead. 2010. *A Sociology of Religious Emotion*. Oxford: Oxford University Press. https://doi.org/10.1093/acprof:oso/9780199567607.001.0001.

Roach, Kent. 2010. "'The Supreme Court at the Bar of Politics': The Afghan Detainee and Omar Khadr Cases." *National Journal of Constitutional Law/Revue nationale de droit constitutionnel* 28, 1: 116–55.

Robert, Anne-Marie, and Tara Gilkinson. 2012. *Mental Health and Well-Being of Recent Immigrants in Canada: Evidence from the Longitudinal Survey of Immigrants to Canada*. Ottawa: Citizenship and Immigration Canada. https://www.canada.ca/content/dam/ircc/migration/ircc/english/pdf/research-stats/mental-health.pdf.

Rochelle, Safiyah. 2013. "Whether Angel or Devil: Law's Knowing and Unknowing of Veiled Muslim Women in the Case of R v. N.S." Master's thesis, Carleton University. https://curve.carleton.ca/system/files/etd/e7d845d7-1bf2-4541-8778-8e1466591433/etd_pdf/153933f3fb58d595922bbe93b5deec53/rochelle-whether angelordevillawsknowingandunknowing.pdf.

Rothenberg, Celia E. 2010. "Wilful Overlooking: Stories from the Islamic Diaspora and the Palestinian West Bank." *Anthropology and Humanism* 35, 1: 101–11. https://doi.org/10.1111/j.1548-1409.2010.01055.x.

Rousseau, Cécile, Taïeb Ferradji, Abdelwahed Mekki-Berrada, and Uzma Jamil. 2013. "North African Muslim Immigrant Families in Canada Giving Meaning to and Coping with the War on Terror." *Journal of Immigrant & Refugee Studies* 11, 2: 136–56. https://doi.org/10.1080/15562948.2013.775892.

Roy, Oliver. 2002. *Les illusions du 11 septembre: le débat stratégique face au terrorisme*. Paris: Édition du Seuil.

Ruby, Tabassum. 2004. *Immigrant Muslim Women and the Hijab*. Saskatoon: Community-University Institute for Social Research. https://www.usask.ca/cuisr/sites/default/files/Ruby.pdf.

Ryan, Daniel. 2010. "International Law and Laws of War and International Criminal Law – Prosecution of Child Soldiers – *United States v. Omar Ahmed Khadr*." *Suffolk Transnational Law Review* 33, 1: 175–86.

Sagan, Aleksandra. 2016. "Canada's No-Fly List Is 'Very Mysterious' and Leaves Targets Little Recourse, Says Critics." CBC News.ca, January 6, 2016. http://www.cbc.ca/news/canada/no-fly-lists-in-canada-1.3389929.

Salomon, Noah, and Jeremy Walton. 2012. "Religious Criticism, Secular Critique, and the 'Critical Study of Religion': Lessons from the Study of Islam." In *The Cambridge Companion to Religious Studies*, edited by Robert A. Orsi, 403–20. Cambridge: Cambridge University Press.

Sanchez, Raf, Barney Henderson, Rob Crilly, and David Millward. 2014. "Gunman and Two Hostages Killed in Sydney Siege: As It Happened." *Telegraph*, December 16, 2014. http://www.telegraph.co.uk/news/worldnews/australiaandthepacific/australia/11293694/Islamists-take-hostages-in-Sydney-cafe-siege-live.html.

Sanders, Carol. 2015. "Immigration Minister's Comments 'Devastating': Islamic Community Leader." *Winnipeg Free Press*, June 17, 2015. https://www.winnipegfreepress.com/local/Immigration-ministers-comments-devistating-308033701.html.

Santa Ana, Otto. 2009. "Did You Call in Mexican? The Racial Politics of Jay Leno Immigrant Jokes." *Language in Society* 38, 1: 23–45. https://doi.org/10.1017/S0047404508090027.

Saris, Anne. 2014. "La burqa au Québec: entre droit et valeurs, qui élabore le droit commun." In *Quand la burqa passe à l'Ouest ... Enjeux éthiques, politiques et juridiques*, edited by David Koussens and Oliver Roy, 177–79. Rennes, France: Presses Universitaires de Rennes.

Saris, Anne, and Samia Amor. 2011. "Femmes musulmanes et divorce à Montréal: fatalité subie ou liberté acquise." *Revue scientifique de l'AIFI* 5, 2.

Saris, Anne, and Sofie Daoust. 2014. "Polygamy Inherently Harmful to Children? The Impacts of Canadian Criminal, Civil, and Child Protection Law." In *Of Crime and Religion: Polygamy in Canadian Law*, edited by Marie Pierre-Robert, David Koussens, and Stéphane Bernatchez, 159–89. Sherbrooke: Éditions RDUS.

Saris, Anne, and Jean-Mathieu Potvin. 2010. "Sharia in Canada. Family Dispute Resolution among Muslim Minorities in the West: Analysis of a Case Study of Muslim Women, Counselors and Civil Actors in Montreal." Draft. https://www.brandeis.edu/hbi/gcrl/images/AnneSarisWP.pdf.

Saris, Anne, and Jean-Mathieu Potvin. 2013. "Canadian Muslim Women and Resolution of Family Conflicts: An Empirical Qualitative Study (2005–2007)." In *Law and Religion in the 21st Century: Relations between States and Religious Communities*, edited by Silvio Ferrari and Rinaldo Cristofori, 339–47. Farnham, UK: Ashgate.

Saris, Anne, and Fatima Seedat. 2009. *Women's Rights in Muslim Communities: A Resource Guide for Human Rights Educators*. Montreal: Equitas–International Centre for Human Rights Education. https://equitas.org/wp-content/uploads/2010/11/research_EQUITAS_Sharia.pdf.

Scharff, Christina. 2011. "Disarticulating Feminism: Individualization, Neoliberalism and the Othering of 'Muslim Women.'" *European Journal of Women's Studies* 18, 2: 119–34. https://doi.org/10.1177/1350506810394613.

Schielke, Samuli. 2009a. "Ambivalent Commitments: Troubles of Morality, Religiosity and Aspiration among Young Egyptians." *Journal of Religion in Africa* 39, 2: 158–85. https://doi.org/10.1163/157006609X427814.

Schielke, Samuli. 2009b. "Being Good in Ramadan: Ambivalence, Fragmentation and the Moral Self in the Lives of Young Egyptians." In "Islam, Politics, Anthropology," edited by Filippo Osella and Benjamin Soares. *Journal of the Royal Anthropological Institute* 15, s1: S24–S40. https://doi.org/10.1111/j.1467-9655.2009.01540.x.

Schielke, Samuli. 2015. *Egypt in the Future Tense: Hope, Frustration, and Ambivalence Before and After 2011*. Bloomington: Indiana University Press.

Schielke, Samuli, and Liza Debevec. 2012. "Introduction." In *Ordinary Lives and Grand Schemes: An Anthropology of Everyday Religion*, edited by Samuli Schielke and Liza Debevec, 1–16. New York: Berghahn.

Scott, David. 2004. *Conscripts of Modernity: The Tragedy of Colonial Enlightenment*. Durham: NC: Duke University Press. https://doi.org/10.1215/9780822386186.

Scott, Joan Wallach. 2007. *Politics of the Veil*. Princeton, NJ: Princeton University Press.

Scott, Joan Wallach. 2011. "Sexularism: On Secularism and Gender Equality." In *The Fantasy of Feminist History*, 91–116. Durham, NC: Duke University Press. https://doi.org/10.1215/9780822394730-005.

Selby, Jennifer. 2012a. "Construing the Secular: Implications of the Ontario Sharia Debate." In *Debating Sharia: Islam, Gender Politics, and Family Law Arbitration*, edited by Anna C. Korteweg and Jennifer A. Selby, 351–76. Toronto: University of Toronto Press.

Selby, Jennifer. 2012b. *Questioning French Secularism: Gender Politics and Islam in a Parisian Surburb*. New York: Palgrave Macmillan.

Selby, Jennifer. 2013. "Promoting the Everyday: Pro-Sharia Advocacy and Public Relations in Ontario, Canada's 'Sharia Debate.'" *Religions* 4, 3: 423–42. https://doi.org/10.3390/rel4030423.

Selby, Jennifer. 2014. "Un/veiling Women's Bodies: Secularism and Sexuality in Full-face Veil Prohibitions in France and Québec." *Studies in Religion/Sciences religieuses* 43, 3: 439–66. https://doi.org/10.1177/0008429814526150.

Selby, Jennifer. 2016a. "Muslimness and Multiplicity in Qualitative Research and in Government Reports in Canada." *Critical Research on Religion* 4, 1: 72–89. https://doi.org/10.1177/2050303216630298.

Selby, Jennifer. 2016b. "'The Diamond Ring Now Is the Thing': Young Muslim Torontonian Women Negotiating Mahr on the Web." In *Muslim Youth and the 9/11 Generation*, ed. Adeline Masquelier and Benjamin F. Soares, 189–212. Albuquerque: University of New Mexico Press.

Selby, Jennifer A., and Lori G. Beaman. 2016. "Re-posing the 'Muslim Question.'" *Critical Research on Religion* 4, 1: 8–20.

Selby, Jennifer A., and Anna C. Korteweg. 2012. "Introduction: Situating the Debate in Ontario." In *Debating Sharia: Islam, Gender Politics, and Family Law Arbitration*, edited by Anna C. Korteweg and Jennifer A. Selby, 12–34. Toronto: University of Toronto Press.

Seljak, David. 2005. "Multiculturalism and Funding for Ontario's Islamic Schools." *Canadian Diversity* 43, 3: 63–66.

Shaben, Carol. 2013. *Into the Abyss*. Toronto: Vintage Canada.

Shaben, Larry. n.d. "Shaben's at Endiang." Undated, unpublished three-page manuscript. Personal collection.

Shahzad, Farhat. 2014. "The Discourse of Fear: Effects of the War on Terror on Canadian University Students." *American Review of Canadian Studies* 44, 4: 467–82. https://doi.org/10.1080/02722011.2014.976232.

Sharify-Funk, Meena. 2009. "Representing Canadian Muslims: Media, Muslim Advocacy, Organizations, and Gender in the Ontario Shari'ah Debate." *Global Media Journal–Canadian Edition* 2, 2: 73–89.

Sharify-Funk, Meena. 2010. "Muslims and the Politics of 'Reasonable Accommodation': Analyzing the Bouchard-Taylor Report and Its Impact on the Canadian Province of Quebec." *Journal of Muslim Minority Affairs* 30, 4: 535–53. https://doi.org/10.1080/13602004.2010.533451.

Sharify-Funk, Meena. 2011. "Governing the Face Veil: Quebec's Bill 94 and the Transnational Politics of Women's Identity." *International Journal of Canadian Studies/Revue internationale d'études canadiennes* 43: 135–63. https://doi.org/10.7202/1009458ar.

Sharify-Funk, Meena, and William Rory Dickson. 2013. "Islam." In *World Religions: Canadian Perspectives – Western Traditions*, edited by Doris B. Jakobsh, 150–200. Toronto: Nelson.

Sharify-Funk, Meena, and Elysia Guzik. 2017. "Muslim Veiling and the Legacy of Laïcité." In *Everyday Sacred: Religion in Contemporary Quebec*, edited by Hillary Kaell, 186–212. Montreal/Kingston: McGill-Queen's University Press. https://doi.org/10.2307/j.ctt1vjqqhp.12.

Sharify-Funk, Meena, and Munira Kassam Haddad. 2012. "Where Do Women 'Stand' in Islam? Negotiating Contemporary Muslim Prayer Leadership in North America." *Feminist Review* 102, 1: 41–61. https://doi.org/10.1057/fr.2012.10.

Shephard, Michelle. 2008. *Guantanamo's Child: The Untold Story of Omar Khadr*. New York: John Wiley and Sons.

Sheridan, Lorraine P. 2006. "Islamophobia Pre– and Post–September 11, 2001." *Journal of Interpersonal Violence* 21, 3: 317–36. https://doi.org/10.1177/0886260505282885.

Sheriff, Robin E. 2001. *Dreaming Equality: Color, Race and Racism in Urban Brazil*. New Brunswick, NJ: Rutgers University Press.

Sheringham, Michael. 2006. *Everyday Life: Theories and Practices from Surrealism to the Present*. Oxford: Oxford University Press.

Shirley, Clive. 2001. "Hazara Ismailis of Afghanistan Arrive in Canada." Ismaili Web, August 6, 2001, updated November 17, 2001. http://www.amaana.org/tajik/hazara.htm.

Shryock, Andrew, ed. 2010. *Islamophobia/Islamophilia: Beyond the Politics of Enemy and Friend*. Bloomington: Indiana University Press.

Silvestri, Sara. 2011. "Faith Intersections and Muslim Women in the European Microcosm: Notes towards the Study of Non-Organized Islam." *Ethnic and Racial Studies* 34, 7: 1230–47. https://doi.org/10.1080/01419870.2011.565779.

Simons, Paula. 2016. "In Honouring Strong Muslim Women, Edmonton School Names Send Powerful Message." *Edmonton Journal,* June 22, 2016. http://edmonton journal.com/news/local-news/paula-simons-in-honouring-strong-muslim-women-edmonton-school-names-send-powerful-message.

Skerrett, Kathleen. 2004. "The Indispensable Rival: William Connolly's Engagement with Augustine of Hippo." *Journal of the American Academy of Religion* 72, 2: 487–506. https://doi.org/10.1093/jaarel/lfh038.

Smith, Dorothy E. 1987. *The Everyday World as Problematic: A Feminist Sociology.* Boston: Northeastern University Press.

Smith, Jane I. 1999. *Islam in America.* New York: Columbia University Press.

Smith, Jonathan Z. 1982. *Imagining Religion: From Babylon to Jonestown.* Chicago: University of Chicago Press.

Smith, Jonathan Z. 1987. *To Take Place: Toward Theory in Ritual.* Chicago: University of Chicago Press.

Smith, Robert. 2011. "The Company One Keeps: The Khadr II Litigation in Its International and Comparative Legal Context." PhD diss., University of Toronto.

Soares, Benjamin, and Marie-Nathalie LeBlanc. 2015. "Islam, jeunesse et trajectoires de mobilisation en Afrique de l'Ouest à l'ère néolibérale: un regard anthropologique." In *Collective Mobilisations in Africa: Enough Is Enough!* edited by Kadya Tall, Marie-Emmanuelle Pommerolle, and Michel Cahen, 67–90. Leiden, The Netherlands: Brill.

Soares, Benjamin, and Filippo Osella. 2009. "Islam, Politics, Anthropology." Special issue, *Journal of the Royal Anthropological Institute* 15, s1:S1–23. https://doi.org/10.1111/j.1467-9655.2009.01539.x.

Statistics Canada. 2001. "Population by Religion, by Province and Territory (2001 Census)." Statistics Canada, Census of Population. http://www.statcan.gc.ca/tables-tableaux/sum-som/l01/cst01/demo30a-eng.htm.

Statistics Canada. 2011a. "Population, Urban and Rural, by Province and Territory (Canada)." Statistics Canada, 2011 Census of Population. http://www.statcan.gc.ca/tables-tableaux/sum-som/l01/cst01/demo62a-eng.htm.

Statistics Canada. 2011b. *Religion (108), Immigrant Status and Period of Immigration (11), Age Groups (10) and Sex (3) for the Population in Private Households of Canada, Provinces, Territories, Census Metropolitan Areas and Census Agglomerations, 2011 National Household Survey.* Statistics Canada Catalogue no. 99-010-X2011032. http://www12.statcan.gc.ca/nhs-enm/2011/dp-pd/dt-td/Rp-eng.cfm?LANG=E&APATH=3&DETAIL=0&DIM=0&FL=A&FREE=0&GC=0&GID=0&GK=0&GRP=0&PID=105399&PRID=0&PTYPE=105277&S=0&SHOWALL=0&SUB=0&Temporal=2013&THEME=95&VID=0.

Statistics Canada. 2013. *Toronto, CMA, Ontario (Code 535) (table). National Household Survey (NHS) Profile. 2011 National Household Survey.* Statistics Canada Catalogue no. 99-004-XWE. Ottawa. Released September 11, 2013. http://www12.statcan.gc.ca/nhs-enm/2011/dp-pd/prof/details/page.cfm?Lang=E&Geo1=CMA&Code1=535&Data=Count&SearchText=toronto&SearchType=Begins&SearchPR=01&A1=Religion&B1=All&Custom=&TABID=1.

Statistics Canada. 2016. "Census Profile, 2016 Census, St. John's, Newfoundland and Labrador." http://www12.statcan.gc.ca/census-recensement/2016/dp-pd/prof/details/page.cfm?Lang=E&Geo1=CMACA&Code1=001&Geo2=PR&Code2=10&Data=Count&SearchText=St.%20John.

Stoker, Valerie. 2007. "Zero Tolerance? Sikh Swords, School Safety, and Secularism in Québec." *Journal of the American Academy of Religion* 75, 4: 814–39. https://doi.org/10.1093/jaarel/lfm064.

Stringer, Martin D. 2013. *Discourses on Religious Diversity: Explorations in an Urban Ecology*. Farnham, UK: Ashgate.

Sue, Christina A., and Tanya Golash-Boza. 2013. "'It Was Only a Joke': How Racial Humour Fuels Colour-Blind Ideologies in Mexico and Peru." *Ethnic and Racial Studies* 36, 10: 1582–98. https://doi.org/10.1080/01419870.2013.783929.

Sullivan, Winnifred Fallers. 2005. *The Impossibility of Religious Freedom*. Princeton, NJ: Princeton University Press.

Sullivan, Winnifred Fallers, and Lori G. Beaman, eds. 2013. *Varieties of Religious Establishment*. New York: Routledge.

Sunier, Thijl. 2014. "Domesticating Islam: Exploring Academic Knowledge Production on Islam and Muslims in European Societies." *Ethnic and Racial Studies* 37, 6: 1138–55. https://doi.org/10.1080/01419870.2012.753151.

Taira, Teemu. 2013. "The Category of 'Invented Religion': A New Opportunity for Studying Discourses on 'Religion.'" *Culture and Religion: An Interdisciplinary Journal* 14, 4: 477–93. https://doi.org/10.1080/14755610.2013.838799.

Taylor, Charles. 2009. *A Secular Age*. Cambridge, MA: Harvard University Press.

Thornback, James. 2005. "The Portrayal of Sharia in Ontario." *Appeal: Review of Current Law and Law Reform* 10, 1: 1–12.

Toronto Muslims. n.d. "Mosques." torontomuslims.com. Accessed December 15, 2015. http://www.torontomuslims.com/listingcategory/mosques/.

Triki-Yamani, Amina, and Marie McAndrew. 2009. "Perceptions du traitement de l'islam, du monde musulman et des minorités musulmanes par de jeunes musulmans(es) du cégep au Québec." *Diversité urbaine* 9, 1: 73–94. https://doi.org/10.7202/037760ar.

Tully, James. 1995. *Strange Multiplicity: Constitutionalism in an Age of Diversity*. Cambridge: Cambridge University Press. https://doi.org/10.1017/CBO9781139170888.

Tully, James. 2000. "Struggles over Recognition and Distribution." *Constellations* 7, 4: 469–82. https://doi.org/10.1111/1467-8675.00203.

Tully, James. 2004. "Approaches to Recognition, Power, and Dialogue." *Political Theory* 32, 6: 855–62.

Turam, Berna. 2015. *Gaining Freedoms: Claiming Space in Istanbul and Berlin*. Stanford, CA: Stanford University Press.

TVA Nouvelles. 2007. "L'érablière présente ses excuses." 2007. TVA Nouvelles, March 20, 2007. http://www.tvanouvelles.ca/2007/03/20/lerabliere-presente-ses-excuses.

Van Quaquebeke, Niels, Daniel C. Henrich, and Tilman Eckloff. 2007. "'It's Not Tolerance I'm Asking for, It's Respect!' A Conceptual Framework to Differentiate between Tolerance, Acceptance and (Two Types of) Respect." *Gruppendynamik* 38, 2: 185–200. https://doi.org/10.1007/s11612-007-0015-6.

Varandani, Suman. 2015. "ISIS Recruitment in Australia: At Least 12 Young Melbourne Women Attempt to Join Islamic State Group." *International Business Times*, May 29, 2015. http://www.ibtimes.com/isis-recruitment-australia-least-12-young-melbourne-women-attempt-join-islamic-state-1943364.

Versi, Salima. "Make This Your Home: The Impact of Religion on Acculturation: The Case of Canadian Khoja Nizari Isma'ilis from East Africa." Master's thesis, Queen's University.

Watters, Haydn. 2015. "C-51, Controversial Anti-terrorism Bill, Is Now Law. So, What Changes?" CBC News.ca, June 18, 2015. http://www.cbc.ca/news/politics/c-51-controversial-anti-terrorism-bill-is-now-law-so-what-changes-1.3108608.

Waugh, Earle. 1980. "The Imam in the New World: Models and Modifications." In *Transitions and Transformations in the History of Religions: Essays in Honour of Joseph M. Kitagawa*, edited by Frank E. Reynolds and Theodore M. Ludwig, 124–49. Leiden, The Netherlands: Brill.

Waugh, Earle. 1994. "Reducing the Distance: A Muslim Congregation in the Canadian North." In *American Congregations*, vol. 1 of *Portraits of Twelve Religious Communities*, edited by James P. Wind and James W. Lewis, 572–611. Chicago: University of Chicago Press.

Waugh, Earle. 2008. "The Aga Khan's Pluralism and Canada's Multiculturalism." In *Ismailis in Canada*, edited by Mansoor Ladha, 37–49. New York: New Press.

Waugh, Earle. 2012. "Muslim Perspectives on a Good Death in Hospice and End-of-Life Care." In *Religious Understandings of a Good Death in Hospice Palliative Care*, edited by Harold Coward and Kelli Stajduhar, 77–98. New York: SUNY Press.

Waugh, Earle H., Baha Abu-Laban, and Regula B. Qureshi, eds. 1983. *The Muslim Community in North America*. Edmonton: University of Alberta Press.

Waugh, Earle H., Sharon McIrvin Abu-Laban, and Regula Burkhardt Qureshi, eds. 1991. *Muslim Families in North America*. Edmonton: University of Alberta Press.

Waugh, Earle, and Jenny Wannas. 2003. "The Rise of a Womanist Movement among Muslim Women in Alberta." *Studies in Contemporary Islam* 1: 1–15.

Waugh, Earle, Jenny Wannas, Maryam Razavy, and Soraya Hafez. 2015. "A Profile of Muslim Growth: Edmonton, a Brief Overview." *Religious Studies and Theology* 34, 2: 145–62. https://doi.org/10.1558/rsth.v34i2.29228.

Wayland, Sarah. 1997. "Religious Expression in Public Schools: Kirpans in Canada, Hijab in France." *Ethnic and Racial Studies* 20, 3: 545–61. https://doi.org/10.1080/01419870.1997.9993974.

Werbner, Pnina. 2013. "Folk Devils and Racist Imaginaries in a Global Prism: Islamophobia and Anti-Semitism in the Twenty-First Century." *Ethnic and Racial Studies* 36, 3: 450–67. http://dx.doi.org/10.1080/01419870.2013.734384.

West, Robin. 1988. "Jurisprudence and Gender." *University of Chicago Law Review* 55, 1: 1–72.

West, Robin. 2003. *Re-Imagining Justice: Progressive Interpretations of Formal Equality, Rights, and the Rule of Law.* Aldershot, UK: Ashgate.

Williams, Jennifer. 2015. "Addressing Multiculturalism in the Newfoundland and Labrador Multiculturalism Policy and in the Everyday Lives of Muslims in St. John's, NL." Master's thesis, Memorial University of Newfoundland.

Williamson, Janice, ed. 2012. *Omar Khadr, Oh Canada.* Montreal/Kingston: McGill-Queen's Press.

Wilson, Erin K. 2012. *After Secularism: Rethinking Religion in Global Politics.* New York: Palgrave Macmillan. https://doi.org/10.1057/9780230355316.

Wilson, Richard J. 2006. "Military Commissions in Guantanamo Bay: Giving Full and Fair Trial a Bad Name." *Gonzaga Journal of International Law* 10, 1: 63.

Wilson, Richard J. 2009. Children in Armed Conflict: The Detention of Children at Guantanamo Bay, and the Trial for War Crimes by Military Commission of Omar Khadr, a Child. Assessing Damage, Urging Action: Report of the Eminent Jurists Panel on Terrorism, Counter-Terrorism and Human Rights. February 2009, last revised April 1, 2009. WCL Legal Studies Research Paper No. 2009-13, American University, Washington, DC.

Wilson, Richard J. 2012. "Omar Khadr: Domestic and International Litigation Strategies for a Child in Armed Conflict Held at Guantanamo." *Santa Clara Journal of International Law* 11, 1: 32–79.

Wong, Alan. 2011. "The Disquieting Revolution: A Genealogy of Reason and Racism in the Québec Press." *Global Media Journal–Canadian Edition* 4, 1: 145–62.

Woodhead, Linda. 2011. "Five Concepts of Religion." *International Review of Sociology* 21, 1: 121–43. https://doi.org/10.1080/03906701.2011.544192.

Woodhead, Linda. 2014. "Religious Other or Religious Inferior." *IIC Quarterly* 40, 3–4: 1–14.

Yegenoglu, Meyda. 2003. "Veiled Fantasies: Cultural and Sexual Difference in the Discourse of Orientalism." In *Feminist Postcolonial Theory*, edited by Rena Lewis and Sara Mills, 542–66. New York: Routledge.

Young, Iris Marion. 1990. *Justice and the Politics of Difference.* Princeton, N.J.: Princeton University Press.

Yousif, Ahmad F. 1993. *Muslims in Canada: A Question of Identity.* New York: LEGAS.

Yousif, Ahmad F. 2005. "The Impact of 9/11 on Muslim Identity in the Canadian National Capital Region: Institutional Response and Future Prospects." *Studies in Religion/Sciences religieuses* 34, 1: 49–68.

Yukleyen, Ahmet. 2010. "State Policies and Islam in Europe: Milli Görüş in Germany and the Netherlands." *Journal of Ethnic and Migration Studies* 36, 3: 445–63. https://doi.org/10.1080/13691830903123203.

Zaman, Saminaz. 2008. "From Imam to Cyber-Mufti: Consuming Identity in Muslim America." *Muslim World* 98, 4: 465–74. https://doi.org/10.1111/j.1478-1913.2008.00240.x.

Zehiri, Mohammed. 2009. "Le débat sur l'implantation de tribunaux islamiques tel que reflété par les journaux québécois *La Presse* et *Le Devoir* (2003–2005)." *Laval théologique et philosophique* 65, 1: 45–54. https://doi.org/10.7202/037939ar.

Zine, Jasmin. 2000. "Redefining Resistance: Towards an Islamic Subculture in Schools." *Race, Ethnicity and Education* 3, 3: 293–316. https://doi.org/10.1080/713693042.

Zine, Jasmin. 2001. "Muslim Youth in Canadian Schools: Education and the Politics of Religious Identity." *Anthropology & Education Quarterly* 32, 4: 399–423. https://doi.org/10.1525/aeq.2001.32.4.399.

Zine, Jasmin. 2002. "Muslim Women and the Politics of Representation." *American Journal of Islamic Social Sciences* 19, 4: 1–22.

Zine, Jasmin. 2006. "Unveiled Sentiments: Gendered Islamophobia and Experiences of Veiling among Muslim Girls in a Canadian Islamic School." *Equity & Excellence in Education* 39, 3: 239–52. https://doi.org/10.1080/10665680600788503.

Zine, Jasmin. 2007. "Safe Havens or Religious 'Ghettos'? Narratives of Islamic Schooling in Canada." *Race, Ethnicity and Education* 10, 1: 71–92. https://doi.org/10.1080/13613320601100385.

Zine, Jasmin. 2008a. *Canadian Islamic Schools: Unravelling the Politics of Faith, Gender, Knowledge and Identity.* Toronto: University of Toronto Press. https://doi.org/10.3138/9781442687509.

Zine, Jasmin. 2008b. "Honour and Identity: An Ethnographic Account of Muslim Girls in a Canadian Islamic School." *Topia* 19, 39: 39–67.

Zine, Jasmin. 2012a. "Introduction: Muslim Cultural Politics in the Canadian Hinterlands." In *Islam in the Hinterlands: Muslim Cultural Politics in Canada,* edited by Jasmin Zine, 1–38. Vancouver: UBC Press.

Zine, Jasmin. 2012b. "Sharia in Canada? Mapping Discourses of Race, Gender and Religious Difference." In *Debating Sharia: Islam, Gender Politics, and Family Law Arbitration,* ed. Anna C. Korteweg and Jennifer A. Selby, 279–306. Toronto: University of Toronto Press.

Zine, Jasmin, and Zabedia Nazim. 2010. *Being a Canadian Muslim Woman in the 21st Century.* Module 1: Educational Framework: An Anti-Racism/Anti-Islamophobia Perspective. Educational Resource Kit. Canadian Council of Muslim Women. http://ccmw.com/wp-content/uploads/2013/05/01-ccmw_being_muslim_toolkit_module1.pdf.

Jurisprudence

Alberta v Hutterian Bretheren of Wilson Colony, [2009] SCR 567.

Canada (Citizenship and Immigration) v Ishaq, 2015 FCA 194.

Ishaq v Canada (Citizenship and Immigration), [2015] 4 FCR 297, 2015 FC 156.

Mouvement laïque québécois v Saguenay (City), [2015] 2 SCR 3.

Multani v Commission scolaire Marguerite-Bourgeoys, [2006] 1 SCR 256.

R v N.S., 2012 SCC 72, [2012] 3 SCR 726.

Index

Motion 103 (Canadian Parliament), to condemn Islamophobia, 38–39
Muhammad, 25, 56, 188*n*3, 191*n*1
Multani v. Commission scolaire Marguerite-Bourgeoys (Supreme Court case), 6–7, 126, 152, 189*nn*8–9
multiculturalism, 15, 75, 126
multiple registers of being, balancing/"cobbling" of, 9, 19, 131–32, 134, 159, 168; at daycare facilities, 135–40, 184–85; in ordering proscribed food, 121–24, 132, 152, 184; when receiving alcohol as gift, 153–54, 176
Muslim Association of Newfoundland and Labrador, 16, 24
Muslim Canadians: as archetypal figures, 17–18, 24–62; assumptions about, 10, 24–26, 37–38, 40–42, 44–48, 57–59, 90–91, 103–7, 117, 119, 129–31, 164, 171–72, 182–83, 215*n*10; as experts/resource persons on Islam, 5, 103–5, 182–83; history/demographics of, 18, 63–88; and mutual respect of dietary requirements, 20–21, 157–77; narratives of everyday life/experiences by, 3–23, 178–87; navigation/negotiation of everyday religion by, 19–20, 121–56; religious identity of, 79–84, 129–31, 180–87; scholarship on, 5, 11–13, 17–18, 59, 63–88, 130–31, 183; in secular society, 14–15, 18–19, 81–82, 89–120. *See also specific topics*; Montreal, Muslims in; Muslim Canadians, in historical/demographic context; Newfoundland, Muslims in; Quebec; St. John's, Muslims in
Muslim Canadians, in historical/demographic context, 18, 63–88; as added to census, 74, 200*n*19; branches of Islam represented by,

74–75; from Confederation to early twentieth century, 68–72; as converts, 15, 45–47, 54, 58, 78–79, 86, 94, 138, 207*n*71; as early immigrants to Alberta, 63–72, 73, 77, 80, 83, 87–88; evolution of scholarship on, 18, 66–68, 75–76, 80–88, 180; gendered experiences of, 80–83; and harsh winters, 67, 72, 77, 199*n*11; as later immigrants to Quebec, 66–67, 76–80, 83, 87, 88, 180; military service by, 72, 81; in 1990s, 76–79; in post-9/11 era, 79–87; in post–Second World War era, 73–76; as proportion of Canadian population, 73, 74(i), 78–79; qualitative research on, 13, 56, 81, 84–87, 127, 180; as "unmosqued," 74–75, 79, 203*n*38. *See also* Alberta, Muslims in; Ibnouzahir, Asmaa; Montreal, Muslim immigrant family's experience in; Shaben, Larry
Muslim Students' Association, 16, 148, 203*n*39; at Memorial University of Newfoundland, 16, 33
mutual respect, 20–21, 157–77; as agonistic, 161, 167–68; vs bounded identities, 159–60, 161; breakdown of, 169–71, 173–76, 177; as dialogical, 160, 163; fragility of, 159, 169–71, 176; and mutual recognition of difference, 158, 159, 160–62, 163–64, 166; as nonjudgmental, 159, 161, 171–73; and power asymmetries, 159, 161, 163, 173–76, 177, 185–87; prior preparation involved in, 157–59, 163–64, 166–67; as process, 160–62, 163–64, 166, 167, 169, 177; as shared, 162–67, 175–76; and "wilful overlooking," 167, 172–73; and willingness to ask "awkward questions," 157–58, 159, 163–64,

193*n*11, 193*n*13, 211*n*7, 213*n*17; vs wish to keep religion private, 36–37, 78–79, 105–12, 127, 209*n*13. *See also* religious identity of Muslims, foregrounding of
request, discourse of: and clothing worn for sports/recreation, 145–52, 181, 213*nn*20–23, 214*n*25; by Foreigner and Good Citizen archetypes, 52–55; and language of accommodation, 125–29; and negotiation of swimming pool use, 3–10, 12, 16, 18, 20, 21–23, 145, 148–50, 181, 213–14*nn*23–24; and prayer space, 102, 103–6, 109, 111–12, 182–83, 184; as resulting in controversy/misunderstanding, 169–71, 176; as resulting in formal request to higher authority, 135–36, 140, 143–45. *See also* reasonable accommodation
Royal Canadian Mounted Police (RCMP), 16, 194*n*17, 194*n*22
Royal Canadian Regiment, 72

Saddy, Mahmoud, 70, 194*n*16
Saddy, Rikia (*née* Haidar), 70, 194*n*16
Schielke, Samuli, 131, 159, 212*n*9, 214*n*2; and Liza Debevec, 147, 156, 169, 213*n*17
scholarship, on Muslim Canadians, 5, 11–13, 17–18, 59, 63–88, 130–31, 183; and early immigrants' stories, 63–72, 87–88; evolution of, 18, 66–68, 75–76, 80–88, 180; and immigrants of 1990s, 76–79; Iranian Revolution and, 75–76; post-9/11 and beyond, 67–68, 76, 79–88, 203*n*43; post–Second World War, 73–76; as qualitative research, 13, 56, 81, 84–87, 127, 180
schools. *See* private Islamic schools; public schools

secularism, 90–93. *See also* secularism in Canada
secularism in Canada, 14–15, 18–19, 81–82, 89–120; and Christmas as "secular" holiday, 18–19, 89–91, 93–100, 129; and invisibility/ privileging of Christianity, 8, 19, 89–100, 105, 119–20, 128, 129, 210*n*16; and norms of social interaction, 18, 112–19; and prayer space, 100–12; and sex education classes, 90–91, 117; and sexuality/ sexual values, 90–91, 92, 114–19, 133–34, 181, 210*n*17
securitization of Muslims, in post-9/11 era, 16, 72, 79–83, 84, 194*n*17, 203*n*38; as sanctioned by use of archetypes, 17–18, 31, 32–33, 38–39, 60
sex education, 90–91, 117, 140
sexuality/sexual values, 92, 133–34, 181; and norms of social interaction, 114–19, 210*n*17; and sex education classes, 90–91, 117, 140
Shaben, Abdul Karim, 69, 70
Shaben, Albert, 70, 71
Shaben, Alma (*née* Saddy), 71, 199*n*14
Shaben, Fatima, 70, 71
Shaben, Hassan, 69, 70
Shaben, Larry, 69–72; and family's migration to/settlement in Canada, 66–67, 69–71, 87; idyllic childhood of, 87–88; and local organizations, 71, 79, 80; marriage/family of, 71; as plane crash survivor, 71, 199*n*14; political career of, 71, 83, 180
Shaben, Lila (*née* Kazeil), 71
Shaben, Mike, 70–71
Shaben, Saleem ("Big Sam"), 69–71, 77, 180
Shafia family, "honour killings" case involving, 42–43, 80
Shahzad, Farhat, 82

38; and post-9/11 securitization, 32–33, 38–39
"Toronto 18," 81, 204*n*50
Trudeau, Pierre Elliott, 200*n*21
Tully, James, 160–61, 163, 172, 185, 186

visible religiosity. *See* religious visibility of Muslims

War Measures Act, 72
"War on Terror," 30–31, 82, 193*n*11
Waugh, Earle, 84, 201*n*26, 207*n*67
Wong, Alan, 82
Woodhead, Linda, 133–34
working consensus, 19, 134–35, 142–52, 154–56; fragility of, 132–33, 142–43, 151, 152, 159; strategies/tactics to support, 133–34. *See also* working consensus, situations involving
working consensus, situations involving: access to Arabic at daycare, 137; dietary adjustment to communal meal, 154–56; opting out of mixed

gym classes, 143–45; wearing of burkini, 149–50, 151; wearing of hijab, 132–33, 134; wearing of hijab in gym class/sports, 142–43, 147, 213*n*20; women-only use of swimming pool, 148–49
workplace: archetypes in, 33–36, 45–47, 61; Christmas parties at, 89–90, 91, 94–95, 97–100; and food/drink issues, 121–24, 165–66, 173–76, 177; Muslims as experts/resource persons on Islam in, 5, 103–5, 182–83; norms of social interaction at, 112–19; prayer space at, 100–12

Yahya, Tooba, 42; and Shafia family killings, 42–43, 80
Yousif, Ahmad F., 76

Zehiri, Mohammed, 82
Zero Tolerance for Barbaric Cultural Practices Act, 43
Zine, Jasmin, 80, 84, 190*n*13, 202*n*36, 203*n*43

Printed and bound in Canada by Friesens
Set in Myriad and Sabon by Apex CoVantage, LLC
Copy editor: Robyn So
Proofreader: Judith Earnshaw
Indexer: Cheryl Lemmens